"Opening the pages of *The SalviSoul Cookbook*, you travel back to your own abuela's, mom's, and tia's kitchen. The smells and sounds return, and your tongue reaches out for the familiar notes. In these pages, Karla Tatiana Vasquez has re-created a homeland, each photograph, each recipe, becomes a window into the reason why a book like *SalviSoul* is so important to world cuisine. Our community has been waiting for this book our whole lives."

—Javier Zamora, author of *Solito*

"*SalviSoul* is not just a cookbook; it's a heartfelt tribute to heritage, a testament to the power of storytelling, and an invitation to savor the true essence of El Salvador, one delicious recipe at a time. Join Karla at the table, where food and memories blend to create an unforgettable journey that celebrates the flavors of home."

—Hawa Hassan, James Beard Award–winning author of *In Bibi's Kitchen*

"There is no one better to write about the food of El Salvador than Karla Vasquez, who has dedicated years of work to ensuring that the work of Salvadoran women in the kitchen is not erased. But for Vasquez, it's not just documentation that is significant: It is effusive celebration along with rigorous research, which is what can be found here in *The SalviSoul Cookbook*. Beautifully shot and gorgeously written, this is a testament to the power of a people's food to provide not just sustenance and survival despite upheaval and political strife, but also love, joy, and connection."

—Alicia Kennedy, author of *No Meat Required*

"*The SalviSoul Cookbook* is a vibrant opus that highlights the strength, resiliency, and soul of Salvadoreño food and the women who nourish a society throughout the generations. These recipes are the perfect example of when food isn't always just food. It would be impossible to share these recipes without sharing the stories that are attached to them. And that's what Karla has done for us."

—Ilyanna Maisonet, James Beard Award–winning author of *Diasporican*

THE SALVISOUL COOKBOOK

KARLA TATIANA VASQUEZ

THE SALVISOUL COOKBOOK

Salvadoran recipes & the women who preserve them

TEN SPEED PRESS

California | New York

Photography by Ren Fuller & Monica Torrento

A molino is a place where grains, like corn, are processed into masa. The one pictured is used by food vendors in Mercado Central in San Salvador.

Para mi Mamá Lucy, mi Mamá Juana, y cada Salvadoreña que ha luchado por el progreso de su familia.

CONTENTS

INTRODUCTION

El Salvador always felt like a movie to me.

It required imagining, editing, and borrowing scenes from films and stories to connect with the country of my birth. The first months of my life took place in the buzzing capital city of San Salvador, but when I was three months old, my family and I became refugees fleeing a war. My roots grew into a distant tale as we found ourselves in Los Angeles, California. When it came to visualizing my homeland, I had to piece together the tape in my mind from whatever exposure to Salvadoran culture I could find.

When my dad shared stories about fighting in the war, I didn't yet have many pictures of El Salvador, so Hollywood was my reference. Scenes from *Platoon* flooded my mind; watching that movie was my dad's way of understanding the memories he had battled in his youth. Instead of young white American soldiers, my mind projected a youthful version of my dad: a skinny, wide-eyed teenager with dark hair that stuck up from his forehead. I imagined a look of fear on his face. Actors playing soldiers on a set in Vietnam helped me fill in the gaps of what life must have been like for my young father fighting in the jungle. But I learned that movies, however helpful, were not enough. They could never capture the essence of El Salvador—they just gave me fragments. They could not portray the good times, the sarcastic humor, or the endearing aspects of our culture.

When my mother shared her stories, cumbia music filled in the score, its exciting rhythm filled the soundtrack. I saw a light-haired little girl running fast through a Salvadoran marketplace in her school uniform. My mother's stories conjured images of mischievous play, adventures, tree climbing, fruit feasts, and friend-ship—a reimagined *Little Rascals* meets *The Sandlot*, with a touch of *Pretty in Pink*. There was a lightness in her tales, a curiosity, and a sense of playfulness that clashed with what my father told. Their experiences were polar opposites, yet they were both true.

My parents told these tales at the table, over frijoles licuados, crema, queso duro blando, and Salvi tortillas. There was hardly a time when eating family dinner didn't involve recounting memories about El Salvador; I came to expect a side of story to be passed along with the tortillas. I realize now how crucial those moments were in my formation. As the food nourished my physical form, these stories nourished my soul—the truly hungry part of me, the part that wanted to

Karla's great-grandmother's delantal, family photos from Karla's upbringing, and Karla's oven mitts.

understand the land I had left as an infant. The movie I constructed in my mind gradually faded, and food, family, and Salvi friends helped me put flesh and soil into El Salvador from afar.

Each evening's menu told me what kind of stories we would hear at the dinner table. Pollo Guisado con Aceitunas (page 158) meant I might hear about my grandmother and how she learned to cook while working as a housekeeper for upper-middle-class Salvadorans in the 1960s. I listened intently as I curated each perfect spoonful of chicken, rice, and olives and chased them with bites of Salvadoran green salad—a platter of sliced radishes, cucumber spears, watercress stems, and fresh lettuce.

One of the chilaterias in Colonia Malaga, San Salvador, a very famous destination for traditional Salvadoran antojitos.

If, by some miracle, someone managed to forage the national flower of El Salvador, flor de izote, in Los Angeles, my mom would cook it for breakfast. She would sauté onions and tomatoes before adding the petals and scrambling in eggs. Over all the sizzling, she would say, "Cómole gusta la flor de izote a tu papá." She served it with frijoles Salvadoreños, fresh tortillas, and aguacate. "Mmmm, que rico, ¡flor de izote! ¿Quién encontró la flor Tere?" my dad would ask.

It was during one of those food-and-story sessions that my dad said, "When you go to college, you can't forget where you came from. I'm going to make sure of that."

Afraid that I would forget mis raíces, my papito told me when I was seventeen that we would take our first trip back to the homeland. He didn't know about the movie I had constructed in my mind as a child, nor did he fully comprehend the stories I had archived to piece together my identity. My Salvadoran roots were already as impossible for me to forget as my own name, but I knew this trip would encourage them to grow deeper.

This trip was a pilgrimage, a visit to the holy places and sites where my family had lost their innocence and joy and taken up the burden as survivors. I'd already been doing the work of remembering when my father urgently decided it was time to go back: *Trust in the Lord. Remember what He has done for you, Karlita. Remember what He has done for our family. Don't forget what happened. Don't forget who you are. Don't forget our pain. Don't forget the joy we fought for.*

I felt most Salvi when I was surrounded by family and food. I felt rich, eating dishes from our roots and listening to my parents talking about fincas (farms), arboles de mango (mango trees), and their many adventures in bachillerato (high school). Salvadoran food and flavors brought my life a sense of grounding and belonging.

When I was in elementary school, asking my mom about our traditional recipes became a habit. She often found my curiosity frustrating because I was looking for an easy answer to something that had taken her whole life to develop. As I got older, I tried different methods. I asked her to dictate her techniques so that I could write them down. She'd roll her eyes and say, "Ay, Karla."

She defaulted to the tried-and-true custom of passing down recipes, techniques, and tips orally; at other times, she suggested hands-on practice.

"¿Mami, cómo sabes que le falta?" I asked.

"Ay, Karlita, solo sabes. Tu paladar te dice que es lo que falta," she said. How did she know what was missing when she tasted a dish she was cooking? Her palate was her answer.

My pressing curiosity about Salvadoran cooking led me to the internet, where I was shocked to discover that—in this country where more than two million Salvadorans reside—Amazon listed only two Salvadoran cookbooks. One was in Spanish and published in El Salvador, while the second was in English and self-published. This severe lack of representation fueled me to take matters into my own hands. I decided to interview the Salvi women in my life and record their recipes because their stories were too precious not to document and share. And this documentation became the start of my life's work.

Anhelo, Yearning for Home and Healing

Anhelo is a word that I often use to describe my experience with writing this book. It means a longing, or a longing to know or have. It became my go-to feeling based on how I saw my family talk about Salvadoran food. Cravings. Antojitos. Afternoon snacks. Street foods. Fruits ripe for picking off the trees. Constant anhelo, to bite into a piece of home. This work is about food.

But really, I didn't mean for it to be. In reality, I think I was looking for a safe place to do some healing. I was looking for a way to touch those parts that hurt, that confused me, that made me feel lost. Food helped create a buffer zone between the hurt and me, a bridge to myself. To my stories. To my pain. To my family. To their stories. I don't know if there would have been another way to tell this story if it hadn't been around food. That's the guiding star of this project. It was not a career move (although later it became one for sure), but it truly began as a way to heal. The Karla who started this project is not the Karla who finished this book.

Back then, I was crying a lot, feeling a lot. Beating myself up to be a certain way, to look a certain way, to sound a certain way, to speak Spanish more of the time than English—all in an effort to feel some sense of belonging. This agony was the tether to home that I didn't realize was all I needed to let me know who I was. When my grandmother passed, I could not stand it; I had lost my citizenship to the only place that mattered.

When I returned to El Salvador as a seventeen-year-old, I hoped to feel some belonging. But I didn't find that. It was the proverbial quest to find home, but it left me with more questions, ambiguities, and distance than I'd hoped for. Still, I held on to those memories—fervently, because they were tokens that told me where I was from.

When I went to El Salvador again, this time to do research for *SalviSoul,* it was a different story, thank goodness. But during the days leading up to my trip, I waited for anxiety and panic to find me. I was ready for the other shoe to drop, but nothing happened. I even went into a desperate period of cleaning and organizing my home because I felt that if anxiety were to descend, it would at least find me busy.

These butterflies of nervousness showed up for a moment at the airport gate in El Salvador. But the minute I stepped out of the airport that evening, the breezes that greeted me were warm and inviting, welcoming me home. The air smelled like tamales de elote—so delicious. I felt like biting into the fragrant air around us. I felt so good. I thought, *I am home. I belong here.* All I really experienced was an abundance of love, serenity, and peace.

Perhaps for some folks, El Salvador is of no consequence; it is a small place in this world, a tiny corner. But it's been the biggest question in my life. I am from a captivating place. And I've been captivated ever since.

Flor de izote petals bought at Mercado Dueñas.

WELCOME TO SALVISOUL

Bus stop on route to Mercado
Dueñas in Santa Tecla.

I turned to my grandmother first because she wanted to share her knowledge of El Salvador's food culture with me. While she chopped radishes and let meat sizzle, her memories filled the kitchen stronger than any seasoning. As she offered anecdotes about her childhood and surviving the war, her heartaches and laughter were laid out on the cutting board. It quickly became clear that my recipe documentation would have to be bigger than any dish.

Later, when I was in cooking school, a classmate asked our instructor, "Why do we use French words like *omelette* and *sauté*?" Our instructor's response changed me forever: "It must be because the French were the first to document that technique." Documentation is power. It affords permanence and ubiquity. In countries such as El Salvador, many recipes have not yet had the chance to be definitively named, categorized, and documented because of such events as war and family separation.

Food is an anchor and safety net when documentation, distance, and language are challenges. This book was born from my upbringing and from being a witness to my family's survival and efforts to build a new life in the United States, all the while passing on what they remembered of their war-torn home. Since food is one of the vessels by which identity is formed, documenting these foodways guarantees access to the culture and cuisine for future generations.

The initial task that began in my family's kitchen has grown into SalviSoul, which encompasses both this cookbook and a platform for multimedia storytelling. Our mission to document Salvadoran cooking continues to grow and now includes a plethora of Salvadoran women who are entrepreneurs, community leaders, and expert cooks. This project is rooted in recipes, but these women and their stories of resilience are the key ingredients. Without the custom of oral storytelling and these women practicing their foodways on a daily basis, Salvadoran cuisine and knowledge would not be able to flourish the way it does in North America.

Why is it so hard to find Salvadoran narratives and even harder to find Salvadoran recipes?

As I've unpacked this question, I've come to accept that the Salvadoran community is still healing and trying to move forward from long episodes of imperialism, poverty, and post–civil war consequences. The road to documenting our culture will be long. However, the sacrifices of our mothers and fathers have forged a unique point in our history. My generation wants things to be different. We want to remember, and we want to cement who we are in this digital era. We want to tell our stories.

Now, when I ask my mother for her recipes, her response is different. She makes time for me to ask questions and request clarification; she even allows me to record her consejos, recetas, and tips. When I asked her recently why she thought my documentation was important, she replied, "Bueno, es importante, porque todo tiene raíz, y tu raíz es tu existir. Entender tu raíz es entender tu existir." (It's important, because everything has a root. Having a root means you exist. Understanding your roots is understanding why you exist.)

This book is a way to include more people in the conversation and to continue the tradition of food, family, and storytelling around the table. It reflects the stories, culture, and love passed down to me as an immigrant kid trying to figure out my own identity and place, and—most of all—who we are. Everyone in my family has a sister: my mom, my tía, my cousin, my grandmas, my dad, and my grandpa. In the way that things worked, I saw that sisters stay together—at least the sets of sisters I grew up with. They were compatriotas. The friend you'd always have,

Storefront in Plaza Central in Santiago de María, Usulután.

for better or worse. I think losing my grandmother hurt so much because she was my sister in a way and also because she was my friend. She could have been any way she wanted, but she treated me like a friend at a time when making friends was hard and my relationship with my mom was difficult.

Growing up, my mother intimidated me. I feel like I've often heard this dynamic around immigrant kids and their mothers—that mothers are a force to be reckoned with. Their survival required a level of grit to which I (we) couldn't relate. Their traumas and life-coping mechanisms separated us and got in the way of a more tender mother-daughter relationship. My mother was brash, strong, and strict, and if you were looking for her soft side, you were not going to find it. This has now changed. She is a much gentler person from what I remember. But when I was a child, an adolescent, and even a young adult in my twenties, my relationship with my mother required me to make room for *her*, not the other way around.

My grandmother was different. She made time for me. Her greetings were always sweet and loving. Once I remember her calling me her tamalito, her little tamale. As a chubby fifth grader, I thought her nickname for me was cute. I think that's why I've become obsessed with making relationships with women, particularly in the kitchen. My grandmother was a bridge to my homeland, to my own mother, and to the female relationships I wanted to experience as a young person.

Even though I was afraid of my mother, I admired her so much. I distinctly remember the times when I saw her standing in front of the congregation at our church in Pico-Union and being fully herself. I had always heard in church that women were not supposed to preach, be seen, or be leaders, but there were times when announcements were made and my mom would rise, wearing her superfly outfit. Strutting in high heels, a tight pencil skirt, and a button-up shirt, with her hair done, makeup on, and jewelry on display, she looked completely proud, unapologetically feminine, and fierce. Seated in the pew, I'd look up at her from my awkward teenage self, and I couldn't see myself in her. I felt as if I could never be like her. But now I am following in her footsteps. For years, she organized women's retreats for the church we attended as a family. For decades, she counseled women that it was healthy to leave their family responsibilities for just one weekend and take care of themselves.

There was no proverbial fireplace, but whenever and wherever these women gathered, there was the feeling of sitting down, paying attention, and learning. I lived for that! I wanted to learn their stories, to belong to that women's space. To be feminine and fierce felt one and the same. There is something so unique about the chambre among women when we tell our stories, make our judgments, and cackle, all the while making something yummy. I wanted to re-create that in this book.

The Women of SalviSoul

My eyes opened. I felt my cozy, fuzzy blankets beneath my sleepy eight-year-old body. I could make out the soft, gentle hum of a guitar strumming and sweet Spanish lyrics. The stereo was on.

What is this? What time is it? I wondered. *Why is music blasting from the living r—?* Before I could finish my thought, the answer came to mind. It was Saturday. My mom cleans on Saturday mornings and, by the looks of it, it was almost afternoon. I jumped out of bed, quickly brushed my teeth, changed out of my camisón, and quietly rushed to the living room. Stepping out, ready to look like I had been awake all morning, I heard the lyrics that had awoken me finally come into focus.

"Suena una guitarra cada día . . ." (A guitar sounds every day . . .)

Street vendor selling fresco de ensalada, a beverage made from tropical fruits.

I saw my mom at the sink in the kitchen. To my relief, she hadn't noticed me yet, and she was in good spirits, singing along. If this song was playing, she was feeling light and happy. I was safe from a regañada, a scolding. Phew!

She loves this song, I thought. She once told me it was her favorite because it was the hit song when she was a teenager. I think she must have heard it when she was in love with some young man back in El Salvador, which is why she'd become so happy. It's a romantic song, a love song.

"Cada vez que sonríes, late mi corazón." (Every time you smile, my heart beats.)

It is so sweet and innocent. And it's how I see my mom. She *is* sweet and carries this innocence that I've never seen anywhere else, even though she is also a force to be reckoned with. She survived a civil war that took the lives of many of her friends and neighbors and gave her a childhood consumed with fear, violence, death, and constant anxiety. She survived migration as a refugee to North America, wherein she sacrificed her only home for her future and left behind all the things that made up her life. She had seen so many scary things, experienced deep fear and persecution, and yet there she was, singing in the kitchen. She was singing because of her memories. Wearing her Saturday clothes, she gently swayed to the beat of the song. Shifting her weight from hip to hip, with a little tap of her toes.

"Escucha mi canción, nace del corazón. No sé si te das cuenta, que te quiero. No sé si me comprendes de verdad. No sé si me comprendes de verdad." (Hear my song, it comes from the heart. I don't think you realize that I love you. I don't think you truly understand me. I don't think you truly understand me.)

Through my eight-year-old eyes, her singing meant that I was off the hook. Now, through my adult eyes, her singing means so much more. It means perseverance, resistance, and love, in spite of the many nasty things that life threw at her. In this memory of my mom, she never turned to look at me, but that wasn't the point. She is the woman who carried me across countries. She is the woman who raised me, who loved me, who fought with me, and who definitely called me greñuda, messy hair, desordenada, unorganized, and, every now and again, huevona, lazy, but she is my mami, mi amor.

When I hear this song, I think of my mom only in this way. Whatever association she has between it and a young man or her youth in El Salvador, it's now my love song to her. It's in this unique place of overwhelming love, mixed with gratitude, inspiration, and a touch of sadness, that *SalviSoul* was born. It fills me up inside. It feels like melancholy, a space where my childhood memories live. And in them, my parents are sharing their stories, and so their memories now become my stories. In listening to these memories, I've learned how to live.

They've shaped me, taught me how ugly life can be and how precious it is all at the same time, and that it's always worth fighting for. My mom singing, in spite of all life's efforts to silence her, is proof of that. *SalviSoul* is where together we learn to appreciate those love songs and recipes passed on to us.

SalviSoul was an Instagram account and a website, but not yet this book. Even though my goal was to ultimately publish a cookbook, I knew I had no way of making it happen in the immediate future. This is why I went to my grandmother. She was Mamá Lucy. When I was in elementary school, she worked as a costurera, a garment worker. I don't remember what her working conditions were like in that factory, only that some of my happiest memories happened there after school. The building was across from my school, Hoover Street Elementary, which I attended from the third to fifth grades because the private school I was going to became too expensive for my family. This school was so close to my grandmother's workplace that the factory became my makeshift after-school program. I remember climbing the stairs from the back of the building. She had a sewing machine in the right corner of the room, next to a large window. There were no toys. In my backpack, I had only my school supplies, homework, and whatever else made it in there when I was eight. But I learned to create my own toys in that factory.

Using discarded pieces of cloth and loose threads, I would make dolls. The factory also threw out the cardboard rolls that the thread was spun on, and I'd find different sizes of spools and imagine them as different characters. From the multicolored threads on the floor, I would fashion makeshift wigs for my dolls. Then I sometimes drew on the cardboard to give them faces, but not all the time, since I knew they were trash; they would all be swept up and dumped into the garbage bins that night. My grandmother knew I'd play with these things, and I think she was glad that I could entertain myself while she finished her work shifts. At home, four different families lived in the house we rented. At one point there were at least fourteen of us, so peace and quiet were scarce. Those moments at the factory were like gold to me.

It was on the playground at the school that I realized that I did not belong. Someone asked us as a group where we were all born. I knew that my answer was not going to be like theirs. I was not born at Mount Sinai or at Los Angeles General—instead, it was at El Seguro Social in San Salvador, Apopa, to be precise. I learned that this kind of answer invited other kinds of questions, like "Does this mean you're a wetback?" "Is your family here?" "Do you have a green card?"

Which, at that time, I did not. But in that factory, I had my own space to decompress as a kid. I didn't have to do homework. I didn't have to keep a vigilant eye on intrusive questions that I perhaps wasn't prepared to answer. In that factory, I had time to play, and that was what I will forever associate with my grandmother. Among the chaos of a young immigrant family coming to a new country, she created pockets of peace for me. Pockets of play. Pockets of laughter. Pockets of ease. In some ways, *SalviSoul* is a playground I've made for myself now—a safe place to explore so many things that before were too scary or overwhelming to poke at.

As I matured, this is also why it pained me to know how much my grandmother had suffered in this life. Her suffering was because of my grandfather, whom I'd been raised to love and protect. My love for him, although she supported it, felt like a betrayal to her. Asking my grandmother to contribute to this book was an obvious place to start. I remember exactly where I was. We were in my car. My husband was driving, and my cousin Luis was sitting behind him. I was in the passenger seat and Mamá Lucy was behind me. I gave her the very first *SalviSoul* pitch. This was, of course, before I had a name and a fleshed-out concept for my book. But my grandmother understood immediately, even without many details. She said, "Claro que sí entiendo esto se trata del legado de la mujer Salvadoreña." (Of course I understand, this is about the legacy of Salvadoran women.) She was a humble woman who had gone only as far as second grade in school, then dedicated herself to work and her family. I understood that *SalviSoul* was not only about documenting her food but also preserving her legacy.

In one of my interviews with her, Mamá Lucy had just left the hospital, and it was raining. We were alone in her living room when she began to tell me about her life— her loves, her pains, her sorrows. There came a time when I could no longer bear the pain I felt for her. I didn't want to cry in front of her, so I told her, "Mamá, I'm going to make you some tea. Stay here, I'll be right back." I went to the kitchen, began making the tea, and felt my emotion subside when I heard the soft shuffle of her feet and the glide of her oxygen tank coming closer to me. Momentarily, I felt frustrated because I had told her to wait in the living room. Then Mamá Lucy quietly said, "Wait, I forgot to tell you why I did everything I did, why I endured so much. I did everything for progress, hija. The progress of my family." Although it hurts me so much for her not to see the book that she helped me start, Mamá Lucy already did her part, and now it's my turn.

I started this project because I was afraid of losing my connection to my homeland and my roots. I had seen what could happen to country folk who would assimilate and se perdian, as my family would say—get lost. Those words haunt me. I don't want to *be* lost. It felt like we were already lost, being so far from our homeland, and for an anxious kid like me, to lose yourself in an identity that wasn't even your own was all I needed to feel spooked. So I began from a place

Pupusodromo El Triángulo in Olocuilta, a shop famous for their comal pupusas.

of fear, and I continued the project because of my fear of losing my grandmother forever. Her health was progressively worsening by the time I quit my job to work on this book.

Mamá Lucy was my first interview for this book, and she took the idea that I felt no one was going to understand or care about very seriously and she not only gave me permission to dream it but she shared it with me and helped me cultivate the confidence to start. Because of her, I had the courage to leave a job to pursue this project and dedicate myself to interviewing and learning about other Salvadoran women. After my first interview with my grandmother, it felt necessary to keep finding women who had been practicing these foodways for decades and to create a platform where they could share their own stories and recipes. So I went to the internet. It was the easiest way to find the people who, like me, had also looked for a Salvadoran cookbook and couldn't find it.

In October 2017, one week after I had left my job, I put out a call for interviews.
I made a flyer in a Microsoft Word document (what did we do before Canva?) and
decided to post it all around town, or at least all around the internet. I posted
on Twitter, Instagram, Facebook, and YouTube. I filmed a video so people could
see my face. It felt important that they hear my case and see it was coming from
someone real, from a Salvadoreña who wanted to do something about this lack
of voice in the cookbook publishing world.

I cannot express this enough: I have moved *SalviSoul* forward primarily on the
belief that this work is important and that it must live out loud. I did not know
what would catch me if it didn't work. Imagine a ladder: all the rungs I could see
were only the ones my hands were on, and as I reached out, I only hoped something would be there.

Here is what this has meant to me: I've had to evolve to finish this, to understand
my grief, and to explore my emotional life around womanhood and my family.
I started this as a granddaughter who grew up in the shadow and strength of
her matriarchs. Now I am a matriarch myself, a keeper of our stories, a keeper of
our ways. Someone who, like my Mamá Lucy, gives a feeling of belonging. Who
is strong because she was strong. Who is kind because she was kind. Who says
"no jodas" when chided about something because she did the same.

I don't have children of my own, but I don't need to be a mother to be a matriarch.
I have their language of endurance in these stories, recipes, and foodways. Here
are women who survived, who loved, who laughed, and who made fortifying,
soulful food.

The Stories and Recipes

There are thirty-three stories of Salvadoreñas in *SalviSoul*. How each one came
to be in the book is a tale in itself, and the process was an organic one. First,
in meeting with these women, I learned not to have an agenda, or even a set of
questions—just curiosity. I have seen the emotional cost of interviewing my own
family members about their traumatic experiences. I never wanted to take anything from these ladies; I wanted only to offer them the space to share. There were
times when their own grown children suggested that I ask about particular stories; but when I did, I quickly learned those were sore spots meant only for family.
I respected those boundaries. These matriarchs taught me not to pay attention
to any suggestions from anyone else but instead to listen only to the storyteller.
Their stories belonged to them alone, and I was going to get only what they felt
like sharing. I enjoyed this a lot; it felt like a new movie was being played every
single time and I was just along for the ride.

In these sessions, we chatted for hours. Sometimes I spent a whole afternoon or even an entire day with the women and their families. These were beautiful times that I will never forget. For that, I am eternally grateful, and they've all changed me for the better—no doubt about it. From there, I would listen to my recordings, then transcribe and translate some of the pieces that jumped out at me. Vivid images sprang up in my mind as I listened to the women recount their experiences, and it became exciting to write down their stories and try to capture scenes of what happened. *Chispas* is what I called them later, sparks. There were moments when obvious sparks would fly, and these were the ones that I chased as stories for this book.

I am not telling any of the women's entire life stories. I am giving you only a glimpse, mere sneak peeks that teach us something about living, humanity, love, or loss—and just a moment to see the women as they were in those moments. These stories were not curated to impress any reader or even to fit a genre but only to express the essence of each individual. Some stories have nothing to do with the recipes contributed; some do, but it's a small percentage. The reason is simple: it's the most organic approach. The recipes sometimes served as the crank in a children's jack-in-the-box toy; the lid would pop open and the memory would spring out. These stories are the soul of the book and the reason I would linger at the dining room table with these women.

I am related to six of the women. They are my great-grandmother Mamá Juana, my grandmother Mamá Lucy, my mother Teresa, and my tías Patricia, Morena, and Estela. Then, there are the Salvadoreñas I met because of my circle of friends and family. They are Laura, Maria, Carmen, Rosa Elvira, Suyapa, and Marta Rosa. And finally, there are the women I met online: Ruth, Estelita, Zoila, Bartola, Maricela, Isabel, Carolina, Wendy, Miriam, and Gabby.

When I started this project, I was often told that publishers wouldn't take an interest because this was a compilation type of cookbook, and those don't sell well. While I understood this concern, I saw this trait as a great asset. This is the first exclusively Salvadoran cookbook published by a major publisher in the United States of America. It only feels right that the people guiding us and making the proper introductions are the women who have devoted decades of their lives to cooking these foods for their loved ones in several countries: their homeland and their new home in the United States. Congregating these experts in one physical kitchen would be impossible, but here in this book, the expertise, knowledge, and technology they've kept practicing in their own kitchens are what makes these pages immeasurably important and valuable.

SALVADORAN FOODWAYS

Local panadería in Santiago de María, Usulután.

It was March 2014, and we were at the Los Angeles Central Library. I didn't know exactly where to tell my boyfriend, my now husband, we were starting our search. One of us decided that this library's history department was as good a place as any. He lunged forward, grabbing both sides of the moving handrails, and swung his legs down the escalator while mouthing a silent *woohoo!* I could tell that he felt a curious urgency too. We were both powered by an impulse to find out what we could about the history of Salvadoran food.

Searching the aisles, we found books on other topics within Mesoamerican history. Most of them were written by historians and archaeologists with European-sounding names, and none of them contained research on food. I told the librarian that I was looking for information on ingredients or cooking techniques—anything about culinary history from El Salvador. She clicked around on her computer, disappeared into a back room for about three minutes, and then returned with a determined look on her face. She typed many things into her computer. Finally, she turned her head toward us and said, "Well, it appears that if you want a book about the history of food in El Salvador, you're going to have to write it yourself."

Salvadoran Food History, a Personal Pilgrimage

All my curiosity about Salvadoran recipes eventually led me to a pilgrimage of my own. While I already knew that I would eventually return to El Salvador at some point in this journey, I realized that I could not rely on a secondary relationship with the country of my birth. For my own sake, my own healing, and my own identity, I needed to choose what kind of woman I wanted to be. *Heritage* is sometimes a word that rubs me the wrong way. It feels passive, dormant, like an inherited relic that I take out for the holidays. I don't want to interact with Salvadoran culture in that way. I have made a choice to constantly be at El Salvador's doorstep to learn, question, and observe. Obviously, my vantage point will always be informed by my being raised in the United States, which makes me aware of certain privileges for which I am responsible, especially when considering the nature of the United States' involvement in Salvadoran history and politics. So when I traveled back to El Salvador, I went with a specific intention to sit at the feet of the culture and let it inform my work, just like I sat at the feet of my grandmother.

One of the places I thank my lucky stars that I got to experience was the Museo Nacional de Antropología, or National Museum of Anthropology (also called MUNA). I first heard about this institution from an Instagram follower on the SalviSoul page. They mentioned that an exhibit on Salvadoran gastronomy was happening, and I immediately knew that I would have to see it. How I eventually got to the museum, met the curator, and even had a private audience with the staff turned out to be very serendipitous.

Around my third day in the country and prior to this museum visit, I met with some editors from a publishing house in San Salvador. As we were saying our goodbyes, they happened to ask what was next on my schedule that day. I mentioned MUNA. They laughed and said, "That's where we are going too! To talk to the curator of the gastronomy exhibit." It was a wonderful feeling to discover this shared interest. Once we all arrived at the museum, I took a few minutes to walk through the exhibit while we waited for the curator. I found myself simply overwhelmed by gratitude to be exactly where I was. For years, I had been talking about Salvadoran cuisine, how worthwhile it was to study, and how important it was to document these foodways. Now I was standing in a room that uplifted that very cause.

As I strolled through the exhibit, I recalled my experiences of looking for books at the library and doing searches on Salvadoran gastronomy, only to be shown results about Spanish artist Salvador Dalí, or, at best, the cuisine of Salvador, Brazil. I kept thinking that perhaps I wasn't the best at researching, but after years of this, I came to understand that Salvadoran knowledge was simply not

View of Volcan de Usulután on the way to Santiago de María.

as accessible. One vivid memory is of sharing this frustration with someone, and their trying to comfort me by suggesting that I just needed to travel to El Salvador to do the research. I am privileged to now have the documentation required to go back and forth, but at one point in my life, this travel was impossible. Some Salvadorans can never return to their homeland.

I was deep in a pool of these memories and feelings when finally I heard the editors say, "Hay viene, la doctora. Dr. Claudia Moisa." I turned around with tears already welling up in my eyes. I had no words to express my gratitude to her. Another Salvi food–obsessed Salvadoreña. The editors saw my emotional response and got teary-eyed themselves. Soon a cryfest of Salvadoran people finding one another ensued as we realized how much we valued our roots and our history. I finally gained some composure as Dr. Moisa began talking about the uphill battle that creating the exhibit had been. It was like the saying, "Birds of a feather flock together." After I shared with her about how my research on Salvadoran food was always coming up short, she validated my experience by telling us that that was very common and that, unfortunately, the organizers needed more funding to continue this work.

We embraced one another and then the editors and I started our private tour of the exhibit. This is where I learned more about one of El Salvador's most important archaeological treasures, La Joya de Cerén, also known as the Pompeii of America. Similar to Pompeii, this farming community was buried under fourteen layers of ash when the Laguna Caldera volcano erupted circa AD 600. Because the exceptional conditions and the ash perfectly preserved the buildings, remnants, and culture, it left clues for archaeologists, and us, about what Central American populations were eating at the time.

According to archaeologists, the evidence suggests that the eruption happened during a major cultural celebration, but that it wasn't a violent event, like Pompeii, because people had time to leave. The remnants revealed their diet: archaeologists found fruit trees, edible plants, animals, certain species of fish, cacao, maíz, yuca, beans, and chiles. An interesting tidbit was that there was no evidence of a comal, which has been traditionally used to this day to cook tortillas. Most of the maíz foods were atoles, or tamales. In one of the fogónes, or fire pits, inside a building that could have been a kitchen, archaeologists found baskets with beans, squash, chiles, painted morro shells, tools made from bones, and even the remains of grilled mice.

Walking deeper into the exhibit, Dr. Moisa talked about the importance of maíz for the Nahuat Pipil community, the Indigenous people who lived in what we now refer to as the nation-state of El Salvador. Their diverse diet included many staples that modern-day Salvadorans still consume, like squash, cacao, tamales, and even cusuco, or armadillo. I was always told yuca was not from Mesoamerica, but Dr. Moisa pointed to artifacts and photos that proved otherwise.

In garbage found in Ciudad Vieja, which was established in 1528 and is another Salvadoran archaeological site, more clues and influences inform us about the mestizaje of Salvadoran cuisine, including how pork, beef, and chicken were among the first animal proteins introduced to the diet. Meats such as dog, rabbit, deer, turkey, and frogs were also found, as well as catfish and crustaceans.

Further into the exhibit, we learned about the merchant ships that traveled to and from the port of Acajutla on the coast. These ships brought goods such as porcelain, crystal, textiles, and spices from Asia, Africa, and Europe. Citrus, wheat, barley, sugarcane, onions, garlic, cinnamon, nutmeg, rice, mangoes, and plantains also came in through that port. And from Mesoamerica to the world, there was pineapple, maíz, sweet potato, papaya, guavas, yuca, avocado, squash, tomato (my absolute favorite food in the world), and chiles. Suffice it to say that by the end of our hour-long visit, I was swimming in a whole new sense of wonder, gratitude, information, and happiness—and I was completely blissed out. As I said my goodbyes to the editors and the curator, we all knew something special had just happened. When I exited, I noticed one last panel graphic. It was the conclusion to the exhibit, named *Gastronomia Salvadoreña, Una Fiesta de Sentidos*, or *Salvadoran Gastronomy, a Party of the Senses*. The last paragraph of text summed up what was an exquisite experience learning about my roots and what this book is all about:

"La gastronomía es la resistencia de las costumbres y prácticas que niegan en desvanecerse . . . la gastronomía es la memoria traducida en sabores, colores y olores." (Gastronomy is the resistance of customs and practices that refuse to fade . . . gastronomy is memory translated into flavors, colors, and smells.)

The Salvadoran Kitchen

Whether bouillon or broth comes in the form of Knorr powder, cubitos, or liquid concentrate, the use of prepared soup seasoning in Salvadoran cooking is highly common. Sometimes it's brought up with shame and embarrassment in hushed whispers. I once chatted about the topic of cooking with a Latina señora who was not Salvadoran. We had finished talking when she added, "Yo no uso esas cosas como el cubito. Yo cocino natural." She prided herself on being someone who did not use Knorr or bouillon cubes and relied only on fresh ingredients. I didn't press the issue with her, but I point this out because a lot of stigma is associated with

using this ingredient, and often the people who carry this burden are women. I find it immensely unfair.

When I went to cooking school, it was an unspoken rule: We don't use that dried, granulated chicken-flavored powder with its addictive, well-rounded flavor notes of MSG umami, salt, and acid. Mostly, I found that homemade chicken or vegetable broth was used in place of prepared bouillon. But such bouillon is a quick, effective way to add flavor to meals and often the secret ingredient that many matriarchs share with those who want to know. But it can also be used as another way to shame people who have experienced poverty. While most of the women in this book have endured poverty and are now financially better off, they still use this ingredient in their kitchens today because it's a nostalgic food ritual.

Most of the recipes in this book were developed and documented with these SalviSoul participants, and this is their space, so we've chosen to use powdered or cube bouillon throughout. Feel free to replace the combination of water and bouillon with your preferred broth or stock. If you make it from scratch, that's amazing. But using a shortcut makes it easier, relatively low-cost, flavorful, and delicious.

Ana Concepción del Valle de López, owner of Sopa de Patas La Tía in Mercado Tinetti, well known by locals for their sopa de patas.

The Foundational Base

At cooking school, I learned about mirepoix, the foundational base of French cooking that is made up of onions, carrots, and celery. It got me thinking about whether there was a similar foundation for Salvadoran food. Then I realized it was tomato, onion, and chile verde (green bell pepper)—the basic sofrito. It was one of those things that just made me feel silly for not recognizing it before.

Apart from these foundations, Salvadoran cuisine is very vegetable-forward and likes to hang out in the form of many tart, sour, and funky flavors. There is also an appreciation for bitterness—this can make it an acquired taste that you wouldn't ever think to disguise or remove; it's very "if you know, you know." I once told my mom that I was trying to make a dish with pacaya, an edible flower native to El Salvador, but that I was going to figure out how to make it less bitter. She got so offended. "Why would you do that? Then you can't taste the pacaya!" she responded. Some edible flowers are so perishable that they can be consumed only in El Salvador, but six popular ones in the cuisine are available to the diaspora. They include flor de izote, pacaya, chufles, lorocos, pitos, and flores de ayote. They can often be found in the freezer section in Central American markets or Latino stores. I have often been able to find them fresh from local street vendors in Los Angeles.

Vegetarian Habits

The common narrative that Salvadoran cuisine is very meat-forward simply isn't true. But to be honest, I don't think I started hearing that false portrayal until my early twenties. In fact, I grew up hearing stories that most of the country relied on vegetarian staples for daily sustenance. Although I don't know precisely what eating habits were like before the war, from what I've been told, most folks hit hard times and consumed verduras, monte, frijoles, and tortillas. If they were fortunate enough to afford meat or dairy, it was a treat. Not only does this mean that Salvadoran cuisine is flexible but also that there is an appetite for vegetable-forward meals. Salvadorans need no convincing to see the benefit—it's evident in our history.

Beans

When I refer to beans in this book, I'm referring to frijoles Salvadoreños, also known as frijoles rojos de seda, or, in English, red silk beans. They are not to be mistaken for red kidney beans, the texture and consistency of which will not render the same results as frijoles Salvadoreños. However, black beans come close and are the second-best choice. They can be used interchangeably for some recipes, although the flavors will not be quite the same. Frijoles Salvadoreños are very special. I have relatives who bring back pounds of them from family in El Salvador, and they're always a welcome gift.

As for methods to cook beans, I have tried many. There are those who soak the beans, and those who never soak them. I grew up only having to sort through the beans and then dump them straight into a pot to cook. It is important to soak older beans; soaking affects their cooking time and prevents them from bursting through their delicate skins. Often with dried beans, you may not know how old they are, so that will affect the amount of cooking time. If you are purchasing your beans from the store, the bag may have a best-by date. If you grab from the bulk bin, bank on your cooking time being on the longer side. If you are fortunate enough to have beans straight from El Salvador, I have found them to have the fastest cook time, which I suspect is because they come from the source more quickly than an imported brand. Here in Los Angeles, we are fortunate that, sometimes in the El Salvador Corridor around September, you see street vendors who are selling fresh beans picked off the vine in front of you. These are a real treat and the cook time is minuscule compared to that of dried beans.

Some of the recipes in this book require that you use beans that have already been cooked and are sitting in broth. This is because it's very common to cook a pound or two for the week so that food is always at the ready. You can enjoy a whole journey of dishes throughout the life of one pot of beans. Start off with a soup, then use some whole beans for Casamiento (page 59). Use them the next day for Frijoles Amelcochados (page 41). And if you still have some left over and have already planned your meals, you can puree the last bit of frijoles and combine them with ripe plantains for Plátanos Fritos con Frijoles Licuados (page 69). If you still have frijoles licuados by the next day, well then, you can cook those down so they are not as saucy but become like refried beans—perfect for Pupusas de Frijol con Queso (page 98)! Beans just keep on giving.

Frijoles salvadoreños
in a rural house.

Corn

For most of these recipes, when corn masa is being used, I am referring to corn flour that can be rehydrated with water to make tortillas, tamales, and even atoles. Some brands that I have used are Maseca, a very popular staple in many homes; P.A.N., which is seen more in South American homes but is very delicious; and Bob's Red Mill, which is a solid choice. In recent years, I have also bought from Masienda, an heirloom corn and masa harina company that creates beautiful products. What product I'll use often depends on what dish I am preparing,

Street vendor selling nances, semillas de paternas, plantains, and bananas in La Libertad.

so experiment and see what you like. Think of it like wine: Some wines you cook with, some you drink on a Monday after work, and others you enjoy on very special occasions.

Some recipes call for whole dried corn, like Chilate (page 223) or Atol Chuco (page 122), because this is how the recipes were taught to me and I want to respect their integrity. This ingredient can be purchased in most Latin American markets, where it is usually available in bulk bins or barrels.

Oils

Throughout this book, different oils are used. In recipes developed with SalviSoul moms, I have defaulted to the oil they prefer, which is why you'll see such a variety. An oil with a high smoke point is advisable for the many fried dishes included. In most Salvadoran kitchens, vegetable oil is the standard for its comfortable price point.

Relajo

Relajo is a blend of spices and seeds that is toasted, ground, and added to sauces. The word also means "chaos," which I find endearing. So it can be used in a sentence to describe a situation, as in "¡Ay Dios mio, que relajo!" (Oh my God, what chaos!)

Some Salvadoran cooks in this book make their own blends, while others purchase prepackaged versions that are available in Central American and Latin American markets. Such options are labeled "relajo para tamales" or "mezcla para tamales." Of course, using prepackaged relajo blends can lend varying results, or they might not be sold near you. So, for some recipes, I have standardized the ingredient amounts. Typically, you'll find it made with raw white sesame seeds, pepitoria (pumpkin seeds), peanuts, cumin, cloves, oregano, and achiote seeds or powder. I used to wonder if a specific ratio of ingredients was needed in a relajo but have since learned it is all up to the individual cook. I've met cooks who completely bypass the sesame seeds (which for me are indispensable) because the seeds give them heartburn. Some never use cloves; others leave out the oregano. Still others would never think to add achiote. What I do know for sure is that some version of relajo is always present in Salvadoran cooking.

Salsa Inglesa

I once read an article in the *Wall Street Journal* about how salsa Inglesa, also known as salsa Perrins or Worcestershire sauce, became so popular in Salvadoran cuisine. It first arrived in El Salvador in 1912, thanks to trade via the Panama Canal. But it didn't become readily available until the 1950s, and only then because of an FBI agent whose American-born daughter really missed Worcestershire sauce when they moved to El Salvador. The story goes that this agent persuaded different companies to send him the sauce so that he could import and sell it. This is, of course, only one version of history. There is also salsa negra in El Salvador, which is made from fruit and vinegar and is therefore quite different from salsa Inglesa; nonetheless, it is very popular and you will see it used a lot in Salvadoran cooking.

Salvi Spellings

Salvadoran, *Salvadorian*, and even *Salvadorean*—why so many spellings exist to refer to our nationality will always constitute some of the low-hanging-fruit conversation within Salvi circles. As are debates about which one is more "right." For this book, we will be using *Salvadoran*.

This interesting linguistic detail, however, repeats itself in some of our ingredients and many spellings you'll see in the book. For instance, *chuco* versus *shuco*,

CONSEJO

*You may choose
to toast the ingredients
separately. I've done it both ways
and found that as long as you're
right by the stove as you're moving
the spices around on the comal,
you will be able to keep an
eye on them and not let
them burn.*

RELAJO

Set a comal, griddle, or cast-iron skillet over medium-high heat. Once it's hot, sprinkle with a little water to check if it is ready; the water should quickly evaporate. Add the sesame seeds, pumpkin seeds, peppercorns, cumin seeds, oregano, achiote powder, bay leaves, guaque pepper, and cloves and toast until you smell the fragrant spices and see and hear the sesame seeds jumping and popping (the hallmark of relajo getting prepped), about 5 minutes. Transfer to a bowl or plate to cool completely, then transfer to a clean coffee or spice grinder and process into a powder. Store the relajo in an airtight container at room temperature for up to a month.

¼ cup raw white sesame seeds
2 tablespoons raw pumpkin seeds
¼ teaspoon black peppercorns
½ teaspoon cumin seeds
1 teaspoon dried oregano
½ teaspoon achiote powder
3 large dried bay leaves
1 guaque pepper
2 whole cloves

which is a fermented atol. Or *guacal* versus *huacal*, a cooking utensil and vessel made from morro trees. Some of these differences can be attributed to accents or pronunciations from Indigenous groups who lived in what is now recognized as El Salvador. Another reason is due to how Nahuat has been españolizado. In other words, Indigenous languages have been Spanish-ized. I point this out in an effort to make it clear that there are many ways to say or spell certain words.

This book's recipes are meant to be cooked at home to remind us of our mothers and grandmothers. Cooking is not something to be feared. It's not something unattainable, especially in the diaspora. But a recipe is also not meant to replace instinct, experience, family customs, or even intuition. So much of what I've learned about cooking is that nobody can decide for you how you like something. You develop your preferences, and that is probably the most tricky and important thing about cooking.

Fisherman showcasing the catch of the day to customers.

Wholesale tomato vendor in Central San Salvador.

Plastic containers filled with different curtidos and salsas, and an empty sugar container.

Any protagonist worth their salt in a story has a crew, a team, or a sidekick that makes the journey fun and creates memorable value for the lead. The accompaniments in this section do just that for the main meals in the chapters that follow. Curtido brightens the bite of any fried food, rice soaks up any savory sauciness, and tortillas, whether fresh, day-old, or nicely toasted, become a vessel for so many good eats. These accompaniments lend so much value to the main meal that they become just as important.

TORTILLAS SALVADOREÑAS

MAKES 6 TORTILLAS

2 cups masa flour
1 teaspoon kosher salt
2 cups lukewarm
    (about 98°F) water

It's customary to make a stack of fresh tortillas Salvadoreñas at every mealtime, with a few exceptions. For example, it's common to eat tamales with pan francés instead of tortillas. In my family, a person could eat three or four tortillas each, if not more. I always like to use a manta, or kitchen towel, to keep the masa covered while I'm making the tortillas. It's what I was taught, especially if you're making many of them; if your masa is sitting without a cover, it dries out.

For tortillas Salvadoreñas, prepare to make a thicker tortilla. It eats more like a flatbread; think naan. But to call it just a thicker version of something else, though, is a travesty. It would be like calling a French roll the same thing as a baguette—it's technically the same but different. The eating experience is more nuanced. It's also a rite of passage—albeit often a gendered one. As illustrated in some of the stories by the SalviSoul moms, making a Salvadoran tortilla is as important as knowing the geography of where El Salvador is.

Personally, I can't put away more than two. Toast one up real good, low and slow, until the color on the edges has darkened and scraping it with a fork makes that scratchy, crisp sound. Sprinkle it with a pinch of salt, and it's good enough to satisfy any hungry belly. It's also been a beacon of strength for many Salvadorans who suffered wartimes with little or no food. For those who could not afford meat or even frijoles, it was "por lo menos, hay tortillas"—(at least, there are tortillas).

Some places in El Salvador, like Santa Ana and La Unión, offer different versions, and employ expert tortilla makers who can make thin versions without a tortilla press. These are as thin as fabric but still quite large. Another variety that is mentioned in the following story is called a chenga, which is made in cafetales, or coffee haciendas, where the workers were often fed these large, plate-size tortillas. In my family, the standard for tortilla making was my great-grandmother Mamá Juana. She had an even tempo and incredible muscle memory; her tortillas were perfectly circular and uniformly thick.

•

In a large bowl, using the tips of your fingers, gently combine the masa flour and salt. Gradually pour in 1 cup of the water. Using your hands, thoroughly mix the water with the dry ingredients. Slowly add the remaining 1 cup water and keep mixing until the dough reaches the consistency of Play-Doh. It should feel cool to the touch and evenly moist throughout. Cover with a manta and set aside.

Set a comal or griddle over medium-high heat. Once it's hot, sprinkle with a little water to check if it is ready; the water should quickly evaporate. Turn the heat to medium.

Fill a small bowl with water. Separate the dough into six golf ball–size portions, 3 to 4 ounces each. Roll them into balls and dip the fingertips of both hands into the water and raise them upward, allowing the water to drip down and spread across both of your palms.

Take out one ball and cover the remaining dough with the towel to keep it from drying out. Center the dough ball in the palm of your nondominant hand and secure it by cupping your hand. Using only the fingers of your dominant hand, pat the ball into a disk that is ¼ inch thick and about 5 inches wide. Gradually uncup your hand until it is flat, and rotate the disk as the dough flattens out. Once you've patted down the dough, rotate the tortilla upward so it's standing on the palm of your hand. Using the index finger on your dominant hand, smooth out the rounded edges of the tortilla, which should be as evenly thick and round as possible.

Carefully place the tortilla flat on the comal and let cook for about 5 minutes on each side. Turn the heat to medium-low so the tortilla doesn't get too toasted on one side. Using a spatula or your hand, turn the tortilla over. When it puffs up, it is finished cooking. Repeat for the five remaining dough balls, keeping an eye on the heat and adjusting it so that the comal never gets so hot that it burns your tortillas or so low that the tortillas take too long to cook.

Transfer the finished tortillas to a basket and cover with a manta to keep warm before serving.

Left: Prepared masa for tortillas on a piedra para moler, an ancient tool for grinding nixtamalized corn. *Right:* Typical scene during sunset in Barrio Santa Anita in San Salvador.

LA NIÑA EVA

Three tortillas per employee. With the caporales and all the campesinos, including los cipotes, that would come to at least six hundred tortillas to make a day. Between Niña Eva and the rest of the women who worked in la cocina, Juana thought they might be able to handle it. Well, they *had* to handle it, no había de otra. There wasn't an alternative or choice. This was Juana's job, and she was grateful.

If Niña Eva hadn't asked Juana about joining the kitchen at the finca, Juana wasn't sure what she would have done. The pay for working the fields was not enough, and the labor was brutal. So many mornings, with the complete exhaustion Juana felt, she couldn't get out of bed. Some days she managed to go to work despite her fevers and sickness. She knew the truth: if you didn't show up, you wouldn't get paid. Or worse, their housing would be compromised. The one perk of the job was housing, and her body was the currency she paid for her family's survival. She knew that, so she was diligent.

Despite her small frame, she was strong and still young, just forty years old. She lifted her cobijas off, swung her legs from the bed, and slowly called on her body to help her through. If the burden of the work didn't kill her, the stress of surviving would. She worked because it helped her feed her grandchildren. When the physical toll of the labor kept her in bed, her grandson volunteered to take her place in the fields. "No, Mamá Juana, no se levante yo le voy a hacer la tarea," Javier would say to his grandmother. (I will go in place of you.)

"I'm here for my grandmother because she is sick," he'd say to the foreman. The foreman would reply, "Esta bien, este es el surco que vas a trabajar," assigning him a furrow to work for the day. If you could strategize your connections or charm the foreman, Juana knew you could win favor with him. But that was a slippery slope she didn't want to entertain. Easy work could be possible, but at what cost?

So she kept working until Niña Eva asked her if she wanted to work in the kitchen. Niña Eva taught Juana the routines that kept everything going in a cocina in a finca. The finca was responsible for feeding everyone who worked the land. The meals were never grand, but they fortified the strength of the workers. Sometimes thick tortillas were made for the campesinos, who each received three every day. Other times, the mujeres made chengas, a different variety of tortilla that was sometimes more than a foot long. They used them as plates and served frijoles on top of them.

Sometimes the day started at two in the morning. Getting the fire started was first on the list of to-dos. Then it was preparing a hot dish of avena, oatmeal, for the workers. When that was complete, the prep for the next meal service began, such as finishing the corn that needed to be cooked for the masa. The finca had its own molino, so it could process large amounts of masa for the tortillas. Huge comales were heated to cook the tortillas. Finally, there was the sorting, washing, and cooking of the frijoles for the afternoon. Before they knew it, from the team of mujeres en la cocina came a symphony of *pat, pat, pat, pat, pat* for as long as it took them to finish.

By the afternoon, the tired crowds of campesinos, their kids, and anyone else at the finca would come in to exchange a vale, a voucher, for their serving of food. Juana would spot her grandkids in the crowd talking to the other children of the finca. Muscle memory had gotten her through all the tortilla-making as she ensured their survival for another day.

Older woman making tortillas before lunch hour in Mercado Dueñas.

BASIC OLLA DE FRIJOLES

MAKES 4 TO 8 SERVINGS

1 pound dried frijoles rojos
    de seda, sorted for
    debris and rinsed
½ yellow onion, peeled
6 garlic cloves, peeled and
    left whole
2 dried bay leaves
Kosher salt

A basic pot of beans is crucial in Salvadoran cooking, as it's a foundational ingredient in so many dishes. This is a guide that can lead you to many other recipes, like Casamiento (page 59) or Frijoles Amelcochados (page 41). Cooking times may vary depending on how old the beans are, but most dried beans should be ready in 3 hours (see page 28).

I like to have my pot of beans out on top of the stove so they are at the ready for any meal. To avoid spoiling, I boil the beans twice a day, in the morning and before going to bed, in addition to the times that I heat them up for a meal. You may also choose to cook your beans, allow them to cool, store in an airtight container in the fridge, and then only take out what you will eat, but I find that with this technique, I can't take advantage of the convenience of having food already made on the stovetop.

●

In a large pot over high heat, bring 8 cups of water to a boil. Add the beans, onion, garlic, and bay leaves. Once the beans start to boil, turn the heat to low and let simmer, uncovered, until they become tender, about 3 hours. Check the beans and stir them every 30 minutes, adding more water to cover as needed; do not let them burn.

When the beans are tender, season with salt. Allow them to cook a few minutes longer until they have reached the saltiness that you prefer before serving.

Frijoles nuevos or fresh
Salvadoran beans still
on the vines.

FRIJOLES AMELCOCHADOS

There are so many ways to enjoy frijoles. There are frijoles fritos, licuados, sancochados, maltrajados, guisados, borrachos, sopa de frijoles, and even frijoles Santanecos, but my absolute favorite version is frijoles amelcochados. *Amelcochado* means a lot of things in Spanish, but in this context, it means super-soft, melt-in-your-mouth, saucy frijoles. This method takes the longest to prepare because the best frijoles amelcochados are the ones that have been sitting in their broth for at least a day, if not longer.

In El Salvador, we eat many kinds of beans, but the most popular is frijoles rojos de seda, also known as frijoles Salvadoreños, or red silk beans or Salvadoran beans. It's the standard in most Salvadoran homes. If I'm making beans at my house, ten times out of ten it's going to be frijoles rojos de seda. You can find them at most Latin American markets. If you're lucky enough to have a Central American market near you, especially one that is Salvadoran-specific, you'll probably see a bulk bin full of these beans so you can buy them by the pound, rather than in branded bags. I always keep at least a pound of them in my kitchen.

Since it's common to make a big pot of beans for the week, the cooked frijoles are usually still whole by the third or even fourth day, but because they've been sitting in their own broth, they have become super-soft and creamy. For this recipe, you don't need to wait days to enjoy them, but if you do, it will be so worthwhile.

•

In a large pot over medium heat, warm the neutral oil until it shimmers. Add the tomato, onion, and bell pepper and sauté until they are tender and cooked through, about 2 minutes. Add the beans and their broth. Season with salt and cook until bubbly, about 7 minutes, stirring occasionally to keep the beans from sticking. Turn the heat to medium-low and cook for 5 minutes more before serving.

MAKES 4 SERVINGS

1 tablespoon neutral oil (such as canola oil)
1 medium tomato, chopped
¼ medium red onion, chopped
¼ medium green bell pepper, cored and chopped
1 cup cooked frijoles rojos de seda (see page 27), or black beans, with broth
Kosher salt

CURTIDO

MAKES 1 QUART

The combination of cabbage, onion, carrot, spice, oregano, and vinegar in Salvadoran cuisine is what we lovingly call curtido. The word is derived from *curtir*, meaning "to age," because by the time it's enjoyed, curtido has aged with the help of vinegar or citrus juice. Some describe this accompaniment as a slaw while others compare it to pickles. No matter the name, curtido has a very specific job. Its crunch and hit of acid offer brightness and texture to traditional dishes, like pupusas, pastelitos, yuca frita, and even tamales, but it can also be eaten in salads and in burgers, or by itself as a simple snack.

Methods for preparing curtido vary. Some prepare a hot brine that is poured over the vegetables and spices and allowed to sit for at least an hour after cooling. Others parboil or massage the vegetables with salt and then submerge them in a cold brine mixture. Because the vegetables keep their texture, and their flavor stays bright and punchy, curtido is deeply satisfying on the Salvadoran table.

Here in Ruth's recipe, she massages the vegetables and then adds the remaining ingredients to the mixture. This is the exact technique she and her mother, Delmy, have used for their pupusa stand, Delmy's Pupusas. They were the first to sell pupusas at farmers' markets in Los Angeles.

Curtido is ready to eat shortly after it is made, but like most things, its flavors deepen and develop with time.

1 small or medium head green cabbage, thinly sliced
1½ small red onions, thinly sliced
1½ cups grated carrot
2 tablespoons kosher salt
2 teaspoons dried oregano
2 teaspoons crushed red pepper flakes, or 1 jalapeño chile, halved
2 cups water
1 cup apple cider vinegar

In a large bowl, combine the cabbage, onion, and carrot and mix until thoroughly combined. Set aside.

In a second large bowl, combine the salt, oregano, and red pepper flakes. Stir in the water and apple cider vinegar.

Pour the spiced vinegar mixture over the vegetables and knead until the vegetables have softened, about 5 minutes. Let sit for 10 minutes at room temperature before serving.

Store the curtido in an airtight container in the refrigerator for up to 1 month.

ESCABECHE DE COLIFLOR Y REMOLACHA

MAKES ABOUT 2 PINTS

3 medium beets, peeled
1 tablespoon extra-virgin
   olive oil
1 large head cauliflower,
   cut into 1-inch pieces
2 medium carrots, sliced into
   2-inch-long matchsticks
8 ounces green beans,
   ends trimmed
1 medium white onion,
   quartered
3 fresh bay leaves
1 habanero chile, halved
1 teaspoon black peppercorns
½ teaspoon dried oregano
2 cups water
½ cup apple cider vinegar
1 tablespoon kosher salt
1 teaspoon granulated sugar

This escabeche is something that my grandmother Mamá Lucy made. Over the years of researching Salvadoran cuisine, I have learned that escabeche in El Salvador can be a few things. There is an escabeche escolar that is similar to Curtido (page 43), only with mayonnaise, and it reminds me of coleslaw. This recipe has remolacha, or beets, which gives it a glorious magenta color and sweetness. I grew up eating this as an accompaniment for pupusas—we used it even more than curtido.

Here's the usual way I enjoy it: Armed with a fork in one hand and a piece of remolacha or cauliflower in the other, I take a bite of my food and then chase it with a bit of the escabeche. It perfectly completes any mouthful.

●

In a small pot, combine the beets with enough water to cover. Set over medium-high heat, bring to a boil, and cook until the beets are tender, 30 minutes. Remove from the heat, drain, and allow to cool. Then cut the beets into wedges and set aside.

In a large saucepan over medium heat, warm the olive oil until it shimmers. Turn the heat to low, add the cauliflower, cover, and cook for 7 minutes. Do not allow the cauliflower to brown. Add the carrots, green beans, onion, bay leaves, and habanero and sauté until the vegetables are cooked through, 7 minutes more. Add the peppercorns, oregano, water, apple cider vinegar, salt, sugar, and beets; turn the heat to medium-high; and bring to a boil. Remove the pan from the heat and allow the escabeche to cool before serving.

Store the escabeche with its liquid in a glass jar in the refrigerator for up to 2 weeks.

EL LAZO DE LUCY

There were no preparations. There was no celebration, just one last plea: a wedding before God with family, and a pastor to marry them.

My grandmother, at age seventy-six, days before her death, finally became a wife, taking the name of the man she had been with since she was a teenager. After six decades of partnership with my grandfather and getting bad news from the doctor, it was now or never. It wasn't supposed to be this kind of wedding, though. There were tears, "I love you's," "te amo's," hugs, and smiles, yet this wasn't the wedding my grandmother deserved. But it was what she was getting.

Rushing from my job at the *Los Angeles Times*, I stopped at my apartment, hurried inside, turned on every light I saw, and frantically searched for something. It was from my own wedding years before—a marriage lazo, a symbol of love for eternity. It was still in the little fragile box where I had placed it after I got married. There were three rites that my husband and I had done at our ceremony, but I didn't know which ones could be performed in a hospital room. My grandparents' marriage had been laced with tragedy long before this wedding day. As soon as I grabbed my marriage lazo, I felt foolish. It weighed so heavily in my bag, its presence so loud in the hurried car ride through L.A. evening traffic.

Turning the corner of the hospital hallway, I didn't know what I would find. Would she still be there? There was no alegria, happiness, in the air, just an urgency held together by sorrow. Seeing my grandmother's body on the hospital bed triggered a memory of another time she had lain motionless in front of my grandfather. It was nighttime, and there were no lights on at home. My grandparents had just arrived at the house where I and many of my other family members lived. He was hitting her. I remember seeing her body lying across the black metal-screen front door, her weight pushed against it as my grandfather kicked over and over again and hearing the sound of her striking the door frame again and again. I can still hear her crying, "No, Roberto!"

My grandmother taught me what love was and is, and what it wasn't—and how complicated that can often be. How imperfect, how dark, how light, and how it fills you with joyful laughter sometimes and with anxiety and terror other times.

Now she was wearing white. She looked like a bride, even if it was a white hospital gown and white bedsheets fixed lovingly around her tired body. The nurses, moved by my grandmother and her situation, thought to place small blossoms—baby's breath, I think—in her weak hands. Lucia, or Lucy,

Flor de Izote in a market basket set on the stairs at the entrance of a small home near Volcán de San Salvador.

as everyone affectionately called her, was getting married. Surrounded by family with tired faces riddled with fear and worry. Faking small smiles because this was the day. This was Lucy's long-awaited wedding, the day she finally became a wife.

CHILE CASERO

Even though Salvadoran cuisine isn't known for its spice, this condiment is used by many Salvi cooks. My family often says, "Voy hacer un chile para tener más hambre." (Let's make a chile so that we can be more hungry.) It opens up your appetite and makes eating even more enjoyable. This chile recipe is by my mother, Teresa. Often requested by our family, it's never missing from the table, especially if there is a sopa on the menu. Its spicy kick and brightness lift all the earthy flavors in such soups as Arroz Aguado con Carne de Tunco (page 153) or even Sopa de Frijoles con Masitas (page 150).

●

In a small bowl, combine the onion, chiles, lemon juice, and salt. Mix thoroughly and let sit for at least 5 minutes before serving. The longer it sits, the better it gets, as the chile infuses the lemon juice.

½ medium red onion, minced
¼ cup finely chopped red and green chiles
½ cup lemon juice
½ teaspoon kosher salt

ENSALADA VERDE

MAKES 4 SERVINGS

2 medium English cucumbers,
    sliced into ¼-inch rounds

3 medium tomatoes, quartered

1 bunch watercress, rinsed
    and dried

1 bunch radishes, ends trimmed
    and halved lengthwise

1 head romaine lettuce, leaves
    separated

Flaky sea salt (optional)

2 limes, quartered

In my view, the Salvadoran table is not complete if it doesn't have a vegetable platter on it. Growing up in my parents' household, washing and prepping the ensalada was my job. Not only does an ensalada verde add a lot of freshness and color to Salvadoran dishes, but the crunchiness of the radishes, the acidity of the tomatoes, and the peppery kick of the watercress complement main dishes such as Pollo Guisado con Aceitunas (page 158), Salpicón de Res (page 170), and so many others.

•

On a large platter, arrange the cucumbers, tomatoes, watercress, radishes, and lettuce leaves neatly in separate piles. Season with salt, if desired.

Serve the ensalada with the lime wedges, for squeezing, on the side.

ARROZ FRITO

As much as Salvadorans love tortillas and pan francés, it cannot be denied that arroz is also a necessary ingredient in the Salvadoran kitchen. I recommend using white jasmine rice for this dish; it's what I use in my kitchen, as do most of the women in my family. My mom told me that while I saw Uncle Ben's used in my childhood years, she, as a child, saw her own mother using San Francisco's arroz blanco, a Salvadoran brand of parboiled rice. As soon as she shared that name with me, I went searching and found it. Instead of an orange bag, this one was blue, with an image of San Francisco, or Saint Francis, in the center. I found the tagline at the bottom of the logo humorous: "¡Una bendición a la hora de cocinar!" (A blessing at the time of cooking!)

This savory dish is the go-to starch accompaniment for entrées that beg for a rice to soak up a sauce. Pairing this rice with Chumpe con Recaudo (page 199) during the holidays is a perfect match.

●

In a colander, rinse the rice under running water.

In a large saucepan over medium heat, warm the grapeseed oil until it shimmers. Add the tomato, bell pepper, onion, and garlic and cook until the vegetables turn fragrant, about 4 minutes. Add the rice and cook, stirring frequently so it doesn't burn. When it begins to deepen in color, dries out from the rinsing, and smells toasty, 3 to 5 minutes, add the water and salt and stir to combine. Cook, uncovered, for 10 minutes, then turn the heat to low, cover, and cook for 10 minutes more. Once all the water has been absorbed, remove the lid and let the rice cook for about 3 minutes more. Once each rice grain is cooked through and esponjadito, it's ready to serve.

2 cups uncooked white
   jasmine rice
1 tablespoon grapeseed oil
1 medium tomato, minced
½ medium green bell pepper,
   cored and minced
½ medium white onion, minced
2 garlic cloves, minced
3 cups water
1 teaspoon kosher salt

CONSEJO

If you are not serving the rice immediately, do not cover it, since the residual heat may overcook it. Instead, place the pan lid ajar so that the steam escapes, therefore leaving the rice perfectly cooked and warm until you're ready to eat.

SALSA DE TOMATE

MAKES 1 QUART

5 very ripe Roma tomatoes
½ medium red onion, root end
    cut off, peeled
2 garlic cloves
1 teaspoon dried thyme
Kosher salt
Freshly ground black pepper
1 teaspoon neutral oil (such as
    canola oil)

While doing salsa research for this recipe, I came upon a YouTube video where someone shared, in the comments, that growing up, when they were sent to the market to get tomatoes for salsa de tomate, they specifically asked the merchant for tomatoes para salsa, because these were the tomatoes that were super-ripe, almost fermenting. It was because this salsa needed to be robust, packed with flavor, not insipid, and definitely not chunky.

Later, during a trip to a Salvadoran meat market, I was talking to the carnicero and he was just as excited as I was about the nuances of making a good salsa de tomate. He shared that he finally figured out the clave, the key, to making it pop: "un toque de tomillo, solo el tomate maduro y tantita agua"—a touch of thyme, just the ripe tomato, and a little water. I ran back to my kitchen to make the most delicious salsa. Suffice it to say, now I'm that person—the kind who eats out and says mine is better.

In a large pot, combine the tomatoes, onion, and garlic with enough water to fully cover. (You don't want anything to be protruding above the water line.) Set over medium-high heat and bring to a boil. Keep an eye on the tomato skins; once they begin to split and peel off, the vegetables are ready and the heat can be turned off, about 7 minutes.

Using tongs or a large slotted spoon, remove the tomatoes, onion, and garlic from the water and place in a blender. Reserve ½ cup of the cooking water. Add the thyme, 2 teaspoons salt, and ⅛ teaspoon pepper to the vegetables and blend until smooth. Place a sieve over a mixing bowl and pour the salsa through the sieve into the bowl.

Add the reserved cooking water to the blender. Seal the blender shut, remove the pitcher from the base, and shake the pitcher so that the water knocks all the pulp and salsa off the inner walls and collects at the bottom. Pour the contents through the sieve into the bowl. Taste the strained salsa and adjust the seasoning to your liking.

Place a dry saucepan over medium-high heat. Once the pan is warm, add the oil. It is important that the oil not get too hot at this point. Dip your finger into the salsa and flick a bit of it into the oil. If the salsa sizzles a lot and looks like it will burn, turn down the heat—we're looking for just a little sizzle. When the oil reaches the proper temperature, pour the salsa into the pan. When bubbles appear across its surface, about 3 minutes, the salsa is done.

Store the salsa in an airtight container at room temperature for up to 4 days, or in the refrigerator for up to 1 week.

CHIRIMOL

Here's the thing, I grew up saying "chimol." The various names for this recipe can be confusing. They depend on what part of El Salvador you're from and, even then, there isn't an exact consensus on the right name for this salsa. Historically, the term is from the Nahuat word *chil-muli*, *chil* meaning "chile," and *muli* meaning "salsa." Discovering, through crowdsourcing, what most folks call this accompaniment has been a fun experience. I've learned that it goes by *chilmol*, *chimol*, *chirmol*, *chirimoy*, *chirimol*, and even *chismol*.

The dish is made from raw vegetables such as tomatoes, onions, radishes, cucumbers, and cilantro, seasoned with lime and salt. It's customary to eat it with grilled foods, but you can add it to all kinds of things, like rice, soups, salads, or any food that needs a kick of freshness and acid. My research into the various names for this recipe revealed a few theories for the confusion. One theory is the accents of Indigenous languages represented in the area. The Pipils, Izalcos, and Lencas all had different ways of pronouncing the dish. The second reason lies in the preparation. If the vegetables are cooked (such as boiled, or roasted to amp up the flavor), then it is called *chimol*. If the vegetables are prepared raw (as in this version), then it's referred to as *chirimol*, which is how I've chosen to list it in the book.

I'll be honest, though. With those in my family at a barbecue or a dinner party, if I'm passing dishes around, I'll be asking if they want chimol, because that's what we all know it as. Serve it as the perfect accompaniment to many Salvadoran dishes such as Sopa de Frijoles con Masitas (page 150), Salpicón de Res (page 170), and Conejo Parrillado (page 205).

●

In a medium mixing bowl, combine the tomatoes, cucumber, radishes, and onion. Pour in the lime juice, add the salt, and mix everything gently to incorporate.

Chirimol is best served the day it is made. Once stored, the vegetables lose their crunch, so transfer to an airtight container and refrigerate for no more than 2 days.

MAKES 1 PINT

2 medium Roma tomatoes, finely chopped
1 medium cucumber, peeled and finely chopped
½ bunch radishes, finely chopped
½ medium red onion, minced
Juice of 2 large limes
½ teaspoon kosher salt

ALGUASHTE

Alguashte is one of the ancestral seasonings and connections that modern-day Salvadorans have to Indigenous communities from the region, and it is also shared with other Central American countries. The word comes from the Nahuat, and it literally means "squash seeds"—semillas de ayote. These seeds are toasted, ground, and then added to many foods. It is also used as a base in other Salvadoran dishes, like Atol Chuco (page 122), Punches con Alguashte (page 196), certain fish tamales, and even alguashte con garrobo, iguana with alguashte. You also use this classic Salvadoran topping to "Salvi up" snacks (especially cut fruit), many dishes, and even drinks, like the SalviSour (page 218). My personal favorite way to enjoy it is over fruit because it adds a wonderful depth of flavor to mango verde, cucumbers, or jicama.

MAKES ABOUT 2 CUPS

2 cups raw whole pumpkin
    seeds
2 teaspoons kosher salt

●

In a dry medium frying pan over low heat, toast the pumpkin seeds until they have turned mostly brown but are still golden in some spots, 5 to 7 minutes, depending on the size of the seeds. Remove the pan from the heat and allow the seeds to cool for about 5 minutes. Then taste one of them; it should have a toasty, nutty flavor. If it doesn't, toast the seeds a bit longer. Add the salt and mix until well incorporated.

In a blender or coffee grinder on high speed, grind the toasted seeds into a fine powder, about 8 seconds. Place a fine-mesh sieve over a bowl and sift the powder through the sieve to separate any unground pieces. Regrind if necessary.

The alguashte can be stored in an airtight container at room temperature for several months.

CUAJADA

Cuajada is a popular fresh cheese that accompanies most mealtimes. As a snack on a toasty tortilla Salvadoreña, it is especially wonderful. The most common cheeses in the Salvadoran diaspora are shelf-stable and dry-aged because they can be shipped more easily. But cuajada is special because it is made at home and commonly wrapped in banana leaves. In this recipe, after making the cuajada, the cheeses are shaped so they can be served individually. While lemon juice is used to coagulate the milk in this recipe, you may use rennet to make this cheese; it should not alter the taste much.

I remember seeing my grandmother make this cheese in her kitchen when I was younger, but I hadn't seen it again until I made it with Estelita in her kitchen. Estelita explained how much the process reminded her of how her own grandmother did it.

Most Latin American markets carry banana leaves year-round, so they should not be too difficult to source. However, if you can't find them fresh, wrap the cheese in plastic wrap.

●

In a large pot, combine the milk and salt and stir to dissolve the salt. Place over medium-high heat and bring the mixture to a boil. Turn the heat to medium-low. Add the lemon juice and stir to combine. Keep stirring until the milk begins to curdle; you should see the fat start to separate from the liquid whey, 10 to 15 minutes.

Place a fine-mesh strainer over a large bowl. Drape a cheesecloth over the strainer and place about half the cheese curds in the strainer. Using a wooden spoon, gently press the curds against the strainer until all the liquid has drained. The cheese should feel moist but not wet. Repeat with the remaining curds. Discard the whey, or save it for other uses (see Consejo).

Cut eight banana leaves (or plastic wrap) into 4-inch squares. Form the cheese into eight oval shapes and completely wrap each inside the banana leaves.

This is fresh cheese so it's best served within a few days of making. Store the cuajada in an airtight container in the refrigerator for up to 5 days.

MAKES 8 SERVINGS

1 gallon whole milk
1 tablespoon kosher salt
½ cup lemon juice
8 banana leaves

CONSEJO

Once it's completely cool, the leftover whey can be used in your garden. I've poured it on roses, trees, and houseplants and they all seem to enjoy the extra boost of nutrients. You can also use it for baking or even in smoothies.

TOMATADA

MAKES 4 TO 6 SERVINGS

1 teaspoon extra-virgin olive oil
½ medium red onion,
    thinly sliced
1 pint cherry tomatoes
1 medium green bell pepper,
    cored and thinly sliced
½ cup water
1 jalapeño chile, cut in half
    lengthwise (optional)
½ teaspoon kosher salt

Tomatada is a very soulful dish for me. It's saucy and all about making you feel great. It reminds me of breakfast with my mom. The breakfasts where, when I get out of the bedroom, the smell of coffee is already in the air and the aroma of frying onions is mixed in with that coffee fragrance. I'm motivated to get the day going, and usually it's tomatada that's calling me to the kitchen.

The tomatoes used for this dish are a very intentional choice. Cherry tomatoes are the juiciest and most tangy, with a super-bright flavor. Tomatada is for a sit-down, relaxing breakfast or weekday dinner. It's not an "in a rush, gotta go" dish, but a "ya esta el cafe, sentate and contame what's going on" meal. On nights when I worked a 9-to-5 job, life was hard, and my daydreams of *SalviSoul* becoming a reality were what kept me going, this was the easy dish I would turn to. Cracking some eggs into the sauce, I'd toast some Salvadoran tortillas I had in the fridge, and it kept me nourished for the journey ahead.

In a medium saucepan over medium-high heat, warm the olive oil until it shimmers. Add the onion and cook until it is tender and slightly browned, 2 to 3 minutes. Add the cherry tomatoes and bell pepper, cover, and let cook until all the tomatoes have softened and burst, about 5 minutes. Add the water, jalapeño (if using), and salt and cook until the vegetables are saucy, about 5 minutes more.

Serve the tomatada immediately.

CASAMIENTO

The combination of rice and beans is iconic across Latin America. Depending on the country, the name and preparation are unique. In El Salvador, it's called *casamiento*, or "marriage." The name has always been considered cute; however, this dish is a perfect example of that marriage between rice and beans. It's considered a mestizo dish, as the beans come from our side of the world and the rice was introduced to Mesoamerica through Spanish colonization. It is cultural syncretism, the fusion of two things becoming one. In certain areas of El Salvador, the dish is also known as arroz curtido.

Casamiento is a terrific dish because it contains protein, carbs, and fats (it's fried)—and so much flavor. When it's made, it signifies that the cook of the house had both rice and beans, and the leftovers were brought together in this second life. A good casamiento must have more beans than rice; if it's got too much rice, it's not a great one. The dish's dominant color comes from the bean broth, which transforms the rice's color. So the end result is not quite an equal marriage. Maybe that's what whoever named this dish believed—and perhaps the name is more tongue-in-cheek.

This is a great food for any meal. I've had it for breakfast, dinner, and even a quick snack, with a fried egg on top.

●

In a large saucepan over medium heat, warm the olive oil until it shimmers. Add the tomato, onion, and garlic and cook until they soften and become fragrant, about 2 minutes. Add the bean broth, turn the heat to medium-high, and bring the mixture to a boil. Stir in the beans and rice and cook for 5 to 7 minutes more.

Serve the casamiento immediately.

MAKES 4 TO 6 SERVINGS

1 tablespoon extra-virgin olive oil
1 medium tomato, peeled and diced
¼ medium white onion, diced
1 large garlic clove, minced
½ cup bean broth, plus 3 cups cooked frijoles rojos de seda, or black beans (see page 27)
1 cup cooked white rice

PAN DE DIOS, LO MUTICHADO Y LO FIADO

"Niña, niña Mercedita dice mi mamá que sí le fía."

In shock, Niña Mercedita gasped loudly and dramatically, "Merlín, pero ya tiene la cuenta bien grande. Ay, mamillita, ya la tienen . . . y no me han venido a pagar." Niña Mercedita was in disbelief that once again Merlín's family was asking for food on credit. Sure, she had a soft spot for this family, but it was a large account now, and they had paid not one centavo. Now Merlín was back with her younger cousin Teresa.

"My mother says we're going to pay this week," Merlín promised.

"Aja, así me dijiste la semana pasada dile a la niña Lupe que ya después se le va a confundir," Niña Mercedita said. (Aha, that's what you told me the week before. Tell your mom that later she's going to get it confused.)

"No, we know what we owe you. Look, that's the truth, for real," came Merlín's reply.

Quite reluctantly and sternly, Niña Mercedita quipped, "¿Cuánto quieres?" (How much do you want?)

Merlín responded quickly, "Dos colones de chorizo." (Two colones worth of chorizo.)

"Well, I'm only going to give you one colon," Niña Mercedita snapped back.

"And two pounds of cheese," Merlín added.

"I'm only going to give you one pound!" Niña Mercedita said.

Merlín's and Teresa's mothers already knew that Niña Mercedita wouldn't give them the amount they asked for. So when they sent their daughters to the market, they took into account what Niña Mercedita would take away. Teresa and Merlín knew that was why their mothers always doubled the order. They happily looked at each other and walked back to the house.

Teresa was satisfied with the groceries they had collected at the mercado, and with all the food that she and her siblings gathered from mutichar, it would be a wonderful lunch and dinner at their Tía Paola's house. She enjoyed mutichando with her family. It was an old tradition in El Salvador, where those in need could go into the fields and pick the excess left after harvest. Corn, squash, squash blossoms, beans, melocotones, guisanperes, and various fruits. They were happy

to have this abundance because, with Teresa's grandmother Mamá Juana, and her siblings, they already had five mouths to feed. Add Tía Lupe's kids, plus Tía Paola's grandchildren from her son, and it totaled twelve people. One of the young cipotes even asked when he saw Teresa and her family arriving, "Well, what are we going to eat today? There are so many of us."

As soon as Merlín and Teresa got back to the house, they joined the women who were already at work. One tía was making the tortillas. Another would start cooking the vegetables. "¿Tía porque no hace frijoles amelcochados?" Merlín would ask. The saucy, extremely tender, almost creamy bean dish was a crowd favorite. A simple dish, made from beans stewed days before, was finished in a sofrito of tomato, onions, and bell peppers—if they had them.

For lunch, they would eat chorizos. For dinner, the frijoles would be ready.

These were the family trips to Apopa, visiting their Tía Paula, spending time together, taking what they found from mutichando and fiando at the mercado. Once Teresa heard her grandmother Mamá Juana say that Tía Paula was "un pan de Dios" because, in their most vulnerable moments, she always took care of them by opening her home and never making them feel bad for adding more mouths to feed. Showing up at Tía Paula's house meant they would eat.

Butifarras, a type of Salvadoran sausage, being sold in Mercado Central in San Salvador.

SALVADORAN ESSENTIALS

Traditional Salvadoran market baskets, large pots, and water pails in Usulután.

Salvis joke that the sound of rainfall always inspires hunger because of how similar it is to the sound of plantains frying. Nothing feels more Salvi than waking up to the sizzling of ripe yellow plantains in a hot frying pan.

Food has been the only flag that I've felt comfortable flying high. When documents could not determine where I belonged, when language could not help me feel like I belonged, food was my guide, especially breakfast foods. I've pledged allegiance for years to its rulers: the women in my life who have fed me. Plátanos, frijoles, tortillas, and queso duro were the four main points on my compass; they told me I was home.

The staples of Salvadoran cuisine are the dishes that are most often enjoyed by the diaspora worldwide. They are the recipes made during the week, the foods that make up early-morning weekend breakfasts or casual lunches with family. They are synonymous with the feeling of being home. These foods are the identity of the country, offering the bounty and splendor that make up El Salvador.

In this chapter are not only breakfast foods but also approachable and satisfying lunch foods, plenty of corn-based foods, and comforting dishes that are pivotal to the cuisine. A good portion of the recipes are vegetable-forward, with some including flowers and buds native to El Salvador. These dishes take me back to that warm feeling of waking up to a house full of family, the sound of coffee being poured into big mugs, and full heavy plates being set down. Most of all, it is the feeling of safety and satisfaction waiting for me at the table.

MAMASOS

MAKES 4 TO 6 SERVINGS

2 cups masa flour
Kosher salt
2 cups lukewarm
    (about 98°F) water
2 cups cuajada (see page 57)

Traditionally made with fresh cheese and torn bits of fresh, hot tortillas, mamasos are special to those who knew them as children. For those growing up in El Salvador, these are the fast, satisfying, easy snacks provided by moms busy whipping up dinner, or lovingly prepared by grandmothers for their grandkids. In this recipe, Estelita shares this beloved snack that her grandmother made for her as a child.

Some cooks also prepare mamasos for soups. Adding them to a nutritious sopa de frijoles is a way to fortify the soup into a complete meal with the addition of tortillas and cheese. My great-grandmother was known for preparing these. When food and money were scarce and she couldn't afford meat or even cheese, she prepared them by using alguashte. These have served as vessels of care and fortitude. To many Salvadorans, this kind of recipe has "grandmother" written all over it—immediately they'll get very misty-eyed and nostalgic.

●

In a large bowl, using the tips of your fingers, gently combine the masa flour and 2 teaspoons salt. Carefully pour in 1 cup of the water. Using your hands, thoroughly mix the water with the dry ingredients. Keep adding the remaining 1 cup water and mixing until the dough reaches the consistency of Play-Doh. It should feel cool to the touch and evenly moist throughout. Cover with a manta and set aside.

Set a comal or griddle over medium-high heat. Once it's hot, sprinkle with a little water to check if it is ready; the water should quickly evaporate. Turn the heat to medium.

Fill a small bowl with water. Separate the dough into six golf ball–size portions, 3 to 4 ounces each. Roll them into balls and return to the large bowl. Dip the fingertips of both hands into the water and raise them upward, allowing the water to drip down and spread across both of your palms.

Take out one ball and cover the remaining dough with the towel to keep it from drying out. Center the dough ball in the palm of your nondominant hand and secure it by cupping your hand. Using only the fingers of your dominant hand, pat the ball into a disk that is ¼ inch thick and about 5 inches wide. Gradually uncup your hand until it is flat, and rotate the disk as the dough flattens out. Once you've patted down the dough, rotate the tortilla upward so it's standing on the palm of your hand. Using the index finger of your dominant hand, smooth out the rounded edges of the tortilla, which should be as evenly thick and round as possible.

Carefully place the tortilla flat on the comal, let it cook for about 2 minutes, and then turn the heat to low, if necessary, so the tortilla doesn't get too toasted on one side. Using a spatula, turn the tortilla over and cook for another 2 minutes. Turn the tortilla a final time. When it puffs up, it has finished cooking.

As soon as the tortilla is cooked through and still hot, quickly tear it into five or six large pieces, to let the steam escape. After 1 to 1½ minutes, put the torn pieces in a bowl and quickly work in ¼ cup of the cheese. Using a wooden spoon (or your hands, but it will be very hot), mix thoroughly until the cheese is fully incorporated. Roll into a ball and set aside. Repeat the process until all the dough and cheese are used.

Serve the mamasos immediately, sprinkled with additional salt.

FRIJOLES CON SOYA

MAKES 4 TO 6 SERVINGS

1 pound dried frijoles rojos
    de seda, sorted for debris
    and rinsed
½ medium red onion, peeled
10 to 12 garlic cloves, left whole
1 celery stalk, halved
¼ medium green bell pepper,
    cored
¾ cup extra-virgin olive oil
¾ cup soy sauce
1 tablespoon chicken bouillon
    powder

Most Salvadorans have a pot of cooked beans ready in their home any given day of the week, and this was no different for Marta Rosa growing up in El Salvador. Her mother always added soy sauce to the beans, and it was one of those things they just did out of costumbre, or custom. This was because her mother was of Japanese descent. The story goes that Marta Rosa's grandmother traveled to Panama to work on the canal and there she met a young man from Japan. They fell in love and, instead of going back to Japan, the young man went with Marta Rosa's grandmother to start a life in El Salvador. So while soy sauce might seem like it doesn't belong here, it definitely does.

●

In a large pot over high heat, bring 8 cups of water to a boil. Add the beans, onion, garlic, celery, and bell pepper. Once the beans start to boil, turn the heat to low and let simmer, uncovered, until they become tender, about 3 hours. Check the beans and stir them every 30 minutes, adding more water to cover as needed; do not let them burn. Using an immersion blender, puree the beans to the desired consistency.

In a large saucepan over medium heat, warm the olive oil until it shimmers. Add the pureed beans, stir in the soy sauce and chicken bouillon, turn the heat to low, and cook until the mixture has thickened, about 20 minutes.

Store the frijoles in an airtight container in the refrigerator for up to 1 week.

They both knew this would be the last time they would share a bed. The last time they would take comfort in each other's warmth on a cold night. What other bond is like that of a grandmother and granddaughter? As young as she was, Estelita knew that her time with her grandmother was special. She knew this because out of all the cousins, she was the only granddaughter to ever live with Mamá Linda, the matriarch of the family. Mamá Linda had birthed ten children, and of the many grandchildren, Estelita was the only one put in Mamá Linda's care. And now it would all change. Mami had finally sent for her to come to the United States, and it was time for Estelita to leave her nest, without Mamá Linda.

The thin cotton-knit cobijas could not hide Estelitas's emotion on her face and the pain in her throat. With sadness disguised as anger, Estelita said, "No se vaya olvidar de mi, Mamá." (Don't ever forget about me, Mamá.) She felt the tightening of her throat when she said it.

Against the quiet night, they hugged as close as they could before their eventual goodbye in the morning. "Como crees mi niña, que me voy a olvidar de ti. Si yo te amo," said her grandmother. (How can you think, my love, that I could forget you. I love you.)

More quiet moments passed when finally Mamá Linda admitted, "Cómo lamento haberle dicho a tu nana." She lamented having written to her daughter, Estelita's mom, on the worsening circumstances in El Salvador. Her daughter needed to send for little twelve-year-old Estelita. The whole country could feel the dangers of the civil war, and in el campo, it was bad enough to force her grandmother to make very hard decisions.

Estelita wished her Mamá Linda had not written to her mother. The adobe house she had grown up in was home. She could name each of the trees on the tereno where they lived. She knew exactly when each one would start bearing fruit and which ones were good for hiding in and climbing. She knew her grandmother's garden so well, from the dahlias to the chipilín. Her grandmother always made cheesy mamasos for her when she came home from school. Would she ever have those moments with her grandmother again?

Eyes moist with tears, Estelita lifted her head and kissed her grandmother's wet cheek. They didn't sleep all night, but they had faith they would see each other again.

PLÁTANOS FRITOS CON FRIJOLES LICUADOS

If plátanos and frijoles were musical recording artists, this dish, fried plantains with pureed frijoles, would be the single that goes platinum. It is a composition of flavors equally masterful and integral, bringing out the best in each other, both in taste and in texture. In other words, name a better duet. I'll wait.

In this recipe, Wendy uses two types of oil: vegetable oil for frying the sofrito for the beans, and coconut oil to add flavor to the plátanos. For this dish, cooking the beans a day ahead is a great idea. Typically, this dish is served with Salvadoran cheese, cream, and avocado slices. I especially love Salvadoran crema; its tanginess pairs wonderfully with the sweet plantains and savory pureed beans.

●

In a large pot over high heat, bring 8 cups of water to a boil. Add the beans and garlic. Once the beans start to boil, turn the heat to low and let simmer, uncovered, until they become tender, about 2 hours. Check the beans and stir them every 30 minutes, adding more water to cover as needed; do not let them burn. When the beans are tender, season with the salt. Allow them to cook until the liquid has reduced by one-third, about 20 minutes more.

In a blender, combine the cooked beans, 2 cups of their cooking liquid, and 2 tablespoons of the onion. Blend until smooth. Set aside.

In a large saucepan over medium-high heat, warm the vegetable oil until it shimmers. Add the remaining onion and cook until tender and slightly browned, about 5 minutes. Remove the pan from the heat and add the blended beans (carefully, to minimize splatter). Return the pan to medium-high heat and cook until the beans are creamy and thick, 10 minutes more. Set aside.

Cut the ends off the plátanos and remove the peel from the flesh. Slice each plátano in half, then each half into three flat slices. Set aside.

In a large frying pan over medium-high heat, melt the coconut oil. In batches, carefully add the plátano slices and fry until the edges caramelize, about 5 minutes per side. Transfer the fried slices to a plate and pat dry with paper towels.

Serve the plátanos immediately with cuajada and crema Salvadoreña on the side.

MAKES 4 TO 6 SERVINGS

1 pound dried black beans, sorted for debris and rinsed
3 garlic cloves, left whole
1 tablespoon kosher salt
½ medium white onion, chopped
2 tablespoons vegetable oil
3 ripe plátanos
½ cup coconut oil
Cuajada (see page 57) and crema Salvadoreña for serving

TORTILLA CON LECHE

MAKES 1 SERVING

2 Tortillas Salvadoreñas
   (page 36)
½ cup milk
1 pinch kosher salt

In my mind's eye, I see a sunrise when I think about tortilla con leche, which is one of the most humble breakfast foods you can find in El Salvador. It is important for me to include it in this book because herein lies the simplicity and elegance of flavors. Mamá Juana and my mom shared that when they lived in el campo, they didn't always heat the milk because they got it fresh from the cow, so it was still warm.

In our peach-colored home in South Central Los Angeles, I would see the colors of the sunrise peeking through the tree branches along the long driveway. Under the fluorescent light of the kitchen that faced the driveway, we waited for my great-grandmother Mamá Juana to tear the tortillas after she had reheated them. As she set the pieces in a bowl, the milk would be heating up. I sat at the glass kitchen table and watched. She's so alive in my memories. I can still see her face and hear the sound of the milk bubbling, the sounds of a quiet kitchen early in the morning. I imagined then, and now, that this simple food is what you, too, would want at dawn if you were getting ready to pick coffee, corn, or any of the other foods that my family harvested in El Salvador.

I did as I saw my family do. As soon as the bowl was in front of me, I reached for the salt shaker. Sprinkling salt all over the mixture, I remember thinking that it might seem odd to someone who hadn't eaten this dish before. I felt like it was "our thing—you wouldn't understand," so I didn't try to explain it to friends.

Later in life, I realized that most Americans eat a version of what I grew up with—Kellogg's cereal, a food also made mostly from corn, then served with cold milk. Only *that* corn comes in different shapes and has added flavors, but still, ours was the real thing. It was rooted in stories of a finca, a comforting food for a rough start to the day, and it was what we shared on those quiet mornings, whether we were heading to work or school.

●

Cut or tear the tortillas into as many bite-size pieces as possible and place them in a serving bowl. In a small pot over medium heat, warm the milk until it begins to bubble and steam starts to rise, 3 to 4 minutes. (Be careful not to scald it.) Pour the warm milk over the torn tortilla pieces and season with the salt before serving.

LOS TRES AMIGOS

Reflecting on her thirty-five years of being a nanny, when it came to handling the competing demands at work and at home, Marta Rosa did it all—alone. She'd gotten better as a single mom in her early thirties, juggling her own two children—a young girl and a younger boy. Unique problem-solving was what was required. She couldn't help her kids with their homework when they arrived home from school, but she could check it in the late hours after she finished her work shift. She couldn't welcome them home after school with a snack, but she could make the snacks the night before. Everything always had to be done the night before. She couldn't ask in person how school was or how they were doing, but she could call them as frequently as possible from her jobs. The three jobs were necessary, but so was capitalizing on the small amounts of time available, even if it was only through notes on homework or the food that she prepared for them for school. Whatever she needed to do, she would do it so they could feel her affection for them.

Responsibility was important to her, such as being on time, doing right by people, and taking care of her duties. But more important were her children. While checking their homework or on her way to the Palisades, where her nanny work often took her far away from them, she'd think about how long she was leaving them alone at home. Hours and hours, so many countless times. But she had to. *Yes, I've left my children alone,* she'd say to herself, but not because of a man or friends or vices. It was to provide them with a home that was theirs, where their comfort would be the priority.

She thinks of the many stories she's heard in her line of work. For instance, nannies whose children must be snapped out of the fantasy that the employer's home or generosity was their reality. She remembers one particular friend whose daughter got the attention of her employer. The woman took to the little girl since she only had boys. In receiving gifts from her, the young girl got confused. "Se le alzaron los humos"—it went to her head. Marta Rosa recalls that the young girl grew to be a "repugnant chica."

Another nanny friend had a twenty-six-year-old son who fell into a bad way. Her friend mentioned that the son had resented being left alone all that time while she looked after other children. She had tried to bring her children to some nanny jobs in previous years, but those were the most stressful times, looking after two sets of children.

Perpetually exhausted, Marta Rosa often slept only three, or maybe four, hours a night for years as she tried to catch up with her children. She could not relent. She had no man, and she didn't need one. The one she once had was a "Salvadoreño machista" who'd had the nerve to say, "Get up, I'm hungry!" when she came home from her night shift.

She loved the children she cared for. It was a very special bond that developed between them, but it was nothing, *nothing*, compared to the love she had for her own children. The children she cared for were her work. While she was great at her job, her own children were everything, her reason for living.

Saturdays were the days when, instead of working as a nanny, she took on cleaning jobs. She brought her children along, not to teach them about finance or honest work, but to spend time with them. She'd pay twenty dollars to her eldest and ten dollars to her youngest. Then would ask them, "What should we do next?" Her daughter would say, "Let's buy a pizza with the money we earned, rent a movie, and go home." Between the three of them, they would get home and divvy up the house chores so they could relax in their clean home together. Marta Rosa recalls that even at breakfast on the weekends when she didn't have to be at work, they would still operate this way. One would say, "Okay, you toast the bread, Mom will make the frijoles, and I'll make the bacon and eggs." It's these memories that she remembers with pride. "Y entre los tres, 'mira qué bonito,' pensé. Y crecieron así y son así." (And among the three of us, 'look how beautiful,' I thought, and they grew up like this and they are like that.) Marta Rosa says, "There wasn't a lot of time, but the little time we did have was quality."

FLOR DE IZOTE CON HUEVOS

MAKES 2 TO 4 SERVINGS

5 cups flor de izote (about a flower stem's worth of petals, or one 32-ounce jar; see Consejo)

4 cups boiling water

1 tablespoon extra-virgin olive oil

1 medium Roma tomato, diced

¼ medium red onion, diced

½ medium green bell pepper, cored and diced

5 eggs, beaten

½ teaspoon kosher salt

There is a saying among Salvadorans that despite the hard times that might fall on us, we'll never go hungry because we eat many things. We are known for consuming the parts of many different types of plants, including buds and flowers. We even eat our national flower, flor de izote, or yuca flower. This white blossom is native to El Salvador and other Central American countries. The petals on the stem face downward, reminding me of the posture of Mother Mary, delicate and precious.

These petals represent not only a nation, a palate, and a craving but also a resolute intention to enjoy the culinary flora of the land. These flowers are a delicacy for most Salvadorans, but some don't care for them. A slightly different variety of yuca grows in Los Angeles, and as I rode on the city's freeways and streets with my parents when I was a child, my ears perked up every time my dad pointed out flor de izote on the hillside along the road. Quickly glancing past the concrete barriers, I would finally spot the blossoms on the tall stalks reaching for the sky. "We eat those flowers—that's real food," my dad would say proudly with a smile on his face. "Son bien ricas." (They are delicious.)

To me, they became a symbol of home in a distant land. Just as these plants could grow and reach for the sky, I could too. This dish is what many people refer to as comida del campo, farmer's food. It's honest, it comes together quickly, and, to me, it showcases the elegance of Salvadoran food. Flowers for breakfast— delicious.

This recipe is by Teresa, my mother; she makes it the most often for my father, Carlos, who loves these blossoms, which can be hard to find fresh. In L.A., I find them at the Salvadoran Corridor around September, being sold by street vendors. If you can't find them fresh, I've really enjoyed using the jarred variety, which are more easily found in markets and online.

•

Rinse the flor de izote under running water to flush out any insects that may be hiding among the petals. Place the flores in a large bowl and pour the boiling water over them. Let sit for 10 minutes, then drain and set aside.

In a large saucepan over medium heat, warm the olive oil until it shimmers. Add the tomato, onion, bell pepper, and salt and sauté until they cook down and soften, about 4 minutes. Add the flores and cook until everything has combined thoroughly, about 5 minutes more. Turn the heat to low and add the eggs. Using a rubber spatula, thoroughly mix the vegetables, flor, and eggs and cook until the eggs are set, just a few minutes.

Serve the flor de izote con huevos immediately.

CONSEJO

If you're preparing fresh flowers, pluck the blossoms off the stems (which can be discarded) and wash them carefully. Now, this part might be controversial to some, but you may choose to keep the inside portions at the center of the blossoms—the pistils and stamens. Some prefer to discard these, as they can taste somewhat bitter. Others, however, would never dream of it, as they add texture and more of the flower's distinctive flavor. Whatever you decide, be sure to thoroughly inspect and clean the blossoms, for little insects can hide among the petals, pistils, and stamens. Some have reported being allergic to the blossoms or being exposed to the toxicity in the pistils and stamens; I have never had a bad experience, but use your own discretion if consuming fresh.

LADRONES

In the bustling streets of San Salvador, Teresa was done. She was over him. She was through. As far as she was concerned, she and Carlos were broken up. Definitivamente. This wasn't just another fight—this was it. He was stubborn. He was tough. He wasn't for her. She hated his haircut.

Walking in the streets with Carlos, Teresa was trapped in her thoughts. *How many ways can I say, "Ya basta, acabamos"* she wondered. *The more it stings the better. I want him to know it's not just a soft breakup, it's a furious one.* Consumed with crafting her speech, she finally realized that two strangers in uniforms were closing in on them. As the two men came up right behind them, they slowly pressed the tips of their fusiles, assault rifles, against both of them.

She glanced at Carlos. He didn't look at her. Quickly, they were guided into a small storefront a few feet away. The store was also a home, which looked a lot like any home in El Salvador. Even the living room looked like hers—compact, with two small rooms that served as the storefront. Her heartbeat quickened.

The men called them all kinds of names, and Teresa saw how the one patting down Carlos was so busy stealing Carlos's wallet that he didn't notice when Carlos raised his arms in submission and unfastened the watch his late father had given him. By the time the men asked them to put their arms down, Carlos had slipped his watch into his back pocket. Teresa saw this and thought, *Listo este tipo.* She was impressed with Carlos's stealth, even if for only one small moment. His late father's watch was safe, at least for now. The men took a gold chain and the wallet from Carlos, which he was happy to give as long as they didn't catch on to the watch.

The men in uniform now shifted their attention to the family who owned the shop. Pointing their rifles, they demanded money. The older woman, frightened, moved as quickly as she could. She handed one of them all the money they had made that day. Twelve colones.

"¡Doce colones! Que no jodan, ¿adonde está el resto del dinero? No lo escondan o les va a ir mal," one of the men exclaimed.

"Joven, no le miento, eso es todo el dinero," responded the woman.

The men wanted more money and demanded that if they didn't get it, they'd have to take a hostage.

Teresa's stomach sank. She held onto Carlos, praying, *I don't want them to take me.* She was only eighteen years old. She explained to me that it was a sin to be

young. If you were a girl, they raped you and then your family had to look for you in the basureros, garbage cans. A volcano of dead people. She didn't want her grandmother to find her body in a dump.

It was in that moment of terror, panic, and anxiety that Teresa realized her anger toward her boyfriend had melted like sorbete on the hot city pavement. *I love this man. This is my boyfriend, and I want to be with him.*

She whispered to Carlos, "I don't want them to take me. Carlos, don't let them take me. If they take me, let them kill me here." Carlos grabbed her hand really hard and told her, "No one is going to take you anywhere, but you have to relax."

In the end, the men were thieves dressed as soldiers, armed with grenades, rifles, and real uniforms. When they saw that no more than a gold chain, a wallet, and twelve colones were their loot, they said, "Saben que cerotes, hechencen al piso." They ran away without taking anyone.

"God has a plan," said Teresa. "From ages fifteen to twenty, I think if I say I was exposed to being killed, say, fifty times, it would be too small a number. They put the gun to me, like, three times, and shots were fired in the air. When a bomb explodes, the earth trembles—I lived through all of that." In the end, she didn't break up with her boyfriend. "I trusted Carlos. Since that time, I have never been afraid when I am with him. Never. Since that day, I always felt very safe with Carlos."

YUCA FRITA CON PEPESCAS

There is no doubt about what you're cooking when you open a plastic box of pepescas. People talk about the funky cheese that Salvadorans love, but in my personal opinion, the smell of these tiny dried sardines when fried is incomparable. I like to file them in the category of "so delicious to eat, but not so great to prepare." They are potent, but so right as an accompaniment to yuca, followed with bites of tangy curtido and zesty watercress.

An option in many places in El Salvador is skipping frying the yuca altogether and only salcocharla (boiling it with garlic, onion, and salt) until it turns fluffy. This fluffy yuca with salty bits of fried pepescas is also a manjar, a heavenly delight. Either way, your home will know what you're up to as soon as you open the pepesca package.

Yuquerias are a dominant culinary tradition of the Mejicanos neighborhood in San Salvador. Just like there are pupuserias, there are yuquerias that serve only items showcasing the gastronomic range of yuca, which covers a lot. They feature two main savory specialties: fried and boiled. In recent years, eleven festivals have been held to honor this cuisine and promote cultural tradition in different areas of the municipality.

This offering also takes various forms. Some versions come with chicharrón and others with fritada, a mix of organ meats stewed in a sauce. But this one celebrates the wonderful—albeit pungent—pepescas. Isabel fries the yuca and pepescas and makes her own version of salsa roja with curtido.

You will need six banana leaves to line the serving plate. Most Latin American markets carry banana leaves year-round, so they should not be too difficult to source.

●

In a large pot over medium-high heat, bring 6 cups of water to a boil (or enough to cover all the yuca). Add the yuca, onion, garlic, sea salt, and baking soda. After about 25 minutes, the yuca should be tender; drain and pat dry with paper towels. Discard the onion and garlic.

In a large pot over medium-high heat, warm the avocado oil until it registers 350°F on an instant-read thermometer. Add the yuca pieces and fry until they turn golden brown, about 2 minutes per side. Set aside.

continued

MAKES 4 TO 6 SERVINGS

3 pounds yuca (see Consejo),
    cut into 2-inch pieces
½ medium yellow onion, peeled
4 garlic cloves, left whole
1 tablespoon sea salt
1 pinch baking soda
1 cup avocado oil

Isabel's Salsa Roja

4 medium tomatoes, stemmed
2 medium green bell peppers,
    cored and halved
1 medium red onion, peeled
3 large garlic cloves, left whole
2 chiles de árbol
¼ teaspoon dried oregano
2 tablespoons neutral oil
    (such as canola oil)

Isabel's Curtido

3 cups cabbage, thinly sliced
1 cup hot water
Juice of 1 lemon
½ teaspoon kosher salt
1 cup thinly sliced radishes
¼ red onion, thinly sliced

1 cup neutral oil (such as
    canola oil)
2 cups pepescas
1 bunch watercress
1 large tomato, cut into wedges
6 banana leaves

YUCA FRITA
CON PEPESCAS

continued

Fried pepescas, tiny
fried sardines.

To make the salsa: In a medium pot over medium-high heat, combine the tomatoes, bell peppers, onion, garlic, and chiles and cover with water and bring to a boil. Once it's boiling, lower the heat to medium, stir and cook until the tomato skins fall away from the flesh, about 15 minutes. Reserve about 1 cup of water. In a blender, add the cooked vegetables with the oregano and 1 cup of water and blend to incorporate. Set a fine-mesh strainer over a bowl and pour the vegetable sauce through the strainer.

In a large saucepan over medium-high heat, warm the neutral oil until it shimmers. Add the strained sauce and fry until the color deepens to bright red, about 5 minutes. Remove from the heat and set aside.

To make the curtido: Place the cabbage in a large bowl and pour the hot water over it. Let sit for about 1 minute, then drain and add the lemon juice, salt, radishes, and red onion. Stir to combine and set aside.

Line a large plate with paper towels and set it near the stove. In a large frying pan over high heat, warm the neutral oil until it shimmers. Place a pepesca in the oil; if it sizzles, the oil is ready for frying. Add the pepescas and fry until they turn golden brown, about 5 minutes. It's a good idea to stay close to the pepescas as they can burn very quickly and easily, given their small size. Using tongs or a slotted spoon, transfer the pepescas to the prepared plate to drain and set aside.

Line the bottom of a plate or bowl with banana leaves. Fill it with the yuca, then layer with the curtido, watercress, tomato wedges, salsa roja, and finally the fried pepescas. Serve immediately.

CONSEJO

When you shop for yuca, be mindful of the inside of the root. Most of the SalviSoul women admit that they break the roots to check their condition while still at the market. If you're in a Latino market, you may see this commonly practiced to find fresh, healthy yuca roots. However, some grocery stores won't permit them to be broken, so be warned. If black lines appear in the root, or the yuca appears yellow and not white throughout, it won't be usable.

TALNIQUE, UN LUGAR CON AROMA A CAFE

It still haunts Isabel. Talnique, a town built atop a mountain and known for its coffee farms and estates, was both beautiful and harsh. When she was younger, the town was home, even though it felt oppressive to her and her family. It was there that Isabel came to appreciate the world's immense beauty. In Talnique, it was said that subterranean bees existed. Their honeycomb lay underground, a whole universe of life buzzing underneath her feet. During the rainy season in El Salvador, many of the trees bore blossoms in a variety of colors and later fruit of equally bright flavors. As these ripe fruits fell, they created magical multicolored carpets beneath the trees, flashing with the vivid yellow of nances and the deep orange of jocotes, sprinkled with the highly saturated green of unripe specimens that also dropped from the branches.

The tropical forests of the Salvadoran cafetales, or coffee plantations, were inspiring. "In spite of the fact that it is small, my country has beautiful places," said Isabel. "Our country is a very blessed land, very prosperous. The seeds that fall there germinate, grow, and are fruitful."

Despite all this beauty and her family roots in Talnique, there was something deep inside Isabel that screamed with a visceral sal de allí—get out of there. For all of its gorgeousness, the town was a villain in Isabel's life, a place that brought despair and gloom. She wanted to leave even when she was only seven years old, and that mission felt even more heightened by the fact that only one road existed to get in and out. She and her family were colonos, or settlers, on the finca, with no house of their own. They lived like slaves, Isabel recalls. She and her eldest sister shared the same deep yearning to leave, but they never spoke of it. Her sister departed first, leaving Isabel behind, who promised herself, "Yo nunca me voy a quedar aquí para toda la vida." (I will not stay here for all my life.)

For years, Isabel witnessed what Talnique could do to people, especially women. Her mom was just one example. Dealing with the difficult life in el campo was hard enough, but she also raised twelve children. There was always so much screaming and regañadas. Isabel understands now how a woman like her mother felt anguished by her situation with no way out, and she resorted to controlling her children the only way she knew how.

Isabel and her family also witnessed and heard stories of people in their community getting older—"Llenarse de hijos y morir ahí, trabajando en el campo de sol a sol." This cycle seemed unfair to Isabel: work all your life, get saddled with too

many children, and work from sunrise to sundown.
Sometimes, it was all for only fourteen colones
every two weeks.

The finca's owner was German, perhaps. Isabel
isn't sure. The little details she recalls about him
are few. It seems to her that he was a captain in the
US military. When she was just seven years old, she
learned to lay fertilizer on the young coffee trees,
then hike steep hills for miles before the sun had
risen. Isabel could not forget seeing her father come
home from work in tears after being treated badly
by the caporales, or foremen. Her father did not
know how to adular his superiors, to flatter them.

There were ways to get lighter work. Rumors
circulated in the finca that among the caporales,
one in particular took a liking to young girls. This
was beyond the sphere of consideration for Isabel,
her older sister, or her family, so this meant hard
work, long hours, and plenty of mistreatment.
That's what provoked her to finally leave. *Is this
going to be my life?* she thought. She had seen good
people die from working in the cafetales. *This will
be your life if you don't get out of here.* "Entonces yo
salí, como a los doce años de la casa," she said. So
she left, at age twelve.

Running away was the only option. What haunts
her most of all is that she did not say goodbye
to her mother. Instead, she lied to her that day.
Told her that she could not work at the finca. An
uncle happened to be in town. This uncle was on
his way to the capital, so she took her chance.

And always, she held the intention that she
would work to get the rest of her family out of
there as well.

SÁNDWICHES DE POLLO

During my trip to El Salvador when I was seventeen, a younger cousin, probably now in their twenties, was having a birthday. Sándwiches de pollo were served. We had a group photo taken at the end, and although I remember feeling awkward, I also remember thinking, *This feels nice*. But I had not remembered the sándwiches de pollo until years later, when I was sitting on my patio talking to Bartola, one of the SalviSoul moms, over the phone.

When I asked her what recipes she would want to feature in the book, she replied, "sándwiches de pollo." Feeling the warm breeze coming in as I listened to Bartola mentioning the sándwiches took me straight back to that summer in El Salvador as a teenager. She explained what they were, because I had them confused with panes de pollo. You see, *sándwiches* refers to sandwiches as we in the United States might refer to them: two slices of bread with something in the middle. *Panes*, which translates to "bread," refers to Salvi sandwiches made with a proper pan francés, a roll that is cut open and stuffed. At least this is the pattern I have noticed. As Bartola described them, I vaguely started to remember creamy chicken salad between two slices of white bread (think Bimbo bread). This excited me and I told her, yes, let's do them. She warned me that it would take a while to make them. I didn't truly understand what she was saying, but I just went with it. We decided to meet at her house early on a Saturday morning to prepare them; then we said our goodbyes and hung up.

When I arrived, I noticed that she had several cabbages on hand, and I wondered why. We went through the vegetable and chicken prep and then she put me to work opening a package of napkins so that we would be able to wrap the sándwiches after assembling them. That's when I realized she intended on making ten bags worth of bread—and sándwiches. She laughed at my surprise. She had tried to warn me. She explained, "Ay es que, como les gustan estos sándwiches a mis hijos. Solo en un instante se vuelan tres o cuatro." (Oh, my sons just love these sándwiches, and in just a moment they'll eat three or four.) And it was true—two of her sons emerged from their bedrooms with a few of their friends, and as soon as I finished wrapping the sandwiches and stacking them in a tall pile, they were scarfed down.

If you don't have as many hungry mouths to feed, the wrapped sándwiches can be put in plastic bags and stored in the refrigerator for up to 3 days.

•

2 boneless, skinless chicken breasts
½ medium red onion, peeled
5 garlic cloves, left whole
1 tablespoon kosher salt
Freshly ground black pepper
2 fresh bay leaves
4 tablespoons unsalted butter
1 medium head cabbage, shredded
2 medium green bell peppers, cored and thinly sliced
3 carrots, shredded
2 cups mayonnaise
½ cup yellow mustard
24 slices whole-wheat bread

continued

SÁNDWICHES DE POLLO

continued

In a large pot over medium-high heat, bring 6 cups of water to a boil. Add the chicken breasts, onion, garlic, 2 teaspoons of the salt, ¼ teaspoon pepper, and bay leaves. When the chicken starts to boil, turn the heat to medium and let simmer until it is cooked through, about 10 minutes or until the internal temperature is 165°F. Using tongs, transfer the chicken to a plate and let cool. Discard the onion and garlic. (You can keep the resulting broth for other uses.) Shred the meat and set aside.

In a large saucepan over medium-high heat, melt the butter. Add the cabbage, bell peppers, and carrots and cook until the vegetables are tender, 5 to 7 minutes. Turn the heat to medium, add the shredded chicken, and mix well. Set aside.

In a small bowl, combine the mayonnaise, mustard, remaining 1 teaspoon salt, and a pinch of pepper and stir to make an aioli.

Working with two bread slices at a time, spread a thin layer of the aioli on one side of both slices. Mound one slice with about ¼ cup of the chicken-vegetable mixture and top with the other piece of bread. Repeat with the remaining bread, aioli, and chicken mixture.

Wrap the sándwiches in paper napkins and serve.

"A la gran puta. ¡Qué frío!" Gasping for air, Bartola was barely able to rub the cold water out of her eyes. Suddenly, another splash of icy water hit her face. It drenched her small eight-year-old body, shocking away all the sleepiness and warmth of her bed.

Squinting her eyes, she opened them enough to see her mother filling another cold bucket of frigid torture. Hoisting it into the ready position, Bartola's mother yelled, "Mira cipotilla, asi es como se te va abrir ese cerebro." (Look little girl, this is how that brain of yours is going to open.)

Splash!

It wasn't fair to Bartola. The early 1970s in El Salvador didn't have any treatment options for her learning disability, so Bartola's teacher gave up. He condescendingly broke the news to Bartola's mother about her learning challenges by stating, "She simply cannot learn. She is not capable. She is taking up a valuable seat in class." Her mother took this evaluation with equal amounts of embarrassment and determination. "*I* will make my daughter's mind open," Bartola's mother promised herself. Thus began the cold buckets of water before dawn—every single morning for six years.

Now, as an adult in her sixties, Bartola laughs as she thinks about her teacher. "I'm surprised I didn't cause him to commit suicide. I was a hard student." But she was determined to read. She knew reading could help her become one of the four vocations she had her heart set on: a secretary to the president, a nurse, a psychologist, or a hair stylist. Most of all, she wanted to learn one very important thing: how to tell time. What did the long line mean? What did the short line mean? And what do they have to do with each other, along with all those symbols around them?

In her twenties, Bartola eventually learned how to tell time. She met a painter in their hometown of Ereguayquín, Usulután. A painter who made signs. One day, he finally explained what those hands on a clock meant. He explained the sequence of numbers, the tick-tock, and how together the two hands could hold time.

RELLENOS DE GÜISQUILES

MAKES 4 TO 6 SERVINGS

Salsa de Tomate para Rellenos

4 medium Roma tomatoes, stemmed
½ medium green bell pepper, cored
¼ medium red onion, peeled
3 garlic cloves, left whole
3 cups water
1 teaspoon kosher salt
½ teaspoon chicken bouillon powder

3 güisquiles
1 pinch kosher salt
1 pound queso fresco (see Consejo)
7 eggs, separated
1 teaspoon all-purpose flour
½ cup grapeseed oil
Arroz Frito (page 51) for serving

My first piece of food writing included a recipe for rellenos de güisquiles. At that point in time, few pieces explored what Salvadoran food was in Los Angeles, or even in the diaspora. When I was contacted about submitting an article for an online publication, I was told that I could write about anything I wanted. They requested a 2,000 word essay, a recipe, and photos—all for a hundred dollars. The dollar amount didn't even bother me; I was just thrilled that I had finally landed a real food-writing gig and I would get a chance to do this work. The piece examined the question of why Salvadoran cuisine isn't documented more. It went viral on Salvadoran Twitter, which, back in 2017, felt overwhelming.

Either way, when I needed to decide what recipe I would contribute, I had no doubt it would be this one, taught to me by my mom, Teresa. My mouth is watering just thinking about it. You may know güisquiles as chayote.

•

To make the salsa de tomate: Preheat the oven to 375°F.

Place the tomatoes, bell pepper, onion, and garlic in a roasting pan and roast until the tomato skins have burst and everything has darkened, about 20 minutes. Using tongs, transfer the roasted vegetables to a blender. Add the water, salt, and chicken bouillon and blend until smooth. Set aside.

Wash the güisquiles and trim off both ends, but note which were the stem ends before you cut. Where the stem was on each güisquil, make two cuts angled toward each other, forming a downward-pointing triangle shape in the center. Discard this triangle section; this removes whatever portion of the stem might still be inside. Using a vegetable peeler, peel the güisquiles, then, using a sharp knife, cut six ¼-inch-thick slices from each. Try not to cut them too thin or thick, and be careful because the seeds in the center might be a little hard to slice through at first.

In a large saucepan over medium-high heat, bring 3 cups of water to a boil. Add the salt and güisquil slices, making sure there is enough water to cover them. Boil the güisquiles until they soften, about 10 minutes. Drain the güisquiles, pat dry, and let cool.

Over a plate, crumble the queso fresco until it's completely soft and mashed. Pair the güisquil slices together. Sprinkle about ¼ cup of cheese on one slice, then place the other slice over the top. Repeat for the remaining pairs of güisquil slices and queso.

In a large bowl, using an electric mixer on high speed (or a whisk), whip the egg whites until foamy, about 30 seconds. Add the egg yolks and the flour and continue to whip until soft peaks form. Set aside.

CONSEJO

Any fresh cheese will do for this recipe, as long as it melts well. Salvadoran cooks have been known to use queso fresco, quesillo, mozzarella, or even Monterey Jack cheese.

Line a large plate with paper towels or put a wire cooling rack in a baking sheet and set it near the stove. In a large frying pan over medium heat, warm the grapeseed oil until it shimmers. Using your hands, dip the prepared güisquil into the egg mixture, making sure that all sides of the rellenos are coated. Place the rellenos in the oil and fry until they're golden brown and crispy, about 2 minutes per side. Transfer the fried rellenos to the prepared plate to drain.

Wipe the frying pan clean with a paper towel and turn the heat to medium. Pour in the salsa de tomate, cover, and bring to a boil. Add the rellenos to the pan and cook until all the rellenos are coated in the sauce and have boiled one last time, about 5 minutes more.

Serve the rellenos immediately with arroz.

MASTERS OF THE UNIVERSE

"I have the power! Cringer became the mighty Battle Cat and I became He-Man, the most powerful man in the universe!"

The boisterous, heroic theme song could be heard playing any given day of the week in Teresa's family home in Apopa. It was the 1980s, and she was on a strict diet—one she gave herself—of munequitos, or cartoons. She could not get enough of them when they aired every day from 11 a.m. to 1 p.m. Once He-Man was done hunting for Skeletor, the next giant in the cartoon world would play. The family's small television screen then showed Aquaman and his ability to summon all the sea creatures of the deep. The theater and adventure of the cartoon series swept her away.

Next, she'd switch gears from superheroes defeating evil villains to *Candy Candy* and then to *Heidi*, the story of an orphaned little girl who went to live with her grandfather in the Swiss Alps, where she was brave and learned priceless lessons of friendship. Teresa, much like Heidi, had to be courageous. And she learned to be content, no matter the situation.

Together with her two brothers, sister, grandmother, mom, and dad, Teresa lived in two places during the beginning of the civil war: Patacones, a rural colonia, and Apopa, a municipality known for its clouds. Both were home. However, each time Teresa and her siblings had to pack up their chunches in her father's camión, it was the same heartbreak. If they were driving away from Patacones, she'd cry every single time. If they were leaving Apopa, it was tears, tears, and more tears.

In Apopa, they had more opportunities. At least that's what her father kept saying over and over again. In Apopa, there was more light. Her feet didn't get as filthy from the dirt roads. In Apopa, she could play with dolls with a distant cousin of hers. Not only was her cousin older, which she liked, but she also knew how to sew, which meant custom dresses for her dolls, every week if possible. This cousin eventually taught her how to sew. Then there was the cinema, places to eat, and the best part of all—electricity, which meant television and its larger-than-life characters who captivated Teresa.

Moving back and forth during the war meant that saying goodbye was routine. When her father sensed it was time to move again, he would let them know, and they prepared themselves. Teresa would cry and cry.

In Patacones, you had to take a bus since the roads weren't as nice. Its city planners had not installed systems for potable water or electricity, so there were disadvantages in adjusting to Patacones after being in Apopa. The family kept the TV, of course—"just in case we go to Apopa again."

Once, when Teresa was in Patacones, she remembered praying that the munequitos would appear on the TV. There was no plug and no electricity available, and she knew very little about God, but she knew her munequitos needed some kind of power source so she could see them again. She closed her eyes, prayed what she thought was prayer, and then quickly opened her eyes to check behind the squat television set to see if her munequitos were there. "¿Que estas haciendo? What are you doing?" her eldest brother Javier asked, interrupting her inspection. She whined, "Quiero ver mis munequitos. I want to see my cartoons." Her brother left the room, making her feel like it wasn't going to happen. She missed Apopa.

Two children playing at the Laguna Verde in Ahuachapán.

There were happy memories that came from being brave, though. To satisfy the family's craving for cold Jell-O, her mother realized that los vientos de Octobre could help, since they didn't have a refrigerator in Patacones. When the October winds showed up in the rainy season, her mother would prep the gelatin mix and then one of Teresa's brothers would carry the dish up to the laminate roof to let it sit outside overnight. By morning, to everyone's delight, the Jell-O would have set and everyone would eat it. Teresa filled her days with climbing trees, picking guavas, and playing with the rest of the colonia cipotes.

At Christmastime, if they were in Apopa, they could decorate and light a Christmas tree; they used a coffee tree. In Patacones, Christmas meant no lights for their tree. Instead, they decorated it with guindas, fruits, and blossoms found around their home. Her brother Mario, who was always taking things apart and putting them back together, made a little battery pack and wired some lights that lit up the family tree. Its lights stayed on for less than a minute, but it lifted Teresa's spirits. In these moments, she was happy. She'd forget about her TV and loved the magic her family made together.

Little boy climbing a fruit tree in Laguna Verde, Ahuachapán.

Their life required them to master their reality, making do with what they had and finding laughter when the war got too close to home. They'd walk out of their house in Patacones to see a wall of dead bodies, thrown away like garbage. After curfew was over, bullets filled the night skies and their grandmother could be heard yelping and shrieking when violent sounds went off. "Ay, ay, ay, ay, ay, ay, ay!" They learned to laugh at those sounds and tease their grandmother for the funny noises she made when she was scared.

What Teresa noticed most about their lives in Apopa versus Patacones was their proximity to the war. In Apopa, you could feel it, but when you were in the isolation of Patacones, you lived it.

RELLENOS DE PACAYA

Pacayas are another of El Salvador's edible blossoms. These flowers of the date palm are one of the foods I have tried hard to enjoy; they can often be a touch too bitter for many.

Nevertheless, when you're someone like me, who has longed to belong, you make yourself go through round after round, no matter the cost. Eating pacayas felt like the deep cuts of Salvi cuisine, and I wanted in, to belong to the flower-eating club. One day during the height of the pandemic, when I had not seen my family in months (which is a long time for us), my mom brought something to my doorstep. I saw her from the window, and when I went outside, I retrieved a Tupperware dish that contained rellenos de pacayas.

Bringing them up to my apartment kitchen, I wasn't sure if I was going to like them, but there they were. I took the first bite. I took a second bite, then a third. They tasted glorious. I immediately telephoned my mom. "What did you put in these?" I asked. She must have prepared them differently this time. Did she get a different brand of jarred pacayas? No. She had not done a single thing differently. I guess my taste buds had finally blossomed.

Pacaya is difficult to find fresh in the United States but I have had some luck in small Central American markets in L.A. I will usually rinse them really well and boil them in some water and salt until tender, then rinse them one last time before preparing them for rellenos.

●

In a large pot, soak the pacayas in enough hot water to cover for at least 20 minutes, or up to 3 hours. (This helps with the bitterness; if soaking for a longer time, change the water every 30 minutes.) Transfer the soaked pacayas to a manta or kitchen towel and pat dry. Season with salt and set aside.

Over a plate, crumble the quesillo until it is completely soft and mashed. (If you are using a different, firmer cheese, shred or slice the pieces so you have enough to place in between the pacaya tendrils.) Take one of the pacayas and fit a clump of cheese near the stem and another near the tips of the tendrils. Then braid the tendrils around the cheese. Repeat for the remaining pacayas and quesillo.

In a large bowl, using an electric mixer on high speed (or a whisk), whip the egg whites until foamy, about 30 seconds. Add the egg yolks, one at a time, and the flour and continue to whip until soft peaks form. Set aside.

MAKES 4 SERVINGS

8 jarred pacayas
Kosher salt
1 pound quesillo (see Consejo, page 89)
7 eggs, separated
1 teaspoon all-purpose flour
½ cup grapeseed oil
1 recipe Salsa de Tomate para Rellenos (page 88)

continued

Line a large plate with paper towels or put a wire cooling rack in a baking sheet and set near the stove. In a large frying pan over medium heat, warm the grapeseed oil until it shimmers. Using tongs, dip the prepared pacaya into the egg mixture, making sure that all sides of the rellenos are coated. Place the rellenos in the oil and fry until they're golden brown and crispy, 2 minutes per side. Transfer the fried rellenos to the prepared plate to drain.

Wipe the frying pan clean with a paper towel and turn the heat to medium-high. Pour in the salsa de tomate, cover, and bring to a boil. Add the rellenos and cook until the sauce has boiled again, about 5 minutes more.

Serve the rellenos immediately.

RELLENOS DE PACAYA

continued

Tower of eggs at the wholesale market in Central San Salvador.

RELLENOS DE PAPA

MAKES 4 SERVINGS

3 russet potatoes, peeled
1 pinch kosher salt
1 pound queso fresco
7 eggs, separated
1 teaspoon all-purpose flour
½ cup grapeseed oil
1 recipe Salsa de Tomate para
    Rellenos (page 88)

Rellenos can be traced back to Spanish cuisine. In El Salvador, there are rellenos made from everything, even green beans. This dish is special because it is from a recipe that my Tia Patricia contributed to this project. Once upon a time, she was in an unhappy marriage where she was not given the freedom to express herself, much less her Salvadoranness. This dish was her SalviSoul coming out to shine. Sometimes food comforts us, feeds us, and fights for us. This was the one dish that she knew how to make, so whenever she could, she would make it to remind herself who she was.

●

Using a sharp knife, cut each potato into six slices about ¼ inch thick.

In a large, wide saucepan over medium-high heat, bring 4 cups of water to a boil. Add the salt and potato slices, making sure there is enough water to cover them. Boil the slices for about 5 minutes, then drain, pat dry, and let cool. (They will still be raw in the center, but we're only partially boiling them at this point.)

Over a plate, crumble the queso fresco until it is completely soft and mashed.

Once the potato slices have cooled, pair the slices together. Cover one side of a potato slice with about ¼ cup mashed queso, then place a second potato slice on top. Continue to pair and stuff the potato slices.

In a large bowl, using an electric mixer on high speed (or a whisk), whip the egg whites until foamy, about 30 seconds. Add the egg yolks, one at a time, and the flour and continue to whip until stiff peaks form. Set aside.

Line a large plate with paper towels or put a wire cooling rack in a baking sheet and set near the stove. In a large frying pan over medium heat, warm the grapeseed oil until it shimmers. Using tongs, dip the prepared potatoes into the egg mixture, making sure that all sides of the rellenos are coated. Place the rellenos in the oil and fry until they're golden brown and crispy, about 2 minutes per side. Transfer the fried rellenos to the prepared plate to drain.

Wipe the frying pan clean with a paper towel and turn the heat to medium-high. Pour in the salsa de tomate, cover, and bring to a boil. Add the rellenos and cook until the potatoes are fork-tender and the sauce boils one more time, about 10 minutes more.

Serve the rellenos immediately.

Maybe the earthquake was a warning. She met him on the same day that the ground shook in Los Angeles. The earth's fault lines slipped hard and at the age of fourteen, Patty did too—into the most turbulent relationship of her life.

After arriving in Los Angeles just two years before, Patty was ready to live freely and search for all the love she could find. She spent too many years waiting in El Salvador. Waiting for her mother to send for her, waiting for the civil war to end. Patty's heart was full of longing. At the age of twelve, she traded one heartache for another. She embarked on a search for her mother, leaving her grandmother Juana behind—Doña Juana, who had protected her from the war raging outside the walls of their home in San Salvador.

Talking about that afternoon in L.A. when Patty first set eyes on Julio, she said, "Me enamore en un instante. I fell in love in an instant." She felt a flutter in her belly and a chaos in her chest all because of this seventeen-year-old Mexican boy. The moment felt like an invitation to grab ahold of life.

Earlier that morning, her middle school panicked at the quake and ushered all the students to one area of the campus. Patty thought, "What was the point of staying in school with everyone out of class anyway?"

As Patty and Julio scrambled up the wire fence surrounding the school grounds, they locked eyes. Julio had a look that was one part Menudo band member and one part brown-skinned Billy Idol—even down to the shiny earring in his right ear. Maybe she was drawn to him because he seemed to have the freedom she wanted.

Two earthquakes happened that day by the fence; except one stayed with Patty for more than thirty years. She cleaned up messes, tempers, control tactics, manipulation, and bruises of so many kinds. "Maybe I wanted to feel like a princess. I wanted to be spoiled, to be loved. Since I've been divorced, I've been happy being Salvadoran. Yes, it's sad. When I was married I wasn't able to say 'I'm Salvi' because I wasn't allowed. So the year I got divorced, I went to El Salvador just to prove that I'm Salvi, and that I was proud of it. I can eat what I want from El Salvador without guilt. I used to hide everything. I gave up my culture and family for what, a man?"

MAYBE THE EARTHQUAKE

PUPUSAS DE FRIJOL CON QUESO

MAKES 30 PUPUSAS

2 cups Basic Olla de Frijoles
    (page 40), plus 2 cups broth
½ cup grapeseed oil
2 cups quesillo
5 pounds masa harina
10 cups water, or as needed
Curtido (page 43) and salsa
    roja for serving

Not only are pupusas the most popular traditional food of El Salvador, but they are also its national dish. The 1980s saw an exodus of Salvadorans from the civil war; wherever the diaspora went, you'll find at least a sprinkling of pupusas in that town.

The griddled, filled tortillas are usually made from corn flour and sometimes rice flour. Pupusas are an ancient food legacy that ties modern Salvadorans to the indigenous roots of what is now El Salvador. The Pipils who inhabited the area are credited with bringing this dish, which they called *pupusawa*, to life. They were also said to be in a half-moon shape.

A good pupusa is plump, with its filling extending all the way to the edges. Now, it's quite common to see queso quemadito, the sizzling cheese that oozes out and gets crispy, as a sign of a good one. Perhaps the most controversial part about pupusas is how they are eaten. Most Salvadorans eat them with their hands, as this dish is intended for you to get all the way in, with sleeves rolled up and hair tucked behind the ears and tied at the nape of the neck. Many are offended by the sight of a fork anywhere near a pupusa.

Choosing between three different kinds of pupusas, I would argue the most popular one is frijol con queso followed by queso con loroco (cheese with loroco; see page 103) and revueltas (beans, cheese, and pork; see page 104). Two are vegetarian, and one is for meat eaters. Ruth, the owner of Delmy's Pupusas, guides us through the first two vegetarian pupusas. Preferably, cook the beans a day or two before you want to eat the pupusas.

●

In a blender on high speed, blend the cooked beans and broth until smooth. Set aside.

In a large frying pan over medium heat, warm the grapeseed oil until it shimmers. Pour the blended beans into the pan and bring to a boil; keep them on medium heat and constantly stir until they reach a stiff texture and no liquid remains, about 25 minutes. Remove from the heat and let cool completely.

Transfer the beans to a large bowl. Add the quesillo and mash the cheese into the beans so that no large chunks remain. The mixture should be thoroughly combined and have a uniform color, with no parts too cheesy or too concentrated with beans. Set aside.

In another large bowl, combine the masa harina and water and knead until it reaches the consistency of Play-Doh. (You may choose to do this in batches. Divide the water and the masa harina and mix one batch at a time.) When the dough is pressed, its sides should not tear.

Pour some water into a small bowl and keep it handy for moistening the dough. Roll about 3 ounces of masa (slightly larger than a golf ball) between the palms of your hands until it forms a completely round ball. Then start flattening it with the fingertips of your dominant hand. Rotate the round slightly so that it gets pressed down evenly. Once the round is about 5 inches in diameter, cup your hand so that the pressed-out dough is now a pocket. Put about 3 ounces of filling into the pocket and press the filling tightly inside. Fold the edges of the dough toward the center to seal the pupusa, and twist off any remaining dough. This should now form a filled disk. Using your dominant hand, pat and flatten the disk until it is 6 to 7 inches in diameter. (If the dough cracks at any point, it needs more moisture; add more water and mix into the dough until it becomes elastic again.)

Set a comal or griddle over medium-high heat. When the comal is hot, add the pupusas and cook until they puff up and the exteriors have browned, about 5 minutes per side. Transfer the pupusas to a plate and cover with a kitchen towel to keep them warm. Repeat the process until you run out of masa and filling.

Serve the pupusas immediately with curtido and salsa roja.

HOW TO SLAUGHTER A CHICKEN

Slaughtering a chicken is a lot like catering. It's a job that requires a lot of running around, knife skills, food conservation, and processing. Much like chasing chickens in a coop, Ruth has had to chase many vendors and clients in the food service business.

Hold the chicken in your left arm. With your right hand, grasp its head at the base where the skull meets the neck and snap the head in a down-and-out movement. Hesitation in any of these movements will cause pain to the animal. The sequence is best done quickly and in one movement, resulting in a singular *snap.* Knowing how to turn a live chicken into a meal can also feel like making your own luck; after all, there's always a wishbone to be found along the way.

Ruth and her mother managed to make their own luck by taking their pupusa stand from parks, parking lots, and freeway off-ramps to being the first vendor to sell pupusas in the Hollywood Farmers' Market in the 1990s. Right next to the organic produce, the beekeepers selling honey, and the artisan bread makers were Ruth and her mother, Delmy—after whom their business is named.

"I came to this country barefoot. I had no shoes because they got lost on the journey here. I was eight," says Ruth. These humble roots are an enormous badge of honor for her. How a shoeless cipota was able to position herself in one of Southern California's largest farmers' markets without compromising her food or her culture was because of the luck she made. Now there was another chicken to grab by the neck and snap. This time, instead of the farmers' market, it was the Coachella Music Festival. Ruth was the first pupusa vendor ever to work there, so everything had to run smoothly, efficiently, and perfectly.

Although setting up their Coachella vendor tent was a dream come true, the heat of the Coachella Valley was intense. Salty beads of sweat covered her body. This was nothing like those first days just off the freeway, but it did remind her of the same backbreaking work. Before, it was just Ruth and her mother, setting up the tent, propane tank, and drinks in the coolers. They were not afraid of hard work; their hands will tell you that. Ruth's smile is warm, but her hands know the weight of single-handedly making a way for herself.

It felt like a mammoth mountain of tasks to get to where she finally was. The crowds in the general section were waves of sweaty kids, all parched and with rolled-up bills trying to get some food. Things got easier in the VIP section. These folks had pisto, money. She prayed to sell out. After prepping all the perishables

and planning in Los Angeles, she did not want to bring anything back. Her workers were dazzled by the celebrities. Everyone sweating buckets just the same. The chele gabacho, blonde white guy, from the *Titanic* movie was walking by. Over the loud musical set coming from the main stage, Ruth overheard that he liked pupusas. Who doesn't?

PUPUSAS DE QUESO CON LOROCO

Pupusas de queso con loroco is another classic type of pupusa. The taste of loroco—an herbaceous, slightly bitter but very enjoyable edible flower—is dynamic.

MAKES 20 PUPUSAS

●

In a large bowl, combine the quesillo and loroco buds, mashing the cheese so that no large chunks remain. The mixture should be thoroughly combined and have a slightly green color. Set aside.

In another large bowl, combine the masa harina and water and knead until it reaches the consistency of Play-Doh. (You may choose to do this in batches. Divide the amount of water and masa harina and mix the batch one at a time.) When the dough is pressed, its sides should not tear.

Pour some water into a small bowl and keep it handy for moistening the dough. Roll about 3 ounces of masa (slightly larger than a golf ball) between the palms of your hands until it forms a completely round ball. Then start flattening it with the fingertips of your dominant hand. Rotate the round slightly so that it gets pressed down evenly. Once the round is about 5 inches in diameter, cup your hand so that the pressed-out dough is now a pocket. Put 3 ounces of filling into the pocket and press the filling tightly inside. Fold the edges of the dough toward the center to seal the pupusa, and twist off any remaining dough. This should now form a filled disk. Using your dominant hand, pat and flatten the disk until it is 6 to 7 inches in diameter. (If the dough cracks at any point, it needs more moisture; add more water and mix into the dough until it becomes elastic again.)

Set a comal or griddle over medium-high heat. When the comal is hot, add the pupusas and cook until they puff up and the exteriors have browned, about 5 minutes per side. Transfer the pupusas to a plate and cover with a kitchen towel to keep them warm. Repeat the process until you run out of masa and filling.

Serve the pupusas immediately.

1¾ pounds quesillo
2 cups fresh or frozen
    loroco buds
3½ pounds masa harina
7 cups water, or as needed

PUPUSAS REVUELTAS

MAKES 30 PUPUSAS

2 pounds trocitos (boneless
   pork shoulder)
2 teaspoons kosher salt
½ medium white onion, peeled
1 medium green bell pepper,
   cored and chopped
1 medium red bell pepper,
   cored and chopped
1 medium Roma tomato, peeled
   and halved
14 ounces quesillo
4 cups refried beans
1 cup fresh or frozen loroco
   buds
1 cup queso duro, finely
   shredded
5 pounds masa harina
10 cups water

I have found that pupusas revueltas can be very much open to interpretation. *Revuelta* means "mixed" in Spanish, so presumably the filling is mixed from whatever you have available. I have eaten pupusas revueltas on street corners; at fairs, festivals, and restaurants; and at home, and each has un toque especial— its own unique spin. It's not like a pupusa de frijol con queso, where you know for sure it has cheese and beans.

For this recipe, I consulted with my Tía Cristina, who helped me understand her approach. She is a tía who, when she visits from the East Coast, is guaranteed to leave rimeros de pupusas on your kitchen counters. These stacks of pupusas are a beautiful sight.

Cristina's pupusas are a mix of all your favorite things, essentially. Beans, cheese, loroco, aged cheese (for an extra bite of funkiness), and, of course, pork. Pork and cheese are two products of Spanish colonization. Pupusas are the national food of El Salvador, and pupusas revueltas are definitely seen as the most popular of them all.

●

In a medium Dutch oven over medium-high heat, combine 4 cups of water, the trocitos, salt, and onion. Bring to a boil and then turn the heat to medium-low. Let simmer until the pork begins to cook in its own fat and all the water has evaporated, about 1 hour. Using a spatula, move the pork pieces around so that all their sides brown evenly in the fat. When the pork has finished cooking, transfer the pieces to a plate and let cool.

In a food processor, combine the pork, both bell peppers, and tomato. Blend until everything is in small pieces and looks thoroughly mixed. Transfer the blended pork to a large bowl. Add the quesillo, refried beans, loroco, and queso duro and mix until thoroughly combined. The mixture should be uniform in texture with no clumps of ingredients remaining. Set aside.

In a large bowl, combine the masa harina and water and knead until it reaches the consistency of Play-Doh. (You may choose to do this in batches. Divide the amount of masa harina and water and mix one batch at a time.) When the dough is pressed, its sides should not tear.

Pour some water into a small bowl and keep it handy for moistening the dough. Roll about 3 ounces of masa (slightly larger than a golf ball) between the palms of your hands until it forms a completely round ball. Then start flattening it with the fingertips of your dominant hand. Rotate the round slightly so that it gets pressed

down evenly. Once the round is about 5 inches in diameter, cup your hand so that the pressed-out dough is now a pocket. Put 3 ounces of filling into the pocket and press the filling tightly inside. Fold the edges of the dough toward the center to seal the pupusa, and twist off any remaining dough. This should now form a filled disk. Using your dominant hand, pat and flatten the disk until it is 6 to 7 inches in diameter. (If the dough cracks at any point, it needs more moisture; add more water and mix into the dough until it becomes elastic again.)

Set a comal or griddle over medium-high heat. When the comal is hot, add the pupusas and cook until they puff up and the exteriors have browned, about 5 minutes per side. Transfer the pupusas to a plate and cover with a kitchen towel to keep them warm. Repeat the process until you run out of masa and filling.

Serve the pupusas immediately.

Left: Loroco, an edible and popular flower, being sold in Mercado Central in San Salvador. *Right:* Woman rolling out masa for pupusas in Pupusodromo El Triángulo during breakfast.

RIGUAS

Riguas are a signal of the season. Corn festivals are popular in El Salvador between August and September, and there you'll see riguas, some of which are even stuffed with refried beans. This dish illustrates the depth of traditional Salvadoran cooking. Fresh raw corn is ground and then cooked in a banana leaf so that it won't stick to the cooking surface, because its sugar could easily cause it to burn.

When I first made this recipe, I could not get the texture right. In El Salvador, the corn used is maíz maduro, "older corn." Unfortunately, even in Los Angeles, which has a large Salvadoran community, the right corn for this dish is not always easy to find. The consejo that I heard from different folks, including Zoila, was to buy the good corn. For this, Zoila and I drove to Orange County, where we bought fresh corn from Mexico, right off the back of a truck that had recently crossed the border. This specific type of corn has the sticky starchiness required to make this dish properly; the corn you find in grocery stores is too young—meaning it's really juicy and thus too watery. If you can't find maíz maduro, you can throw in some cheese or flour so the batter doesn't fall apart. Use a mix of young and mature corn to balance it out, or you can simply strain the ground corn so that the mixture isn't too wet.

You will need 15 banana leaves for wrapping the riguas. Most Latin American markets carry banana leaves year-round, so they should not be too difficult to source.

A note about the cheese in riguas: In the archives of El Palacio Nacional in San Salvador, I couldn't find any historical riguas recipe that included cheese. Today cheese is a popular addition to the dish, and it helps to make the masa more firm. Enjoy riguas whichever way you like. They are wonderful by themselves, with crema, or with frijoles.

●

In a large bowl and using a sharp knife, cut the kernels off each ear of corn. In a blender or food processor, blend the kernels, 5 cups at a time, until they become soft. Add the sugar, butter, and salt and blend until well combined. Place a mesh sieve over a large bowl and pour in the blended corn. Press down to squeeze out any excess liquid. The corn mixture should not be dry or strained completely, just wet enough that it doesn't fall apart. Set aside.

MAKES 15 RIGUAS

14 elotes (ears of corn), shucked
¼ cup granulated sugar
5 tablespoons unsalted butter, at room temperature
½ teaspoon kosher salt
2 tablespoons neutral oil (such as canola oil)
Frijoles licuados (see page 69) and crema Salvadoreña for serving
15 banana leaves

continued

RIGUAS

continued

Cut fifteen banana leaves into 8 by 11-inch sheets. Clean each sheet by wiping the front and back with a moistened paper towel and then wiping them dry. Pour the neutral oil on a single paper towel and wipe each leaf sheet from front and back. Note that the underside of each banana leaf is a muted pale-green color with a matte appearance, while the other side is shinier and a more vibrant green.

Set a comal or griddle over medium-high heat. Lay one banana leaf, shiny green side down, on the comal. Place ½ cup of the corn mixture on the leaf just to the side of where the center line would be. Fold the sheet in half to envelope the corn filling, making sure the fold forms a straight edge for the filling inside. Being careful not to burn your hand, gently press down on the leaf to flatten the filling as thinly as you can without forcing any of it out the sides. Turn the heat to medium and repeat the process for wrapping as many riguas as you can fit onto the comal at one time. Cook each side for 5 minutes, until the filling is cooked through and the banana-leaf ribs create charred lines on the corn masa that resemble grill marks. Repeat for the remaining riguas.

Serve the riguas immediately with frijoles licuados and crema Salvadoreña.

Red flags everywhere! Zoila's ex-husband was not the man of her dreams—never in a million years. He was, however, the man with whom she had spent twenty-six years of her life, enduring his tricks, lies, threats, and manipulations.

Her lunches with coworkers had put her on to his schemes. So it's *not* normal for a husband to take all your tax returns? *That's* how your partner is supposed to treat you? He never contributed to the household financially or otherwise. Zoila would come home and still have to serve him. Her findings only confirmed what she knew when she was seventeen. This man was bad.

It was her mother who had chosen him for Zoila back in El Salvador. Even though he was twenty years older than Zoila, her mother approved of him when he came in asking about her young daughter. It was of no consequence that Zoila had a boyfriend at the time, one that she liked. None of that mattered. Zoila doesn't know what words were exchanged between her mother and the older man, only that her family was del campo and he was adinerado, he had money, and that was enough to change her life completely.

All of a sudden, she belonged to her new boyfriend. Years later, when her family migrated north, she couldn't shake him off—even though it was her own mother who sent for her daughter out of fear. The irony. Until the moment the last red flag waved high in the sky. Zoila could not ignore it. It was a tax refund check that broke her and took her over the edge.

Around tax season, her husband would always take the bigger check that was issued to Zoila. For years, this happened. She humored him by saying, "I wonder when the check will get here." He would respond by saying, "It's probably lost. It's probably on its way." Zoila knew he had taken the checks, but she never said anything, even after losing thousands and thousands of dollars. This particular tax season was different. Her fourteen-year-old son had just joined the workforce. He earned no more than $250 every two weeks. It was a good first job and he was excited to go through this rite of passage and receive his tax return, but he never received it.

"Mamá, mi papá me robó mi cheque," he quietly shared with her. (Mom, Dad stole my check.) She had no reason to doubt her son. Her husband had done this kind of thing to her for years. For Zoila, her son's small tax return meant everything. "It was like he stole $20,000 or $30,000 from me. That was worth more than everything he had stolen from me. I told him that this is where everything ends," she said. "The fear is over. All my life I did it alone. All my life. I didn't need him or anyone."

THE MESSAGE

Tamales de Puerco in a rural
mercado in La Libertad.

TAMALES DE PUERCO

I had to call Bartola, one of the SalviSoul mamis and collaborators to whom this recipe belongs, several times to honor her receta as best as I could. It was a most enjoyable process. When I started testing and retesting recipes for this book, an intense heat wave swept Los Angeles, and I decided to move out of my apartment and into my parents' home for a month. Along with my husband and our dog, we packed up our kitchen and brought everything to their house. This meant that I was testing with many family members around, which was incredibly helpful during the eating and sampling process. It also made for many laughs.

This was one recipe that my mom and I were frightened to try at first. She and I had never made tamales before, much less together. We both agreed that it wasn't anything I had learned from her or that she had learned from my grandmother, which is why we called Bartola—we needed her guidance. This recipe is perhaps the perfect example of what I was looking for when I started SalviSoul: community among women. The laughing, eating, and talking over the phone, like so many immigrants do when they call back home to clarify a family recipe. Our Mamá Lucy wasn't there to help us quell our fears about making tamales, but Bartola was. She made us laugh, she reassured us, and she also reminded us not to skip a single step of the process, even though it was "Sí, yo se, es mucho trabajo." It may seem like a lot of work to peel each garbanzo bean, but Bartola explained that the texture of the skin isn't pleasant, so spending a few minutes on the task is worth it. So we didn't skip a single step.

You will need fifty banana leaves as well as fifty sheets of aluminum foil for wrapping the tamales. The leaves impart flavor to the tamales, and are a traditional ingredient for this dish. The foil is used as a second layer so the tamales don't fall apart. Using foil is a more modern way to make the tamales because preparing banana leaves requires an added prep step. However, all cooks recognize how necessary the leaves are, so the inside layer is always a banana leaf. Some cooks prefer to use double the amount of leaves as they prefer not to rely on too much foil for food preparation. If you choose not to use foil, prepare a hundred banana leaves. You can also line the pot with any extra bits of banana leaves before filling and steaming.

●

MAKES 50 TAMALES

4 pounds boneless pork ribs, rinsed and cut into 1-inch cubes
1 medium white onion, halved
3 garlic cloves, left whole
5 dried bay leaves
2 cups dried garbanzo beans, rinsed and soaked in 7 cups water overnight, then drained
2 teaspoons kosher salt
1 pinch baking soda

Recaudo for Tamales de Puerco

4 medium tomatoes, stemmed
1 medium white onion, halved
4 garlic cloves, left whole
¼ cup raw white sesame seeds
1 tablespoon raw peanuts
1 teaspoon unshelled pumpkin seeds
1 teaspoon black peppercorns
½ teaspoon dried oregano
½ teaspoon achiote powder
½ teaspoon cumin seeds
3 large dried bay leaves

4 pounds masa harina
10 to 12 cups water
4 cups lard, melted
1 tablespoon kosher salt
8 medium russet potatoes, peeled and cut into 1-inch cubes
100 banana leaves

continued

TAMALES DE PUERCO

continued

In a large pot over medium-high heat, combine the pork ribs and 6 cups of water and bring to a boil. Skim off any foam that floats to the top of the water. Add the onion, garlic, and four of the bay leaves, turn the heat to low, and cook for about 1 hour. Transfer the pork to a large plate and let it cool. Reserve 4 cups of the broth. Discard the onion, garlic, and bay leaves.

In a small pot over medium-high heat, combine 8 cups of water, the garbanzo beans, salt, and remaining bay leaf. Once the water is boiling, add the baking soda, which helps tenderize the garbanzos. Turn the heat to medium-low, cover, and cook until the beans are tender, about 45 minutes. Remove from the heat and drain. Once the garbanzos have completely cooled, peel and discard the skin from each one.

To make the recaudo: In a large pot, combine the tomatoes, onion, and garlic with enough water to fully cover. (You don't want anything to be protruding above the water line.) Set over medium-high heat and bring to a boil. Keep an eye on the tomato skins; once they begin to split and peel off, the vegetables are ready and the heat can be turned off, about 7 minutes.

In a small dry skillet over medium-high heat, combine the sesame seeds, peanuts, pumpkin seeds, peppercorns, oregano, achiote powder, cumin seeds, and bay leaves and toast until they turn fragrant, making sure to stir and shake them in the pan so they don't burn.

Using tongs or a large slotted spoon, transfer the tomatoes, onion, and garlic to a blender. Add 2 cups of the cooking water and the toasted spices and blend on high speed into a smooth sauce. Place a fine-mesh strainer over a large pot and pour the sauce through the strainer. Add the cooked pork to the pot, set over high heat, and cook until the mixture boils, about 10 minutes. Remove from the heat, transfer the meat to a plate, and set the sauce aside.

In a large bowl, combine the masa harina and water, using about 3 cups of water per 1 pound of masa. The masa should be well mixed and runny. Set a fine-mesh strainer in the sink and add the masa to strain out any grumos, or clumps. Transfer the masa mixture to a large pot, stir in the lard and salt, set over low heat, and stir vigorously until the masa becomes thick and reaches the consistency of Play-Doh. Add the reserved 4 cups pork broth and 1 cup of the sauce and keep stirring constantly to prevent the masa from sticking to the bottom of the pot. Cook until the texture is not too loose and not too tight, like pudding, about 20 minutes. It should come to a boil, which you'll know when little bubbles rise to the surface and pop like molten lava in a volcano. Remove from the heat and set aside.

Cut fifty 8 by 11-inch sheets each of banana leaves and aluminum foil. Arrange everything you'll need in its own container with its own spoon or utensil in the order of assembly: banana leaves, foil, masa, pork, potato, garbanzos, and reserved sauce.

Wipe a banana leaf with a moistened paper towel, then pass the leaf over medium-high heat to make it bendable without breaking. (Look for the leaf to change color to a brighter green.) Place the leaf on top of a sheet of foil and spoon about ½ cup of the masa in the center of the leaf. Add about 2 tablespoons of the pork, followed by a piece of potato and three garbanzo beans. Finish with a bit of sauce. Pull the bottom edge of the leaf up and over the filling, tucking it over and under the filling. Next, roll the leaf all the way toward its top edge. Following this motion, fold in the edges of the leaf. Repeat this process of wrapping all the tamales until you've run out of filling.

In a large pot with a steamer basket, add at least 3 inches of water. Place the prepared tamales upright in the steamer so they stand next to one another. Once you've added all the tamales, place a manta or kitchen towel over the mouth of the pot and then top with the lid. Set over medium-high heat, bring to a boil, and steam for about 1 hour. Transfer the tamales to a platter and allow them to cool completely.

The tamales are best served the following day to allow them to set. They will keep in the refrigerator for up to 7 days, or in the freezer for up to 1 month. Remove the aluminum foil wrapping and individually reheat each tamale in the microwave.

CONSEJO

Stirring the masa is what some folks have said is the trickiest part of this process. I recommend using a few things to ensure that the desired outcome is achieved. A wooden paleta is advisable, which can be purchased at most Latino marketplaces. It makes stirring a lot more doable. Three other tools that might not be traditional but do allow you to suffer less grief are a stepladder, a blender, and a metal balloon whisk. Sometimes to stir tamale masa better, it's not our skills that are missing but maybe just proper leverage. A stepladder is advisable, especially if there isn't a willing volunteer who is tall enough to help. A blender can also be helpful to mix the masa and water more completely and with less trouble. The last two things you want to avoid in your masa are grumos (clumps) and burning. You can avoid the burning by stirring, which should also help with the grumos. But if it doesn't, you can use a large metal whisk, which I've found handy many a time. Tamales can be mysterious but they are fun, so try to enjoy the process.

TAMALES DE POLLO

MAKES 50 TAMALES

6 pounds chicken, preferably
    thighs and breasts
6 cups water
½ medium red onion, halved
5 garlic cloves, left whole
5 dried bay leaves
1 bunch cilantro, coarsely
    chopped
2 celery stalks, cut into
    6-inch slices
1 tablespoon chicken bouillon
    powder
Kosher salt
2 cups dried garbanzo beans,
    rinsed and soaked in
    8 cups water overnight,
    then drained
1 pinch baking soda

**Recaudo for Tamales
de Pollo**

2 pounds Roma tomatoes,
    stemmed
1 medium green bell pepper,
    cored and halved
¼ cup raw white sesame seeds
1 tablespoon kosher salt
1 tablespoon chicken bouillon
    powder
1 tablespoon raw peanuts
1 teaspoon raw pumpkin seeds
1 teaspoon black peppercorns
½ teaspoon dried oregano

When I started this SalviSoul journey, I began with my grandmother. She sent me to Vermont Avenue in Los Angeles, which is home to a Salvadoran cultural food hub. When I asked her how she cooked as a recent immigrant in the country in the 1980s, she said, "Fui a la Vermont." (I went to Vermont.) I'm so glad I followed her tip because I found a wealth of Salvadoran food and a world of street vendors there.

It gives me so much pleasure that the last person who was added to the list of *SalviSoul* contributors was Maricela, a longtime vendor in El Salvador and in Los Angeles. Maricela makes her livelihood selling many different kinds of Salvadoran street foods in one of the most iconic corners of Salvadoran culture in L.A. I met her while I was reporting and investigating the uncertain future of this street market. Without her, this book would not be complete. When I asked her what recipe she'd like to contribute, tamales de pollo was one of her top suggestions. As with most labor-intensive recipes, you must make many of them to justify the work involved; this recipe yields fifty tamales.

Tamales are a super-important cultural heritage and legacy. Tamales de pollo are for every occasion. Birthdays, New Year's, Easter, funerals—you can't go wrong. Mostly, it's a feeling that no matter what's going on, tamales make the occasion worthwhile.

Peeling the garbanzo beans may seem like a lot of work, but it is worth it. All the Salvadoran cooks that I've spoken to about this agree: not peeling them is like not rinsing your rice. You could bypass that step, but the end result is much more enjoyable if you don't skip it.

You will need fifty banana leaves as well as fifty sheets of aluminum foil for wrapping the tamales. The leaves impart flavor to the tamales, and are a traditional ingredient for this dish. The foil is used as a second layer so the tamales don't fall apart. Using foil is a more modern way to make the tamales because preparing banana leaves requires an added prep step. However, all cooks recognize how necessary the leaves are, so the inside layer is always a banana leaf. Some cooks prefer to use double the amount of leaves as they prefer not relying on much foil for food preparation. If you choose not to use foil, prepare a hundred banana leaves. You can also line the pot with any extra bits of banana leaves before filling and steaming.

●

continued

TAMALES DE POLLO

continued

½ teaspoon achiote powder
½ teaspoon cumin seeds
3 large dried bay leaves

8 medium russet potatoes,
    peeled and cut into
    2-inch cubes
4 pounds masa harina
10 to 12 cups water
4 cups vegetable oil
1 tablespoon kosher salt
50 green olives (optional)
50 banana leaves

In a large pot over medium-high heat, combine the chicken and 6 cups of water and bring to a boil. Turn the heat to medium-low; add the onion, garlic, four of the bay leaves, cilantro, celery, chicken bouillon, and 1 tablespoon salt; and cook until the chicken is cooked through, about 25 minutes. Transfer the chicken to a large plate and let it cool. Reserve 4 cups of the broth. Separate the meat from the bones, shred it, and set aside.

In a small pot over medium-high heat, combine 8 cups of water, the garbanzos, 2 teaspoons salt, and remaining bay leaf. Once the water is boiling, add the baking soda, which helps tenderize the garbanzos. Turn the heat to medium-low, cover, and cook until the beans are tender, about 45 minutes. Remove from the heat and drain. Once the garbanzos have completely cooled, peel and discard the skin from each one.

To make the recaudo: In a large bowl, combine the tomatoes, bell pepper, sesame seeds, salt, chicken bouillon, peanuts, pumpkin seeds, peppercorns, oregano, achiote powder, cumin seeds, and bay leaves. Add 2 cups of the reserved chicken broth and stir to combine. Pour the sauce mixture into a blender and blend on high speed until thoroughly mixed, about 3 minutes. (This may need to be done in batches.)

Place a fine-mesh strainer over a large pot and pour the sauce into the strainer. Add the cooked chicken and the potatoes to the pot, set over medium heat, and cook until the mixture boils, about 10 minutes. Remove from the heat, transfer the chicken and potatoes to a plate, and set the sauce aside.

In a large bowl, combine the masa harina and water, using about 3 cups of water per 1 pound of masa. Transfer the masa mixture to a blender and blend on high speed to ensure that no grumos, or clumps, remain. While the blender is running, add the vegetable oil, salt, and 1 cup of the sauce and blend to the consistency of pancake batter.

Transfer the masa mixture to a large pot, set over low heat, and stir vigorously until the masa becomes thick and reaches the consistency of Play-Doh. Add the remaining reserved chicken broth and keep stirring constantly to prevent the masa from sticking to the bottom of the pot. Cook until the texture is not too loose and not too tight, like pudding, about 20 minutes. It should come to a boil, which you'll know when little bubbles rise to the surface and pop like molten lava in a volcano. Remove from the heat and set aside.

Cut fifty 8 by 11-inch sheets each of banana leaves and aluminum foil. Arrange everything you'll need in its own container with its own spoon or utensil in the order of assembly: banana leaves, foil, masa, chicken and potatoes, garbanzos, green olives (if using), and reserved sauce.

Wipe a banana leaf with a moistened paper towel. Pass the leaf over medium heat to make it bendable without breaking. (Look for the leaf to change color to a brighter green.) Place the leaf on top of a sheet of foil and spoon about ½ cup of the masa in the center of the leaf. Add about 2 tablespoons of the chicken-potato mixture, three garbanzo beans, and an olive. Finish with a bit of sauce. Pull the bottom edge of the leaf up and over the filling, tucking it over and under the filling. Next, roll the leaf all the way toward its top edge. Following this motion, fold in the edges of the leaf. Repeat this process of wrapping all the tamales until you've run out of filling.

In a large pot with a steamer basket, add 3 inches of water. Place the prepared tamales upright in the steamer so they stand next to one another. Once you've added all the tamales, place a manta or kitchen towel over the mouth of the pot and place the lid on top. Set over medium-low heat, bring to a boil, and steam for 1 hour. Transfer the tamales to a platter and allow them to cool completely.

The tamales are best served the following day to allow them to set. They will keep in the refrigerator for up to 7 days, or in the freezer for up to 1 month. Remove the aluminum foil wrapping and individually reheat each tamale in the microwave.

Woman waiting for her pupusas for breakfast in La Libertad.

NOT HOMESICK

Maricela may be far from her original home of Usulután, but she doesn't miss it, even after almost four years. "I don't miss anything from my country because everything is here, in that respect. Not my work, either. Because we have always worked for ourselves, and that's what's better for us," she says.

Street vending has been in her family for several generations. She knows how to make several kinds of atoles, tamales, pan dulces, and other traditional dishes, not because her mother encouraged her to cook but because it was their way of life. For instance, making chuco takes a full week, depending on the weather. She knew all these things because she lived by what her and her mother's hands prepared day and night. The only time she didn't work for herself was after she had newly arrived in this country. She was employed for three long months in a meatpacking plant, processing Burger King patties. The freezing-cold temperatures got to her, and she suffered an injury that took her out of commission for five months. She never went back.

She now sells out of a 10 by 10-foot stall in the heart of Salvadoran Los Angeles, between 11th and 12th Streets, where an impromptu market exists—one that sprang from a bank in a small strip mall. The story goes that the mall's Italian owners decided to lease to Banco Agrícola. An enormous influx of Salvadorans was migrating to Los Angeles, and when the bank set up shop, it was one of the few financial institutions that provided the service of sending remittances back to relatives in El Salvador. Decades later, this is where Maricela set up her blue tent. She feels at home here, despite the market's uncertain future, potential closures, ongoing tickets from the health department, Southern California heat waves, a lack of storage and personal safety, and a flurry of other problems. Through it all, she has continued to vend and greet clients in her endearing Salvadoran sing-songy manner, "¿Que va querer corazon? ¿Que va llevar amor?"

At the market, she's had Salvadoran clients who have requested large orders of food to bring back to their homes in Virginia, Wisconsin, or as far away as Europe. "Why not just own it?" says Maricela. "In every part of the world, there is always a Salvadoran person there. They miss our food." It's become a rite of passage for Salvadorans in the diaspora.

CHILAQUILAS

MAKES 4 TO 6 SERVINGS (ABOUT
2 CHILAQUILAS PER PERSON)

2 cups queso fresco
    (see Consejo, page 89)
12 Tortillas Salvadoreñas
    (page 36)
7 eggs, separated
1 tablespoon all-purpose flour
½ cup grapeseed oil
1 recipe Salsa de Tomate para
    Rellenos (page 88)
Arroz Frito (page 51) for serving

I don't know why this particular dish is not more common in Salvadoran restaurants. I've seen it used on social media as a type of qualifier. One Twitter user said about chilaquilas, "Si nunca comiste chilaquilas con arroz y tortilla no sos #Salvadoreño." (If you've never eaten chilaquilas with rice and tortilla, you are not Salvadoran.) A little harsh, if you ask me, especially as someone in the diaspora. So many dishes exist that I only learned as an adult, never mind making or eating them. This has created panic in me by supporting the narrative that I'll never be Salvadoran enough. I believe we're meant to continually learn about our culture; whether it's from guilt or genuine curiosity, the choice is ours. My choice was to learn it and not let intrusive thoughts interfere in my relationship with what belongs to me: a connection to my homeland and identity.

This chilaquilas recipe was also the first one that my mom and I ever taught to an in-person group. She was nervous. The class had sold out, and we had to add seats. It was hosted in a very well-known Los Angeles location. We had equipment to schlep, and I feared someone would say, "Oh, this is just like Mexican rellenos de chile." Somehow, I felt that drawing similarities between the two dishes would diminish the value of this recipe, which to me was a Salvi insider's cultural touchstone. I felt so insecure. But what happened was something else. No one said anything close to what I feared. My mom, who was a preschool teacher back then, handled a roomful of adults flawlessly. In fact, she thrived. Everyone loved having her there.

The Salvi folks in attendance were grateful to have a place to learn about this recipe, for they had never tried it. They appreciated that SalviSoul carved out a space in downtown Los Angeles where they could learn something that would otherwise be inaccessible. The non-Salvadorans never uttered or confirmed my worst fears. Everyone walked away feeling stronger about their abilities in the kitchen and happy to know yet another way to love corn. At the end of the class, someone did say chilaquilas reminded them of a delicious gourmet pasta dish. At the time, that comment seemed like a compliment; I understand that we sometimes value European dishes far too much. Now chilaquilas are another reminder that when we're in El Salvador, we do things differently, and that makes us unique.

●

Over a plate, crumble the queso fresco until it's completely soft and mashed. (If you are using a different, firmer cheese, shred or slice the pieces so you have equal amounts of cheese to place in the tortillas.) Cut the tortillas lengthwise, then lay them flat and slide the knife blade along the straight edge to cut pockets inside them. Do not cut all the way through. Put the queso in the tortilla pockets. Set aside.

In a large bowl, using an electric mixer on high speed (or a whisk), whip the egg whites until foamy, about 30 seconds. Add the egg yolks, one at a time, and the flour, and continue to whip until soft peaks form. Set aside.

Line a large plate with paper towels or put a wire cooling rack in a baking sheet and set near the stove. In a large skillet over medium heat, warm the grapeseed oil until it shimmers. Using tongs, dip the prepared tortillas into the egg mixture, making sure that all sides are coated. Place the chilaquilas in the oil and fry until they're golden brown and crispy, about 2 minutes per side. Transfer the fried chilaquilas to the prepared plate to drain.

Wipe the pan clean with a paper towel and turn the heat to medium-low. Pour the salsa de tomate into the pan, cover, and bring to a boil. Add the chilaquilas and cook until the sauce has thickened and changed from bright red to a more orange-red, about 5 minutes more.

Serve the chilaquilas immediately with arroz.

Pupusera refers to a cook who makes pupusas; here the pupusera is making sure the masa is well covered with a multicolored manta.

ATOL CHUCO

MAKES 6 TO 8 SERVINGS

2 pounds dried maíz negro
1 pound dried black beans,
    sorted to remove debris
½ small red onion, peeled
2 garlic cloves, left whole
Kosher salt
One 3-inch cinnamon stick
25 chiles de árbol
½ cup alguashte (see page 55)
8 pan francés, toasted

Sometimes when you cook a cultural dish for the first time as an adult, shame is attached to that reality, a growing pain of being an immigrant in the diaspora. "What do you mean you don't know how to make [insert name of cultural dish here]? You must not be a real [insert culture]." That accusation has been thrown at me by my family, the community, and even myself at times. I'm here to say that it's okay. Through the process of creating this cookbook, I've made new dishes that no one in my family had tried before because they also left El Salvador when they were really young. The point is to keep learning for yourself.

This dish is sometimes called comida de las abuelitas, food from the grandmothers. There might be various reasons why, but I believe it's a food that many Salvadorans forget to practice or lose an appetite for but that the abuelitas always remember. This is compounded when some people have lost their elders or been separated from them through war or migration.

This recipe utilizes maíz negro, or black corn, and is from Maricela, a wonderful Salvadoreña who comes from a long line of street vendors both in Los Angeles and El Salvador. This dish takes several days to make and connects us to the Indigenous traditions of the "three sisters"—corn, beans, and squash, as well as chile, which is also native to El Salvador. It's fermented, vegan, savory, funky, and super Salvadoran.

●

Days 1 and 2
Wash the maíz negro thoroughly to remove any debris. In a large bowl or pot, combine the corn and enough water to cover by 2 inches, cover with a manta or kitchen towel, and let soak for 48 hours. After the corn has finished soaking, drain the water.

Day 3
In a blender, combine 2 cups of the drained corn with 1 cup fresh water. Pulse the blender to slowly grind the corn, then transfer to a large bowl. Cover the bowl with a manta and set in a spot at room temperature and allow to ferment for 24 hours. (If the temperature is cooler than 70°F inside your home, Maricela suggests leaving the bowl outside in a warm shaded area where it won't be moved or in the way. Alternatively, place it in the warmest spot in your home, like next to a heater.) By the end of this fermenting period, the ground corn will have a sour smell, and the once-clear water will be cloudy with white foam on its surface.

Rinse the beans. In a large pot, combine the beans and enough water to cover, and let soak for 2 hours.

continued

An atol chuco stand in Barrio Zurita in San Salvador.

ATOL CHUCO

continued

At the end of the soaking time, drain the beans. In the same pot over high heat, bring 8 cups of water to a boil. Add the beans, onion, and garlic. Once the beans start to boil, turn the heat to low and simmer, uncovered, until they become tender, about 2 hours. Check the beans and stir them every 30 minutes, adding more water to cover as needed; do not let them burn. When the beans are tender, remove from the heat, stir in 1 tablespoon salt, and set aside.

Day 4

Place a fine-mesh strainer over a large bowl and pour the fermented corn mixture into the strainer. This separates any solid pieces of corn from the chuco liquid. Discard the solids. In a large pot over medium-high heat, combine the chuco liquid and cinnamon stick and season with salt. Cook until the mixture boils and has thickened, about 30 minutes. Set this chuco aside.

In a medium bowl, soak the chiles de árbol in 1 cup of hot water for 15 minutes. Transfer the chiles and their soaking liquid to the blender and blend until smooth. Place a fine-mesh strainer over the bowl and pour the blended chiles into the strainer. Using a rubber spatula, scrape as much of the pulp from the bottom side of the strainer into the bowl as you can. Set aside.

In a medium bowl, combine ½ cup of the chuco with the alguashte and thoroughly mix. Add more chuco if needed to make this alguashte sauce liquid enough that it pours easily.

In individual bowls or guacales de morro, pour in 2 cups of the chuco and about ½ cup of the black beans. Drizzle 1 tablespoon of the alguashte sauce and 1 teaspoon of the chile over the atol.

Serve the atol chuco as a soup with a side of pan francés.

Maricela knows that if you call chuco "atol rosado" or "atol dulce," you're from her home of Usulután. Cooking in her colonia, she came to understand the flavors that her neighbors preferred over others and those beyond. It has taught her a thing or two about the cultural anthropology of El Salvador.

Once, she led her own controlled-testing survey of sorts and made atol chuco, a saltier popular version in Occidente, the western part of El Salvador, and atol chuco dulce, as she does back home. "Aja, el chuco se me fui asi." Yes, the chuco went like this, she said, snapping her fingers in an upward motion to signal it was the obvious choice for people. The atol rosado didn't move quite as fast. "Aja, es que lo busca la gente de oriente nada más, no la gente de occidente." Are there more Salvadoran immigrants from Oriente, the eastern side of El Salvador, then? She shakes her head. "No, not really. It's about even." To support her findings, she states, "Yo vendo mucho tamal de elote, de sal y dulce y yo vendo mas el de tamal de sal." When she sells tamales de elote, she finds that people prefer the saltier version from Oriente.

These observations have helped her to successfully keep customers. Making these foods is very labor-intensive, with four components that can each take between twenty minutes and five days. Over the years, Maricela has tried shortcuts but doesn't like them because it compromises the end product too much. For instance, for the atol, instead of toasting the corn and soaking it for days (or up to a week, depending on the climate), you could use masa harina, or corn flour. It's a big shortcut, but clumps easily form when cooking the atol. Speaking of corn, the corn for fresh atol has been responsible for breaking too many of her blenders.

During one atol season, she finally made a big investment in her street-vending business and spent more than eight hundred dollars for a Vitamix, that highly reviewed, highly coveted premium-quality blender. She had heard it could pulverize anything. Naturally, she assumed her long nights of making chuco would come to a halt now that she had the right equipment.

Her daydream was short-lived. In her excitement, she may have overpacked the blender and the soaked corn did what it did to all her other blenders—it broke her Vitamix. This is why she doesn't believe in shortcuts.

PASTELITOS DE HONGOS

MAKES 12 TO 14 PASTELITOS

1 tablespoon extra-virgin
    olive oil
½ cup minced white onion
3 garlic cloves, minced
½ teaspoon kosher salt
10 ounces cremini mushrooms,
    finely chopped
5 teaspoons chicken bouillon
    powder
½ teaspoon dried oregano
4½ cups water, or as needed
2 cups peeled and diced
    potatoes
1 cup peeled and diced carrot
1 cup chopped Roma tomato
½ cup chopped green beans
2 cups masa harina
2 teaspoons achiote powder
1 teaspoon baking soda
2 cups vegetable oil or
    peanut oil
Curtido (page 43) and Salsa
    de Tomate (page 52) for
    serving (optional)

When the COVID-19 pandemic began, all my gigs and work dried up and we couldn't continue in-person classes. This opened a huge, obvious opportunity to explore some of my favorite Salvadoran foods with folks through online cooking classes. Throughout those months, students tuned in from France, Canada, Japan, and Belgium, and this recipe was one of my more popular offerings.

This dish is usually made with beef, pork, or chicken, but I love mushrooms and needed to explore them when people requested more vegetarian options. This recipe is the result.

●

In a large saucepan over medium-high heat, warm the olive oil until it shimmers. Add the onion, garlic, and salt and cook until fragrant, about 2 minutes. Add the mushrooms, 1 teaspoon of the chicken bouillon, the oregano, and ½ cup of the water and cook, stirring frequently, until the liquid is mostly absorbed, about 7 to 8 minutes. Transfer the mushroom mixture to a mixing bowl.

In the same pan over medium-high heat, combine the potatoes, carrot, tomato, green beans, 2 teaspoons chicken bouillon, and 2 cups water. Bring to a boil, then lower the heat to medium and let the vegetables simmer until tender, about 10 minutes. Transfer the vegetables to the same bowl containing the mushroom mixture.

In a large bowl, combine the masa harina, achiote powder, baking soda, and remaining 2 teaspoons chicken bouillon. Slowly add the remaining 2 cups water to the masa harina and knead until the dough reaches the consistency of Play-Doh. (When the dough is pressed, its sides should not tear.) Pour some water into a small bowl and keep it handy for moistening the dough. Roll 1½ to 2 ounces of masa between the palms of your hands until it forms a completely round ball. Then start flattening it with the fingertips of your dominant hand. Rotate the round slightly so that it gets pressed down evenly and thinly. Repeat for the remaining tortillas.

Spoon 2 tablespoons of the vegetable mixture onto half of each tortilla. Fold the other half of the tortilla over the mixture and pinch the seam to close it. Repeat for the rest of the pastelitos.

Line a large plate with paper towels and set near the stove. In a large pot over medium heat, warm the vegetable oil until it registers 350°F on an instant-read thermometer. Add the pastelitos, two at a time, and fry until they turn golden brown, about 2 minutes per side. Using tongs, transfer the pastelitos to the prepared plate to drain and cool.

Enjoy the pastelitos on their own, or with curtido and salsa de tomate.

ENCHILADAS DE CARNE DE RES

The first time I heard of Salvadoran enchiladas, I was in southeast Los Angeles, talking to a woman with whom I had connected through her son, who worked at Albright College. He had seen my call for participants in SalviSoul and thought that his mom would be a great candidate for the project. Unfortunately, she was unable to continue with the project, and she never gave me her recipe, so I adapted this based on what I learned after she described it. It was a wonderful experience to then discuss it with my Guatemalan neighbor Claudia, who then also mentioned a similar dish and how Central American it is.

●

In a large bowl, combine the masa harina, achiote powder, and 1½ teaspoons of the salt and mix well. Carefully pour in 1 cup of the warm water. Using your hands, thoroughly mix the water with the dry ingredients. Keep adding the remaining water, ½ cup at a time, and mixing until the dough reaches the consistency of Play-Doh. It should feel cool to the touch and evenly moist throughout. Cover with a manta or kitchen towel and set aside.

Pat the ground beef dry with a paper towel. Allow it to sit for 15 minutes to come to room temperature. In a large saucepan over medium heat, warm 2 teaspoons of the canola oil until it shimmers. Add the beef and, using a spatula, flatten it into a single thin layer in the pan. Sprinkle 1 teaspoon salt over the top and don't move it around, even if you want to. Fry the beef until the edges turn brown and crispy. Using the spatula, flip the beef, sprinkle with another 1 teaspoon salt, and brown the other side. Remove the beef from the pan, sprinkle with the remaining ½ teaspoon salt, and set aside.

In the same pan over medium heat, combine the tomato, onion, and garlic and cook until the onion turns translucent. Stir in the oregano and mix thoroughly. Add the potatoes, green beans, carrot, and beef bouillon and cook for 3 minutes. Add 1 cup water and cook until the vegetables are tender and the water has evaporated, 5 to 7 minutes. Add the browned beef back to the pan and mix well.

In a large pot over medium-high heat, place the eggs in a single layer, add enough water to cover by 1 inch, and bring them to a gentle boil. Remove from the heat, cover, and set a timer for 8 minutes. Fill a medium bowl with 4 cups of ice water. Once the timer sounds, transfer the eggs to the ice water and let sit for 10 minutes. Remove them from the ice water, peel, and cut each egg crosswise into four slices. Set aside.

MAKES 8 ENCHILADAS

2¼ cups masa harina
2 teaspoons achiote powder
4 teaspoons kosher salt
2½ cups lukewarm
    (about 98°F) water
1 pound ground beef
    (80% lean)
2 cups plus 2 teaspoons
    canola oil
1 medium Roma tomato, finely
    chopped
¼ medium white onion, minced
3 garlic cloves, minced
1 teaspoon dried oregano
1½ cups peeled and chopped
    Yukon gold potatoes
8 ounces finely chopped
    green beans
1 medium carrot, finely
    chopped
1 teaspoon beef bouillon
    powder
5 eggs
½ cup Salsa de Tomate
    (page 52)
½ cup Curtido (page 43)
½ cup shredded queso rallado
    (such as queso duro blando)

continued

ENCHILADAS
DE CARNE DE RES

continued

Line a large plate with paper towels and set near the stove. In a large, deep saucepan over medium-high heat, warm 1 cup canola oil until it registers 350°F on an instant-read thermometer.

Fill a small bowl with water. Separate the dough into eight golf ball–size portions, 3 to 4 ounces each. Roll them into balls and return to the large bowl. Dip the fingertips of both hands into the water and raise them upward, allowing the water to drip down and spread across both of your palms.

Take out one ball and cover the remaining dough with the manta to keep it from drying out. Start flattening the ball with the fingertips of your dominant hand. Rotate the round slightly so that it gets pressed down as evenly and thinly as possible, to make a ⅛-inch-thick tortilla. Repeat for the remaining dough balls.

Add two tortillas to the oil and fry until they turn golden brown, about 2 minutes per side. Using tongs, transfer the fried tortillas to the prepared plate to drain, and set aside. Repeat with the remaining tortillas, adding the remaining 1 cup oil as needed and lowering the heat if necessary.

Spoon about ¼ cup of the beef filling on top of each fried tortilla. Top with 1 tablespoon salsa de tomate, about 1 tablespoon curtido, and 1 tablespoon queso rallado. Garnish with two slices of hard-boiled egg.

Serve the enchiladas immediately.

Aluminum comales and pots and hammocks displayed in Usulután.

SOPAS

Two locals eating sopa de patas at Sopa de Patas

A soup is an event. Unless it's a sopa de frijoles—then it's a weekday. But if the sopa de frijoles contains costilla de res and mamasos, it might just be a special day. Of course, if the weather is hot, it's sopa weather. According to some Salvadoran cooks, that's because the only way to cool down on a sweltering day is to enjoy a piping-hot bowl of soup, which signals your body to break a sweat to control its temperature.

It was not uncommon to get an invitation by phone or text from a family member who said, "Come over—tu Mamá Lucy hizo sopa de patas." My grandma, the matriarch of the family, was going to make her famous cow's hoof soup. She was going to throw down in the kitchen and show her skills and sazón for us, her family. You were expected to show up, eat your serving, and hang out until someone said, "Well, I have to work tomorrow, so I gotta go." Other sopas that became events were Sopa de Res (page 134), Sopa de Frijoles con Masitas (page 150), and Sopa de Gallina (page 149). Very rarely, it could even be sopa de cangrejo.

Sopas are a reason to call the family and have a get-together. Sure, it could be 95 degrees outside and the gathering could be hosted by the family member with the smallest kitchen and tiniest living room, but that's beside the point—you showed up no matter what.

Classic Salvadoran soups, like sopa de gallina, are a go-to for wellness and comfort. Sopa de frijoles is the tried-and-true soup that calls you home instead of eating out because it keeps money in your pocket and fills your body with iron. Sopa de patas is for celebrations and special occasions. And finally, sopa de res fortifies and strengthens the body and spirit.

SOPA DE RES

MAKES 4 TO 6 SERVINGS

1½ gallons water
3 pounds chamorro
    (beef shanks)
1 Roma tomato, quartered
1 medium white onion, halved
6 garlic cloves, left whole
1 celery stalk, trimmed
    and halved
1 bunch cilantro, coarsely
    chopped
1 pound yuca, peeled and
    quartered
3 elotes (ears of corn),
    shucked and cut into
    2-inch rounds
3 güisquiles, quartered
1 pound carrots, peeled and
    quartered
1 medium head green cabbage,
    quartered
3 tablespoons kosher salt
4 limes, quartered
Tortillas Salvadoreñas
    (page 36) for serving

My mom can be at home alone and randomly get the urge to make sopa de res. By the time it's done, without her saying a word to anyone else, the whole extended family will have somehow heard about what she is making and show up at her house for the warmth, laughs, and arguments. Sopa de res isn't just a meal—it's an event you don't want to miss.

For contributor Laura, this is also a recipe she associates with her family, her childhood, and a good time. To enjoy sopa de res as a child meant that she went on a family trip to the playa and, on the way back, everyone looked forward to the sopa that would replenish their strength after a fun, hot day at the beach. Her extended family often prepared this dish for everyone who visited.

So while someone's perfect beach snack might be chips, ice cream, or hot dogs, for Laura and other Salvadorans, a sopa de res at the end of the day was the cherry on top.

Some historians have suggested that the addition of potatoes or plantains to this soup is from the influence of Afrodescendants in El Salvador. This is especially true in San Miguel, the part of El Salvador with the highest concentration of Afro-descendants.

In a large pot over medium-high heat, combine the water, chamorro, tomato, onion, garlic, celery, and cilantro and bring to a boil. Using a large spoon, skim off and discard any foam and fat that rises to the surface of the water; repeat as needed.

Turn the heat to medium and let the meat simmer until it becomes tender, about 1 hour. Remove the meat from the broth, cover, and set aside. (At this point, it's important to know if you will be serving the soup immediately after it has finished cooking. Add the vegetables only if the soup is being served right away; otherwise, they'll overcook sitting in the hot broth.)

Add the yuca to the pot, cover, and cook until tender, 15 to 20 minutes. Add the corn, güisquiles, and carrots and cook until they are tender, 5 to 10 minutes more. Next, place the cabbage quarters atop the soup and allow them to sink a bit below the surface. Cover and let simmer for 5 minutes more. Once all the vegetables are tender, add the meat back into the soup and allow it to warm for a few minutes.

Serve the soup hot with the lime wedges and plenty of fresh tortillas.

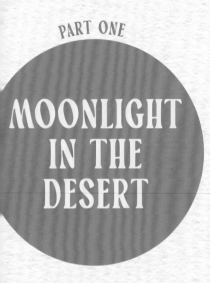

PART ONE

MOONLIGHT IN THE DESERT

To experience the cold desert at night under the light of a mystical full moon was one thing. To experience it under helicopter searchlights—well, that was completely different. Laura was even more afraid and anxious now than when she and her tía left Santa Ana. These birds flying in the chilly, inky-dark sky, with the thunderous sound of their rotary blades roaring and their bright lights spotlighting every part of the desert, were terrifying. As she squinted into the darkness, she made out what could only be a row of houses. A neighborhood.

She grabbed her aunt's hand. The coyote had threatened them—if they got separated from the group or, worse, were caught by anyone, especially the DHS, they were on their own. The stern warning ended with, "You better forget my name too." Not only had they separated from the group but they had also lost Laura's uncle, her tía's husband. "Esto va de peor en peor, Tía," Laura cried out, fearful of the worsening situation. Laura looked at her tía again. "¿Tía, puede corer?" (Can you run?) They had just jumped a fence, and the neat row of homes looked like the only shelter in the desolate landscape. Her tía, visibly tired, crouching, and in pain, nodded a weak yes. She had just started her period and had been dealing with cramps for miles.

As they scanned between the fence and the homes, Laura estimated they were less than a half mile away. They could cover that distance, even in their debilitated physical state. She helped her tía up and they ran. As they got closer to the homes, they spotted a shadow. Under the bright moonlight, Laura made out the face of a young woman, who quickly introduced herself as Elisabeth. As soon as they reached the end of the block, all three started knocking on doors. "¡Auxilio, help! ¡Alguien ayudenos!" Was anyone home? Were they all deep sleepers? Were the three of them not loud enough? Or a more sobering question: Could the people inside these comfortable homes hear them and choose to not care? Laura pushed past those thoughts and kept knocking.

Finally, one door opened. No one came out. They ran inside. It wasn't until she saw the dark shadow of a bearded man with a serious face that Laura was bothered by a new concern—had they just entered the wolf's den? He was an older man. "My wife isn't here right now," he said in Spanish. "But she'll be back. He led them to a bedroom. "Sleep here if you want." Laura glanced inside the neat, tidy bedroom. Her tía and Elisabeth followed her into the room with frightened eyes. They glanced at one another, each thinking the same thing,

Have we put ourselves in more danger by taking shelter in this home? Laura was about to say something when a loud bang came from outside. The DHS officers were knocking on the same door they had entered just moments before. The three of them quickly slid under the bed. From their hiding place they heard the older man's heavy footsteps. When he walked by, they heard two sounds that made Laura's stomach churn. The first was a cock of a rifle. The second was the sound of the bedroom door being closed.

Elisabeth was shaking. Laura's tía cried silently with her eyes closed. Laura was still trying to catch her breath.

SOPA DE ESPINACA CON HUEVO

MAKES 4 TO 6 SERVINGS

8 cups water
1 Roma tomato, quartered
3 green onions, cut into
    1-inch pieces
4 garlic cloves, left whole
1 tablespoon chicken bouillon
    powder
1 teaspoon kosher salt
1 güisquil, quartered
1 cup sliced green beans,
    cut into 3-inch pieces
2 large Yukon gold potatoes,
    peeled and cut into
    1-inch cubes
2 medium calabaza squash,
    cut into 1-inch pieces
8 ounces fresh spinach
6 eggs
4 limes, quartered
Fresh cheese, chopped cilantro
    leaves and tender stems,
    chile casero, and Tortillas
    Salvadoreñas (page 36)
    for serving

In my family, if someone is sick or depressed, this spinach soup with eggs is one of our remedies. When I have a nourishing bowl of this sopa, I think about my bisabuela, my great-grandmother Mamá Juana—this is her recipe. She is known in our family for having been humble, honest, and honorable. She is also the oldest elder I ever got to meet on either side of my family both in the United States and in my homeland.

Instead of spinach, you will see in the story that my great-grandmother used the green leaves of a chile plant. It is common practice to use whatever leafy greens are available. Some Salvadoran cooks also use mora, another green popular in El Salvador. Sometimes I can find mora in Latin American markets, but I usually make this soup with spinach.

●

In a large pot over medium-high heat, bring the water to a boil. Add the tomato, green onions, garlic, chicken bouillon, and salt and stir to combine. Add the güisquil and green beans and cook for 5 minutes. Add the potatoes and squash and cook until they are tender, about 10 minutes. Add the spinach, cover, and cook until the spinach becomes soft and the vegetables are fork-tender, about 2 minutes more.

Carefully add the eggs to the layer of spinach that sits atop the soup. Once all the eggs have been added, spoon some broth over them. Cover the pot, turn off the heat, and let sit until the egg whites are set but the yolk is still runny, about 6 minutes.

Serve the soup hot with the lime wedges, cheese, cilantro, chile, and fresh tortillas.

EL ÁRBOL DE CHILE

There were three things that Juana could do in her sleep.

First, she could braid her hair. She always wore braids as thick as rope. Six sections of hair became two braids, which were tied together with two fasteners that never matched. Sometimes it was a rubber band and other times a piece of cloth ripped off another garment.

The second thing that Juana could do in her sleep was make tortillas. She didn't have to look at her hands while she was making them. She could gaze into the street and let her mind wander to other things; yet her hands were like scales, with the perfect muscle memory for weight, size, and thickness—and for crafting identical, gorgeous tortillas.

The third thing she could do was make a magical meal out of any ingredients in the kitchen. This was required for survival. She was always the machete, never the sugarcane. And during the civil war, Juana was in charge of her survival and that of her grandchildren. They had gone hungry before; this wasn't the first time. Their stomachaches and anxiety surrounding food were familiar to Juana.

One evening, she needed to make magic happen almost immediately. She checked her food storage baskets, hoping to find at least one güisquil, one ayote, or some herbs. There was nothing.

The sounds of her grandchildren playing in the street made her aware of her own hunger. With all the running around they were doing in the colonia, they were working up an appetite. It was in this instant that she saw a small plant outside her simple home, el árbol de chile. She walked out to it and saw it was growing so well, yet it bore no fruit. No chiles to be found. But she plucked one of the leaves, brought it to her lips, and took the smallest bite. It was mild, only a little peppery. Almost like espinaca. She breathed in the aroma of the herb and exhaled. This would have to be dinner.

Taking a small kitchen knife from her delantal, she began to cut larger leaves from the older branches to fill up her apron pockets. She thanked the plant for the inspiration. Inside, she brought water to a boil and added the chile leaves. The smell brought her immediate comfort. It was the smallest semblance of cooking, this combination of some monte and water. But for tonight, it was a meal.

She called her five grandchildren inside and told each of them to visit a different vecina to ask for any small vegetable, eggs, potatoes, or cheese they could spare.

Cocina de leña, a typical rural cooking stove using wood.

"¡No se les olviden decir gracias!" she yelled as they ran off to the neighbors'. (Don't forget to say thank you.) Mario came back with a small chile verde. Teresa had one egg. Patty brought some masa and garlic cloves. Javier returned with another egg and a cup of rice. Juana could make do with this.

With the two eggs, she considered her options. If she fried them, it would feed only two people. If she scrambled them, she could not stretch it enough for the six of them. Feeling unsatisfied, she left it at that and went on to the other ingredients. With the masa, she made small tortillas—enough for everyone to get at least one. The rice she added to the soup along with the green chile and garlic. The anxiety that had filled the air was now being replaced by the delicious aroma of a cooked meal. As the soup finished cooking, it occurred to Juana what to do with the eggs. She placed them in a pot filled with water and soft-boiled them.

To serve the meal, she ladled hot soup into six bowls. Earlier, she had found two limes on a tree outside and some chile that a neighbor had gifted her. She sprinkled the lime juice and chile in the soup; together, their bright flavor, with just enough of a kick, made the most exquisite combination. Cracking the eggs open, Juana sprinkled salt on them. With a spoon, she carefully mixed the yolks with the whites inside the shells.

While everyone slurped their soup, they shared the two soft-boiled eggs by passing them around the table. Each person took turns tearing off a piece of their tortillas to dip into an egg. Juana's granddaughter Teresa remembers, "When we thought, 'Today we're not going to eat because there is no chicken, no meat, no food,' that was when we ate the best."

SOPA DE PATAS

MAKES 6 TO 8 SERVINGS

1 gallon water
3 pounds pata (cow hoof)
2 large tomatoes, chopped
1 large white onion, halved
1 garlic head, cut crosswise
Kosher salt
1 pound panza (honeycomb
    tripe), cut into 3-inch pieces
1 tablespoon achiote paste
2 pounds fresh or frozen yuca,
    peeled and cut into 2-inch
    pieces
3 güisquiles, cut into
    1-inch pieces
3 calabaza squash, peeled
    and cut into 1-inch pieces
3 green plantains, peeled
    and quartered
2 large carrots, cut into
    1-inch rounds
3 celery stalks, cut into
    1-inch pieces
8 ounces green beans,
    trimmed and cut into
    1-inch pieces
3 corn cobs, peeled, and
    halved (optional)
3 tablespoons chicken
    bouillon powder
2 teaspoons dried oregano
1 teaspoon red pepper flakes
1 medium head green cabbage,
    cut into 8 wedges
1 bunch cilantro, coarsely
    chopped
3 limes, quartered

If sopa de res is an event, then sopa de patas is the soup headliner in Salvi food culture. While it is a lot of work to make and often served only for special occasions, like family reunions, it's also just a good excuse to have people over. I once heard Salvadoran cookbook author Alicia Maher mention that cooking is changing, even in El Salvador. She explained that home cooks in some places in the motherland don't use achiote anymore in their sopa de patas. Be assured that the use of achiote paste in your soup will help preserve the tradition and impress Salvi elders.

Although this soup does not contain much meat, it is very rich, thanks to the collagen from nerves and tendons in the patas, or cow hooves. The nerves are what make this dish a delicacy, so the hooves need to be boiled long enough to loosen from the tissue.

Sourcing cow hooves is not as difficult as it may sound. Most meat markets and butcher counters carry them, especially those that specialize in the foods of Latin America, the Caribbean, and Africa. Plenty of cultures around the world know what a delicacy this ingredient is, which makes finding them a bit easier.

To this recipe, Zoila also adds panza, the stomach lining of the cow; it lends texture and body to an already rich soup. To properly prepare it, Salvadoran cooks like to rinse it in a solution of water, lemon, and salt.

In a large pot over medium-high heat, combine the water, pata, half of the tomatoes, onion, garlic, and 1 teaspoon salt and bring to a boil. Using a spoon, skim and discard the white foam that forms on the surface of the soup and cook until the nerves loosen from the hoof, about 1½ hours. Remove from the heat and set aside.

In a separate large pot over medium-high heat, bring 4 cups of water to a boil. Add the panza and cook until it becomes tender, about 30 minutes. Rinse the panza under running water and set aside.

In a blender, combine ½ cup of the pata broth, a cooked onion half, the achiote paste, and remaining tomatoes and blend until the achiote dissolves completely and everything is pureed. Add this mixture to the pata broth.

Set the soup pot over medium heat, add the yuca, güisquiles, squash, plantains, carrots, celery, green beans, corn (if using), chicken bouillon, oregano, and red pepper flakes and cook until the vegetables are tender, about 10 minutes. Add the panza and cabbage, cover, and cook until the cabbage is cooked through, about 5 minutes more.

Serve the sopa hot and garnish each bowl with cilantro. Make sure everyone gets a lime wedge to squeeze over their soup.

WE FOUND LOVE IN A HOPELESS PLACE

It started with rice. Zoila knew how to make rice with her eyes closed—delicious, perfectly seasoned, and fluffy, with every grain cooked through.

Actually, it started first with lunch—that is, work lunch. Every day, a group of colleagues at the factory where Zoila worked would gather during the lunch hour. They would talk and learn about one another, with an added bonus that they'd try each other's homemade lunches, which were often leftover dinners from the day before. Eventually, they went on to discuss cooking and all kinds of food talk, like how to make the best sopa, how to tenderize meat, and how to keep vegetables fresh longer.

That was when Zoila learned that Hugo was in need of rice—specifically, a good-quality rice recipe. Her coworkers told her that he had recently separated from his wife, the mother of his son. She had cheated on him, then left for Las Vegas, leaving him behind with their child and the two daughters she'd had with the partner before him.

"Ya mis hijos ya me están reclamando que porque sólo tortilla tostada en aceite y con huevo les doy todo el tiempo." Hugo knew how to make only fried tortillas with eggs, and his children were fed up with his cooking. Zoila knew a cry for help when she heard it. She herself had also recently separated from an abusive husband and could understand what it was like to come home and still need to feed children since she also had three of her own. So she told him, "Okay, I will teach you how to make rice."

These cooking lessons led to a much-needed friendship between two people who intimately understood what the other was going through. When Hugo needed to move out of the house that he had shared with his ex, he called Zoila and asked if she could use the brand-new appliances he had bought for his wife. He offered Zoila a stovetop, a washing machine, and a dryer, all as a small thanks for her generosity.

When he craved a sweet treat, like atol de elote, he'd call her and ask how to make it and if she could bring some to work. She'd laugh and say, "Of course, how about I swing by your department before I get to mine." And she'd bring with her a thermos full of the atol for him. It went on and on, until a kiss shined a light on feelings they could no longer deny.

As she said, "Since then, we get along perfectly. We do everything together, we go everywhere. Through him, I got to know the cinema, and I go to restaurants

now." Perhaps the biggest difference from her former marriage, she says, is that "If we don't like something, we discuss it. Are we in agreement? There is more liberty. Like the boyfriend you have for the first time. We are totally compatible. We are what we both wanted. We're happy."

As for the cooking, he turned out to be a good student. "If I'm out, he tells me, 'Don't worry, I'll cook.' He makes his sopas, sets up a grill, and roasts the chicken. Everything, everything."

SOPA DE BAGRE

MAKES 4 TO 6 SERVINGS

2 tablespoons unsalted butter

2 tablespoons extra-virgin
    olive oil

½ medium red onion, chopped

4 large garlic cloves, smashed

2 medium tomatoes, roughly
    chopped

1 celery stalk, cut into ½-inch
    pieces

Kosher salt

4 pounds catfish
    (see headnote)

8 cups water

2 green plantains, peeled
    and quartered

1 large carrot, cut into 1-inch
    rounds and halved

2 güisquiles, peeled and
    cut into 1½-inch pieces

1 cup sliced green beans,
    cut into 1-inch pieces

2 calabaza squash, cut into
    1-inch pieces

½ large green bell pepper,
    cut into ½-inch pieces

8 ounces fresh spinach

1 seafood bouillon cube

1 bunch cilantro, coarsely
    chopped

4 limes, quartered

Tortillas Salvadoreñas
    (page 36) for serving

Like so many Salvadoran recipes, this dish has countless versions. The soup has la fama, meaning that it is famous for being very easy to make and taking very little effort or time. Some believe it doesn't necessarily require vegetables, unlike other soups. For many cooks, it's not real sopa de bagre if too many things are added to it. Or so I've heard.

Folks talk about it mostly because of its nutritional value. Mora (an edible black nightshade) is high in calcium, iron, and vitamin C. Whereas other dishes are meant for holding celebrations, having guests over, or creating comfort, this one has the very specific job of treating pain and other ailments. When mora is not available, cooks have been known to replace it with chile leaves or spinach, like I do here.

Ask your fishmonger to clean and gut your catfish. Cut the flesh into 2-inch pieces and save the head and tail for making the stock.

In a large pot over medium-high heat, heat the butter and the olive oil. When the butter melts, add the onion, garlic, tomatoes, celery, and 1 teaspoon salt. Turn the heat to medium-low and let simmer until the onion turns translucent and the vegetables are tender, about 8 minutes.

Using tongs or a large slotted spoon, remove half of the pot's contents and place in a blender. Blend until liquefied and then pour the liquid back into the pot. Add the fish head and tail and the water. Turn the heat to medium-high and bring to a boil. Then, turn the heat to medium-low; add the seafood bouillon cube, the plantains, carrot, güisquiles, green beans, squash, bell pepper, and spinach; and cook for 10 minutes. (You want to get the vegetables cooking since the fish pieces will finish much faster. You may remove the fish head and tail at this point, as they've done their job of flavoring the broth. Some of my family members really enjoy them, so I usually leave them in.)

Turn the heat to medium, add the catfish flesh, and cook until the flesh becomes opaque, loses its raw appearance, and flakes easily, 7 to 8 minutes more. Add the chopped cilantro to the soup at the end.

Serve the sopa hot with the lime wedges and tortillas.

A row of homes in Santiago
de María, Usulután.

SOPA DE GALLINA

Sopa de gallina is a very important part of Salvadoran food culture. However, it's not like American chicken soup, where the meat is left in the broth; instead, the chicken is removed after boiling and later grilled. Some cooks add mustard and seasonings to the chicken before grilling to sear this zesty flavor into the meat. The soup is served with various accompaniments, such as rice, chicken, tortillas, and ensalada verde. When I think of chicken soup in an American sense, it's literally chicken and soup, but here it definitely is not. I've been told that leaving the chicken in the soup is poor form. I've asked around why this is so, but no one seems to know exactly why it's best to serve the broth and meat separately.

This soup uses a gallina, or hen, not a young chicken. Because hens are older (by at least several years), their flavor is stronger. By contrast, chicken sold in the supermarket is usually never older than six months, so the flavor is much milder. Hens are also preferred for this soup as they better withstand the longer cooking time.

Sopa de gallina is the dish for certain occasions, like a birth. My mom shared with me a custom about sopa de gallina. When a woman gives birth to un baron—a boy—the saying goes, "Te ganaste la sopa de gallina." (You earned the sopa de gallina.)

●

Rub the gallina with the salt. Set aside.

In a large stockpot over medium-high heat, combine the gallina, tomato, onion, garlic, bay leaves, and water and bring to a boil. Lower the heat to medium and simmer until the gallina is tender and cooked through, about 50 to 60 minutes. Transfer the hen to a large plate to cool, and set aside.

Keeping the stockpot on medium heat, add the güisquiles, potatoes, and carrots and cook until they are tender, about 10 minutes. Add the zucchini and cook until tender, about 7 minutes more. Stir in the basil and mint.

In a small bowl, combine the mustard, Worcestershire, and adobo. Rub the mustard mixture all over the cooked gallina.

Set a comal or griddle over high heat. Once it's hot, sprinkle with a little water to check if it is ready; the water should quickly evaporate. Place the whole gallina on the hottest part of the grill just long enough for the mustard mixture to form a crust on the outside, about 7 minutes. Using tongs, flip the gallina to make sure all sides get contact with the grill.

Cut the gallina into eight pieces—two drumsticks, two breasts, two wings, and two thighs. Serve the sopa and gallina with ensalada and arroz.

MAKES 4 TO 6 SERVINGS

1 whole gallina (hen)
1 tablespoon kosher salt
1 medium tomato, halved
1 medium red onion, halved
6 garlic cloves, left whole
3 dried bay leaves
10 cups water
3 güisquiles, seeded and
    cut into 1-inch pieces
1½ cups cubed peeled
    potatoes, cut into 1-inch
    pieces
2 medium carrots, peeled
    and cut into 1-inch pieces
2 medium zucchini, peeled
    and cut into 1-inch pieces
4 basil stems
3 mint stems
¼ cup yellow mustard
2 tablespoons Worcestershire
    sauce
1 teaspoon adobo
Ensalada Verde (page 50)
    and Arroz Frito (page 51)
    for serving

CONSEJO

Instead of using mustard sauce before grilling, sprinkle 1 tablespoon salt over your cooked gallina and grill on all sides until it turns golden brown, 7 to 10 minutes.

SOPA DE FRIJOLES CON MASITAS

MAKES 6 SERVINGS

12 cups water, or as needed
1 pound dried frijoles rojos
    de seda, sorted for debris
    and rinsed
½ medium red onion,
    ends trimmed
6 garlic cloves
1 fresh bay leaf
1 pinch baking soda (optional)
Kosher salt
2½ cups masa harina
2 cups chicken broth
¼ cup extra-virgin olive oil
3 güisquiles, seeded
    and quartered
Chirimol (page 53) for
    garnishing

"I thought it was just something my mom made up." That's what I've heard many Salvis say about sopa de frijoles con masitas. Sure enough, it is widely known in the culture. The disconnect is probably because it's a dish that comes from happenstance. If there is extra masa from making tortillas, and sopa de frijoles happens to be on the stovetop, certain things click as brilliant once you see the opportunity in front of you. Here, we've decided to be intentional about it. For those who are unfamiliar with this dish, it is a bit like a dumpling soup.

In a large pot over high heat, bring the water to a boil. Add the beans, onion, garlic, and bay leaf. Once the beans start to boil, stir in the baking soda (if using). Turn the heat to low and let simmer, uncovered, until the beans become tender, about 2 hours. Check the beans and stir them every 30 minutes, adding more water to cover as needed; do not let them burn. After the beans have softened, season with salt.

Meanwhile, in a large bowl, combine the masa harina, chicken broth, olive oil, and 1 teaspoon salt. Knead the dough until it reaches the consistency of Play-Doh. When the dough is pressed, its sides should not tear.

Pour some water into a small bowl and keep it handy for moistening the dough. Roll about 2½ ounces of masa (slightly smaller than a golf ball) between the palms of your hands until it forms a completely round ball, then using your thumb, make a small indentation in the center of the ball. (If the dough cracks at any point, it needs more moisture; add more water and mix into the dough until it becomes elastic again.) Repeat to make a total of eighteen masitas.

When the beans are tender, carefully add the güisquiles and the masitas, dispersing them throughout the soup. (If the soup has thickened, add up to 1 cup water.) The masitas are done when they become plump and buoyant, about 15 minutes. When the güisquiles are tender, the soup is done.

Divide the sopa into individual bowls, with one or two pieces of güisquil and three masitas, and garnish with chirimol. Serve immediately.

ARROZ AGUADO CON CARNE DE TUNCO

You won't find this classic Salvadoran dish in restaurants in the diaspora—instead, it's reserved mostly for the Salvadoran home kitchen. Arroz aguado, also known as sopa de arroz aguado, is similar to rice porridge and is valued for its broth. It is especially known for its use of chipilín, a very common wild green in El Salvador that can be found in Latin American markets. As for a substitute, there is none. My mother's exact words are "I'm sorry, but nothing else compares." In 2012, the *Los Angeles Times* reported that chipilín is one of the "most important edible leaves used by humans globally." Its flavor is earthy, pungent, and a bit sour. It's not typically eaten raw but instead is almost always cooked in pupusas, arroz aguado, tamales, and scrambled eggs. I usually find large bundles of the herb in markets such as El Turco Meat Market in Los Angeles. Sometimes, you can find it frozen; the flavor isn't as potent as fresh, but in a pinch, it can satisfy the craving.

I enjoy this dish with chile casero (see page 49). It's perfect for those days when you're sick or need healing food. It is also a meaningful dish to me, as it is the only recipe I have from women on my father's side of the family. It was taught to me by my Tía Morena, who learned it from my Mamá Angela, my father's mother. Through a series of WhatsApp voice notes, texts, and videos, my tía was able to give me this connection to my grandmother, with whom I spent time during only a handful of occasions.

●

In a large pot over medium-high heat, combine the water and costillas and bring to a boil. Using a large spoon, skim off and discard any foam and fat that rises to the surface of the water; repeat as needed. Turn the heat to medium and let simmer until the pork becomes blanditos, or tender, about 30 minutes. Add the salt, onion, tomato, and garlic and cook until they turn tender, about 10 minutes more.

Add the rice to the pot and cook another 10 minutes. Then add the güisquiles, potatoes, squash, and green beans; cover and cook until they soften, about 10 minutes more. Add the chipilín, cover, and cook until tender, about 7 minutes.

Finally, place the cabbage wedges atop the soup and allow them to sink a bit below the surface. Cover, let simmer for 3 minutes, and then turn off the heat. The residual heat will ensure the cabbage is tender without overcooking it.

Serve the arroz aguado with chile casero and ensalada verde.

MAKES 4 TO 6 SERVINGS

10 cups water
1 pound pork costillas (ribs), cut into 2-inch pieces
2 teaspoons kosher salt
½ medium white onion, peeled
1 large tomato, halved
1 garlic head, halved crosswise
1½ cups uncooked white rice
2 güisquiles, cut into 1-inch pieces
3 medium Yukon gold or russet potatoes, cut into 1-inch pieces
2 calabaza squash, cut into 1-inch pieces
8 ounces green beans, cut into 1-inch pieces
3 cups fresh chipilín leaves, stemmed
1 medium head cabbage, cut into 8 wedges
Chile Casero (page 49) and Ensalada Verde (page 50) for serving

MORENA

It hasn't been until recently that I have been told I look like my mother. All my childhood years were marked by moments when I was reminded that I was the carbon copy of my father. One distinct memory is when I was on the playground, and I happened to have a photograph of my parents. I don't know why I was carrying it, but I was. An opportunity came up for a group of us children to talk about our parents, and then I pulled out this small photo.

Everyone around me pressed closer to see it. "Wow, they look young." "Those are your parents?" "How old are they?" "How old are you?"

"Yes, they were young when they had me," I replied. "Yes." "I think twenty-nine, thirty." "I'm nine."

Then finally someone said, "Wow, your mom is so pretty." A somewhat long pause followed, and then, "Well, you definitely look like your dad."

I always thought my dad was handsome, but these comments left me wondering what they meant. For a time, I interpreted them to mean that I have more manly features. I'm also hairy like my dad. In middle school, my sideburns were a fuzzy reminder that I looked like a man—a handsome man, but nevertheless, masculine. It messed with me. It also begged the question: If I don't look like the women on my mother's side, do I look like the women in my father's family?

This ate at me when I was younger because I did not meet any of the women on my father's side until I was seventeen and took my first trip back to El Salvador. I ached to see their faces. Were they taller like I was? Did their hair frizz up like mine? What did they do with their sideburns? Bleach them? Shave them? But when I finally met my Tía Morena, I loved looking at her. Yes, she is tall—taller than most of the women in my life. I am the tallest female in my family. Her hair is like mine. These days, she opts for parting it on the side.

It wasn't until I was in El Salvador years later to do research that I truly appreciated my Tía Morena. This time, instead of studying her sideburns and her height, I noticed a completely different set of characteristics. Her voice reminded me of mine, the tone and timbre of it. Her temperament, the way she carried herself too. To finally see yourself in a family member calms the nervous system. Something settles inside.

On my last night in El Salvador on this trip, I wasn't sure if I'd be able to see my tía and my cousin Karen, but I did. Along with my cousin—and yes, we look like

cousins; same eyebrows and smile—my tía suggested we find some Salvadoran cookbooks. Seated in the back of my cousin's stick-shift car, we drove into the night in search of them. The traffic was loud, the car windows were slightly ajar, the air was thick, and everyone was sweating and hot, but I was having the best time. In the middle of listening to my retelling of my adventures on this trip, my tía chuckled softly, amused by something. I laughed when she said, "Karlita, sabes que, ahorita que estas hablando, es como que estuviera oyendo a tu mamá," she said. (Karlita, you know what? Right now, as you're talking, it's as if I were listening to your mom.)

"Ay, sí mami, eso iba decir yo tambien, igualita a mi Tía Tere," my cousin agreed. (Oh yes, mami, I was just going to say the same thing, too, just like my Tía Tere.) It remains one of my favorite moments in my life.

Locals waiting for the bus in Central San Salvador.

PLATILLOS FUERTES

Maribel, a chuco vendor in Mercado Dueñas.

Years before I started SalviSoul, I would often meet people who would ask me to describe Salvadoran cuisine. What I gathered from their question and attitude was more along the lines of, "Why couldn't they call Salvadoran food Mexican food?" Their argument was that both cuisines share similar ingredients. It was always an uncomfortable moment for me, and correcting people became the norm.

At the time, I was a young immigrant woman with limited cooking experience. And having spent only a few months in the country of my birth, I would often resort to answers that felt easy. "Have you tried tortillas?" I'd ask. Then I'd explain that Salvadoran tortillas are made by hand and that good ones are thick and round, made by a cocinera who could sustain a steady beat with her patting of the masa. If a curious person wanted more examples, I'd refer them to our national dish—our famous pupusas, followed by their equally famous accompaniments, curtido and salsa roja.

These days, after years of dedicated research, I am a different person with a different answer to these kinds of questions. Salvadoran food is a cuisine obsessed with celebrating the splendor of its native flora and fauna from its land and waters, including abundant vegetables, hearty meats, and delightful seafood. Plus, of course, our ever-present beans and corn. Our flavors are funky, sweet, salty, succulent, sour, and fire-grilled. I am ready to talk about our lesser-known but equally meaningful dishes, like Pescado Seco Envuelto (page 185), Gallo en Chicha (page 174), Punches con Alguashte (page 196), and many others.

POLLO GUISADO CON ACEITUNAS

MAKES 4 TO 6 SERVINGS

⅓ cup yellow mustard
½ teaspoon freshly ground
　　black pepper
½ teaspoon garlic powder
9 bone-in, skin-on chicken
　　thighs
7 Roma tomatoes, stemmed
½ medium red onion, peeled
1 celery stalk, trimmed
4 garlic cloves, left whole
1 teaspoon chicken bouillon
　　powder
¼ cup raw white sesame seeds
1 pound green olives with pits,
　　drained
Arroz Frito (page 51) and
　　Ensalada Verde (page 50)
　　for serving

"Cuidado con las semillas, okay?"—Be careful with the seeds, okay?—is something guests in our home have often heard my mom say as she served them plates of pollo guisado con aceitunas. She was referring to the green olives that always have pits. Much like carne guisada, this dish is a stewed meat, but with chicken and olives. Once everyone has finished eating, the olive lovers in my family count the pits on their plates to determine if anyone was lucky enough to get more olives than everyone else. Everything becomes a competition.

●

In a small bowl, combine the mustard, pepper, and garlic powder. Rub the mustard sauce all over the chicken. Cover the chicken with a manta or kitchen towel or plastic wrap, transfer to the refrigerator, and let marinate for 1 hour.

In a large pot over medium-high heat, bring 4 cups of water to a boil. Add the tomatoes, onion, celery, and garlic and cook until the vegetables have softened and the tomato skins have burst, 8 to 10 minutes. Turn off the heat.

While the vegetables are boiling and the chicken is marinating, in a small dry pan over medium heat, toast the sesame seeds until they turn fragrant and their color has deepened, 5 to 7 minutes. (You'll know they are done when they start popping in the hot pan.) Set aside.

Using tongs or a large slotted spoon, in batches if necessary, transfer the tomatoes, onion, celery, and garlic to a blender. Add 1 cup of the cooking water, the chicken bouillon, and the toasted sesame seeds and blend until a smooth sauce forms. Set aside.

About 30 minutes before you are ready to finish cooking, remove the chicken from the fridge and let come to room temperature.

In a large skillet over medium-high heat, combine the sauce and marinated chicken. Cover and cook for about 25 minutes. Then add the olives, cover, and cook until the chicken has cooked through and the internal temperature registers 165°F on an instant-read thermometer, about 15 minutes more.

Serve the pollo immediately, with arroz and ensalada on the side.

A flower shop selling
a variety of blossoms
in Santa Tecla.

A DEAL WITH REINA

Pat. Pat. Pat. Pat. Setting one more lopsided tortilla on the hot comal, Teresa wiped her sweaty right eye with the back of her hand and then swiped at her nose. She was hungry. She was angry. And she was tired. It had already been three hours of making tortillas and each one looked worse than the last. Sure, she had lied and made arrangements to get out of the chore of making tortillas every day, but her lie had not been so bad.

"Roberto, deja a la bicha, Roberto. Yo voy a tortillar," pleaded Mamá Juana, Teresa's grandmother, as she tried to reason with her son-in-law. Roberto had found out that the tortillas he had been eating every day had not been made by his daughter Teresa. She had lied. It was Teresa's neighborhood friend Reina who had been the whiz at making the perfectly round ones. The spanking Teresa got wasn't as bad as the cólera, anger, she felt for her father.

Teresa comes from a long line of excellent cooks. Her grandmothers, who were both creative and industrious in the kitchen, taught her to appreciate every available ingredient. From one of them, she learned the hard work of picking caña, sugarcane, and how to appreciate vegetables, herbs, and native plants that were always in dependable supply, especially when eggs, cheese, and animal proteins were not. From the other grandmother, she came to understand how to sell nuegados de yuca and chilate in the neighborhood, how to use lard in popular dishes, how to turn a profit, and how to stay tough.

While her grandmothers were versed in street foods, her mother, Lucia, was also a fine cook. She was hired to work in the kitchens of wealthy Salvadorans in San Salvador, making dishes such as paella, salpicón, carne salada, fresh cheese, and anything else her employers wanted. It did require Lucia to live with them during the week, but the advantage was that when she came home on the weekends, she'd bring all the methods and techniques that she had learned in their kitchens.

Even though Teresa enjoyed watching the women in her life cook exquisitely, she herself did not like making tortillas. "Yo no podía con ese pencazo de masa, era un montón," she claimed. It was an intimidating feat. First, the pressure for a young girl to make perfect tortillas was too much. Second, it took too long. Lastly, she'd rather be playing with her friends.

There were eight mouths to feed. Her dad alone consumed at least ten tortillas every day, while each kid could eat up to four. Preparing thirty-eight tortillas was too much! Teresa was torn between the task of making an overwhelming number of tortillas every day and not being able to afford store-bought ones from the tortilleria down the street. So she made a deal with Reina. Reina was her chera, a neighborhood friend who knew what it took to survive in Patacones. In exchange for Reina's superb tortilla-making, she would receive two or three eggs, two potatoes, one avocado, and some tortillas for her own family. Everything had been working out perfectly.

Typically, Roberto would arrive home at his usual time. By then, Reina was gone, Teresa had set the table for dinner, and she was still the apple of her father's eye. Until this day, when Roberto showed up earlier than usual. He caught Reina's manos en la masa instead of Teresa's. Roberto immediately called his daughter into the room to interrogate her. "No jodas, Teresita, no quiero oir que me estas mintiendo otra vez," he scolded. (I don't want to hear that you've been lying to me again.)

"Está bien, pápa," she said. (Okay, Dad.)

"Y además, ¿cuantas veces vino la Reina a ayudarte?" Roberto asked angrily. (And by the way, how many times did Reina come to help you?)

Teresa carefully and quickly answered with "Solo fueron unas pocas veces, pápa." It was just a handful of times, she assured her father. The dust was beginning to settle. Her dad didn't need to know that, in fact, it had been a whole year.

"Vaya pues, que la niña Juana te ayude con las tortillas," he replied, his anger toward his daughter satisfied, which gave Mamá Juana the green light to finish making the rest of the tortillas. Teresa walked away feeling like she'd escaped. All she could hear now was the rhythmic, fast beat of tortillas being made. *Pat, pat, pat, pat, pat, pat. . . .*

Vendor selling spices in Mercado Central in San Salvador.

POLLO CON PAPAS

MAKES 4 TO 6 SERVINGS

2 tablespoons chicken bouillon
    powder
2 tablespoons Worcestershire
    sauce
2 tablespoons ketchup
2 tablespoons yellow mustard
1 tablespoon kosher salt
1 teaspoon freshly ground
    black pepper
1 tablespoon dried parsley
1 teaspoon paprika
½ cup naranja agria (see
    Consejo)
3 pounds bone-in, skin-on
    chicken legs and thighs
1 tablespoon avocado oil
1 large tomato, finely chopped
½ large white onion, finely
    chopped
4 garlic cloves, crushed
2 cups cubed peeled Yukon
    gold potatoes, cut into
    1-inch pieces
One 28-ounce can crushed
    tomatoes
½ bunch cilantro, stemmed and
    coarsely chopped
Arroz Frito (page 51) and
    Ensalada Verde (page 50)
    for serving

Chicken with potatoes is about as classic home cooking as you can get. In this recipe, Wendy uses canned tomatoes to help her get dinner on the table faster. The recipe is terrific for those weeknights when you need to pull out a quick, tasty meal for a hungry family using ingredients from your pantry. In this recipe, Wendy uses naranja agria juice. It means "bitter orange" and is a product you can generally find in the grocery store, typically in the Hispanic/Asian/international aisle. Of course, if you go to a Latino store, it will be where the vinegars and condiments live.

●

In a large bowl, combine the chicken bouillon, Worcestershire, ketchup, mustard, salt, pepper, parsley, paprika, and naranja agria and stir to mix thoroughly. Rub this marinade all over the chicken pieces until they are well coated. Cover the chicken with a manta or kitchen towel and let marinate at room temperature for at least 30 minutes, or in the refrigerator for up to overnight.

In a large skillet over medium heat, warm the avocado oil until it shimmers. Remove the chicken from the marinade and discard marinade. Then sear the chicken until there is visible browning. When all the chicken has been seared, transfer to a large bowl and set aside.

In the same skillet over medium heat, combine the chopped tomato, onion, and garlic and cook until the onion turns translucent, about 3 minutes. Add the seared chicken back into the pan, then add the potatoes, crushed tomatoes, and cilantro and cook until the chicken is cooked through, about 20 minutes.

Serve the pollo with arroz and ensalada on the side.

CONSEJO

If you don't have naranja agria, mix one part orange juice with one part lime juice.

MI PRIMO

That familiar heavy percussion beat began . . . tsch-tsch-tsch-tsch, followed by the hollow sound of the wooden guiro . . . *crrrrgh chkchk crrrrgh chkchk.* Then the bass finally set in with its muddy, boomy sound, while a saxophone note led you to the full blast and rhythm of the horns playing.

"Salvadoreñas que lindas son/Que me han robado el corazón." (Salvadoreñas, how beautiful they are/They've robbed my heart.)

For Wendy, blasting music in the kitchen with her cousin German was their thing. Before he came to live with her, coming home late from work wasn't as comforting or fun. He always liked having the music on full blast. When you entered her kitchen, it was common to see him deftly cutting vegetables for dinner while garlic sautéed, hot pans sizzled, and sauces steamed. It felt like two orchestras were playing full-on all at once—Los Hermanos Flores and German with his cooking.

Sometimes, when Wendy came home, he had pollo con papas ready for her to eat. Stewed chicken in tomato sauce with fresh herbs and perfectly cooked potatoes. If, for whatever reason, he hadn't finished cooking, Wendy would jump in and quickly take to making the rice, both of them laughing, talking, and dancing, stepping from side to side with a quick swing of the hips, rolling with the rhythm of *tsch-tsch-tsch-tsch.* If the energy of the music didn't liven Wendy up, it was German, who was always the life of the party.

When he moved out, Wendy missed him terribly, but every time he came back to visit, the first thing he did was go to the kitchen. "He had so much pride in feeding people," she said.

Things are different now. With German's passing, Wendy now cooks the pollo con papas. Cooking with her daughter one night, Wendy said, "Acuérdate lo que hacía tu tío. Tienes que siempre echarle la mostaza. Acuérdate. Este es el secret ingredient Salvi." Never forget the mustard. It's the secret Salvi ingredient. When asked what she and German talked about, she laughs and says, "Puras picardias." Pure mischief.

Cumbia dancing that happens every day at four p.m. in Plaza La Libertad in San Salvador.

PANES CON POLLO

1 whole chicken (see Consejo), or 5 pounds boneless, skin-on chicken thighs

½ cup yellow mustard

¼ cup white vinegar

Kosher salt

3 celery stalks, trimmed and smashed

3 large garlic cloves, slightly smashed

Recaudo for Panes con Pollo

6 Roma tomatoes, stemmed

1 medium red onion, halved

1 medium green bell pepper, cored and halved

2 celery stalks, trimmed and cut into 4-inch pieces

3 garlic cloves, left whole

¼ cup raw white sesame seeds

2 tablespoons raw pumpkin seeds

1 teaspoon dried oregano

4 whole cloves

½ teaspoon whole allspice

4 dried bay leaves

1 guaque chile, stemmed

1 ciruela chile, stemmed

2 teaspoons achiote powder

2 teaspoons chicken bouillon powder

1 cup water

2 tablespoons mayonnaise

Panes con pollo, the Salvadoran version of a chicken sandwich, is a wonderful way to celebrate a party, birthday, holiday, or just a regular family cookout.

One thing to note is the type of bread used. Some folks say that pan francés and Mexican bolillo are the same and interchangeable; I say for some things, sure, but not for this Salvadoran dish. This sandwich requires a hollow bread that will hold and absorb a lot of sauce. Bolillo can sometimes be too doughy and its crumb doesn't absorb liquid very well, so using it would be a travesty. If you cannot find a good pan francés from a Salvadoran bakery, the next available bread will have to suffice, but I am just giving you the facts. Some Salvadoran cooks add curtido, sliced hard-boiled eggs, and sliced beets to their panes, but this is optional.

If you're eating the sandwich and realize that it's falling apart because of the sauce, that's okay—it just means you're doing it right. I've been to parties where the bread is soaked and whoever is putting the sandwiches together still says, "Oh wait, let me spoon more sauce on there." Once, on Christmas Eve, my brother, my husband, and I were making the holiday family rounds, and a tía whom we went to visit was still cooking and cutting the vegetables for the panes. She told us to wait until they were ready. By the time we needed to leave, she was just finishing but we couldn't stay to eat them or else we'd fall behind in our carefully planned family Christmas tour. My brother got one pan to go, and let's just say it's not a sandwich that travels well. He loved every bite, but he had sauce and crumbs all over him.

●

Pat the chicken dry with paper towels. Set aside.

In a large bowl, combine ¼ cup of the mustard, the vinegar, and salt (1 teaspoon of salt per pound of chicken) and stir to mix thoroughly. Add the chicken and rub this marinade all over the pieces until they are well coated. Insert the celery and smashed garlic between the chicken meat and skin, cover the chicken with a manta or kitchen towel, transfer to the refrigerator, and let marinate in the refrigerator for at least 30 minutes or up to 1 hour.

Preheat the oven to 375°F.

continued

PANES CON POLLO

continued

8 Spanish olives, pitted

1 tablespoon white distilled vinegar or Spanish olive brine

6 pan francés (see Consejo)

1 medium tomato, thinly sliced

4 medium radishes, thinly sliced

½ medium cucumber, thinly sliced

1 bunch watercress, rinsed and dried

1 head romaine lettuce, leaves separated

To make the recaudo: Set a comal or griddle over medium-high heat. Once it's hot, sprinkle with a little water to check if it is ready; the water should quickly evaporate. Add the tomatoes, onion, bell pepper, celery, and whole garlic and grill until the vegetables darken on the outside, about 7 minutes. Using tongs, flip the vegetables and grill another 7 minutes to darken the other side. Transfer the vegetables to a plate and set aside. Turn the heat to medium-low.

In a small bowl, combine the sesame seeds, pumpkin seeds, oregano, cloves, allspice, bay leaves, guaque, and ciruela and stir to mix thoroughly. Transfer the spice mixture to the comal and toast until it turns fragrant, about 1 minute, making sure to stir it so it doesn't burn. Transfer the toasted spices to a blender and add the charred vegetables, achiote powder, and chicken bouillon. Blend on high speed until smooth, adding the water to keep the mixture moving as needed. Set aside.

In a small bowl, combine the remaining ¼ cup mustard, the mayonnaise, and ¼ teaspoon salt and stir to make an aioli.

About 30 minutes before you are ready to start cooking, remove the chicken from the fridge and let come to room temperature. Remove chicken from marinade and discard marinade. Place the chicken in a large roasting pan, pour the recaudo over the chicken, add the olives and vinegar, and cover the pan with aluminum foil. Roast until the chicken juices run clear and an instant-read thermometer inserted into a thigh registers 165°F. Depending on the size of the chicken pieces, this will take 40 to 45 minutes. Remove from the oven and season with additional salt if needed.

Meanwhile, split the pan francés lengthwise, about three-fourths of the way through, so the halves are still connected. Place in the oven right until golden and toasty.

Once the chicken is done and the bread is toasted, slather the mustard aioli inside of the cavity of each pan francés and top with 1 cup of the chicken and a few slices each of the tomato, radishes, and cucumber, as well as some watercress sprigs and lettuce leaves. Drizzle each sandwich with a bit of the recaudo in the roasting pan. There will be a lot, so pour the remainder into a serving bowl.

Serve the sandwiches with the remaining sauce on the side.

CONSEJO

If you are using a whole chicken, debone it and then divide into eight pieces: two breast halves, two thighs, two drumsticks, and two wings. Discard the rest.

Toast the pan francés in the oven right before the chicken is done cooking and while you're preparing all the vegetables.

BISTEC ENCEBOLLADO

In this dish, the beef is given a heavy hand of two of the Salvadoran cook's most favorite condiments: mustard and salsa Inglesa (Worcestershire sauce). The sweet onions, zesty condiments, juicy tomatoes, and tender, thinly sliced beef make this an easy option for an almuerzo, or lunch. I like this dish with rice, but if you ever have any leftovers, a sandwich with pan francés, tomato, bistec, and greens is amazing. This family-friendly recipe is very adaptable; leave out the bell peppers if you don't have them, but keep the mustard, Worcestershire, and onions. Otherwise, it's not bistec encebollado.

When I need certain cuts of beef, I prefer to shop at Latino markets because they'll know what result I'm after. This is a great example. The carnicerias, meat markets, that I shop at will know what I mean when I say I am looking for bistec tierno for bistec encebollado. Often, the top round steak is already thinly sliced to the desired thickness. This is Teresa's recipe and one of her family's favorites.

●

Wash the meat and pat dry with paper towels. Using a mallet, pound the meat repeatedly to flatten it until it is ½ centimeter thick.

In a large bowl, combine the mustard, Worcestershire, onions, garlic powder, and salt and stir to mix thoroughly. Add the meat and rub with the mustard marinade until well coated. Cover with a manta or kitchen towel or plastic wrap, transfer to the refrigerator, and let marinate for 1 hour.

In a large skillet over medium-high heat, warm 1 teaspoon of the canola oil until it shimmers. Working in batches, add the meat with the marinade in a single layer and sear each piece on both sides until a nice layer of browning occurs. Remove the meat from the pan, cover, and set aside.

In the same pan over medium-high heat, add the remaining 1 teaspoon canola oil and the onions with the marinade and cook until they turn translucent, about 3 minutes. Add the bell peppers and cook until they soften, about 3 minutes. Add the meat back to the pan, layering it on top of the onions and peppers, then add the tomatoes. Cover and let cook until the vegetables are softened and tender, 10 to 15 minutes longer.

Serve the bistec encebollado immediately.

MAKES 4 TO 6 SERVINGS

1½ pounds bistec tierno or top round steak, thinly sliced

2 medium white onions, thinly sliced

¼ cup yellow mustard

2 tablespoons Worcestershire sauce

1 tablespoon garlic powder

1 teaspoon kosher salt

2 teaspoons canola oil

1 medium green bell pepper, thinly sliced

1 medium red bell pepper, thinly sliced

4 large tomatoes, thinly sliced

CONFETTI FEELING

So many sighs of relief. We could stay. I remember my naturalization ceremony as if it were yesterday. It was the day I became a US citizen. For some reason, I had thought these ceremonies were much smaller and plainer. I expected a county immigration officer in an office somewhere who would swear me in like I'd seen in the movies. But it is nothing like that. Instead, my mom and dad have driven me from our home in South Central to a warehouse in Anaheim.

I see my shadow as I walk toward a hot parking lot under the peak sun of midday. Hundreds of people are in front of me and behind me, all taking the same steps as I am. I'm wearing a light-blue, long-sleeved shirt with a collar. (I was really into that shirt for a while; I thought it made me look sophisticated.) The day started out foggy and cool, but now the L.A. heat has burned through the fog, and I can feel the sweat in my leggings and skirt. Everything is sticky. I'm on fire.

I walk among the long lines of people for a while, not knowing if I am even going the right way—I just know that I need to keep following the huge crowd. I don't talk to anyone because I don't know anybody in this giant sea of humans. Thousands of people must be getting sworn in today, or at least that's how it feels. A few people chat with one another, but mostly we are quiet, as everyone knows that we are about to become citizens. Everyone is about to belong, and all that strain and hustle to get to this place will soon be rewarded.

When I enter the air-conditioned warehouse, I immediately feel relief. The cool air instantly finds every overheated place on my body. One moment I am burning up and then, bam, the breeze finds me. I notice some dividers, and I start looking for my parents as I follow the crowds. Imagine walking up to a warehouse and when you finally enter it, it's this big place and your eyes go straight up to a ceiling that's been decorated with United States flags. An officer leads us to our seating rows. Finally, I spot my parents on the other side of the dividers. They are looking on, standing on tiptoe behind other spectators, smiling big as if they were at a game and cheering me on from the sidelines. I feel better after seeing them.

This is happening, I think to myself. I look to my left and to my right, wanting to imprint the moment in my memory because I can't believe it. No more green card. No more burning. Now, some relief. No more calling my lawyer and asking, "Hey, is it cool if I go to Tijuana with the volunteer group on campus?" No more burning. Now, some relief. No more panicking about being separated from my family. No more burning. Now, some relief. No more clouds of threats hovering over me.

Like the fog that morning, it will all just disappear. No more burning, just relief.

I look around. To my right stands an older Asian man. His white hair is neatly combed back, and he is wearing glasses, suspenders, and a brown khaki outfit. To my left stands an older Latina. She looks like she is someone's grandmother. Her shoulder-length salt-and-pepper hair is pulled back by a delicate black hairband, and her outfit has a floral print all over it. The three of us probably wore what we thought was best for a naturalization ceremony. I never see their faces straight on, only their profiles, but I know how they feel.

The end of the ceremony feels like the end of a wedding. I don't remember the language the emcee uses, just that there are many smiles and a communal sigh of relief. The song "I'm Proud to Be an American" starts playing. To my utter shame, tears well up in my eyes. *What a fuckin' corny song to tear up to*, I think. I can't look at my parents, who are standing close by, because I know I'm going to cry. They look relieved. Everyone in the entire warehouse is relieved: parents, children, wives, husbands, uncles, grandmas, and grandpas. Whether we are young or old, we can all breathe a little easier now.

In my memory, I keep thinking that there must have been patriotic-colored balloons and confetti falling from the ceiling, but then I rationalize that I must be wrong. No balloons or confetti—surely the government wouldn't want to spend that money on these ceremonies, on immigrants. Honestly, I might be confusing that memory with a scene in a movie I've watched, but it really doesn't matter. The balloons and confetti are how I feel. I am so happy.

The next thing I remember is walking back to my college dorm. The lights are out, my roommate is gone, and I'm happy about that. I had told only a few people about it anyway. Lying on my nightstand, right by my bed, is a CD—a mixtape left for me by a friend. A note on it says, "Happy Citizenship Day, Karla!"

SALPICÓN DE RES

MAKES 4 TO 6 SERVINGS

2 pounds beef (such as eye of round)
1 medium red onion, halved and one half minced
5 garlic cloves, left whole
Kosher salt
1 bunch mint, minced
1 bunch radishes, trimmed and minced
1 cup lime juice, plus more for serving
Arroz Frito (page 51) for serving

This is the dish that got me to call my grandmother and ask her to help me figure out the recipe. It was probably my favorite as a kid because it serves as a savory vessel for lime and salt. Salpicón de res is technically considered a salad because the meat is cooked, cooled, and then minced and mixed with the vegetables and herbs, very similar to a larb. But instead of finishing it off with a lettuce wrap, salpicón is accompanied by rice and beans. There is some variety in which vegetables to use or how fine the minced meat and vegetables should be, but for the most part, most agree, it should have mint and it should have lime. Its flavors are fresh, like a Saturday morning, and everyone feels pretty good after eating it. When we enjoyed this meal, my family was usually together, relaxing on a weekend or after work. It marked the pinnacle of rest.

This recipe typically calls for a lean cut of beef. Using such a cut works because it's affordable and when it's minced and dressed in the lime, the toughness isn't a problem.

●

In a large pot over medium-high heat, bring 8 cups of water to a boil. Add the beef, onion half, garlic, and 1 tablespoon salt. Using a large slotted spoon, skim off and discard any foam and fat that rises to the surface of the water; repeat as needed. Cook the meat until it is tender, 30 to 45 minutes. Transfer the meat to a cutting board and let rest.

In a large bowl, combine the minced onion, mint, and radishes. Set aside.

Using a sharp knife, mince the cooled beef and then add to the onion-mint-radish mixture. Add the lime juice, season with salt, and stir to mix well. Let the salad sit for 10 minutes at room temperature to let the flavors mingle.

Serve the salpicón with arroz and additional lime juice.

CARNE GUISADA CON PAPAS

This stewed beef is a reliable meal in many Salvadoran homes. It is very affordable and adaptable in that you can use many different kinds of vegetables, such as potatoes, carrots, or even green beans. My favorite aspect of these kinds of meals is eating rice with jugito, the sauce. I know the meat is often the highlight, but I love the sauce. This is also a way to feed many people with a substantial, flavorful meal. This is Teresa's recipe.

●

In a large bowl, combine the mustard, Worcestershire, salt, and pepper and stir to mix thoroughly. Add the meat and rub the mustard marinade all over until it is well coated. Cover with a manta or kitchen towel and let marinate in the refrigerator for 1 hour.

In a small skillet over medium heat, toast the sesame seeds until they start popping. Remove from the heat and set aside.

In a large pot over medium-high heat, bring 3 cups of water to boil. Add the tomatoes, onion, bell pepper, and garlic and cook until the vegetables have softened and the tomato skins have burst, 8 to 10 minutes. Using tongs or a large slotted spoon, remove the vegetables from the water and place in a blender, in batches if needed. Add ½ cup of the cooking water and the sesame seeds and blend until smooth, about 1 minute. About 15 minutes before cooking the beef, take it out of the refrigerator and let it come to room temperature.

In a large skillet over medium heat, warm the canola oil until it shimmers. Working in batches, if necessary, add the meat and marinade in a single layer and sear each piece until a browned crust forms, about 2 minutes per side. Transfer the meat to a plate.

Place a fine-mesh strainer over the skillet, pour the sauce through the strainer, and then stir the sauce with a wooden spoon to deglaze the pan, scraping up any browned bits. Add all the meat back into the skillet, cover, and cook until tender, about 25 minutes. Add the potatoes and carrots, cover, and cook until tender, 7 to 10 minutes more.

Serve the carne guisada with arroz.

MAKES 4 TO 6 SERVINGS

¼ cup yellow mustard
1 tablespoon Worcestershire sauce
2 teaspoons kosher salt
⅛ teaspoon freshly ground black pepper
2 pounds carne de res trocitos (beef chuck), cubed
2 tablespoons raw white sesame seeds
3 Roma tomatoes, stemmed
¼ red onion, peeled
1 medium green bell pepper, cored
4 garlic cloves, left whole
1 tablespoon canola oil
4 Yukon gold potatoes, peeled and cut into 1-inch cubes
2 large carrots, peeled and cut into 1-inch cubes
Arroz Frito (page 51) for serving

GALLO EN CHICHA

MAKES 6 TO 8 SERVINGS

1 gallo, quartered

5 medium tomatoes, stemmed

1 medium green bell pepper, cored

½ medium white onion, peeled

1 celery stalk, trimmed

6 garlic cloves, left whole

1 cup raw white sesame seeds

1 tablespoon raw pumpkin seeds

2 guaque chiles, or 2 dried guajillo chiles

1 whole star anise

1 teaspoon whole cloves

1 teaspoon black peppercorns

5 dried bay leaves

One 3-inch cinnamon stick

1 tablespoon chicken consommé

2 tablespoons kosher salt

½ hot chocolate tablet (such as Ibarra brand)

¼ dulce de panela

2 tablespoons Worcestershire sauce

¼ teaspoon ground cumin

¼ teaspoon dried thyme

1 tablespoon chicken bouillon powder

16 ounces chicha (see page 216)

This is one of the recipes for which SalviSoul was created. I was sitting across from Isabel in her kitchen in Santa Ana, California, as we talked about the recipes she could contribute to this book. She mentioned a few that unfortunately were already taken by other women. Then she suggested gallo en chicha, or rooster cooked in chicha, a fermented pineapple beverage. In my voice recording of our interview, you can hear me say, "Gallo en chicha, ¿y eso que es?" It was the first time I'd ever heard of this dish, and as soon as she described it, I thought *Yes!* I knew it was the one, especially when I learned that her mom had taught her the recipe and was the only one in her family who knew how to make it. Isabel then added that it had been years since her family had eaten the dish because her mother didn't cook it anymore for religious reasons, since it contains alcohol.

Isabel said that while most people cooked chompipe, tamales, or panes con pollo for special occasions, her family always used to celebrate with gallo en chicha. When we finally wrote down the recipe, it reminded me a lot of coq au vin, the French chicken dish cooked in red wine. When I made it in cooking school, I did not like it, so I was afraid that gallo en chicha would taste similar, but of course, it didn't. This recipe is so flavorful. The chicha for the recipe is homemade, and with all the spices and herbs, this is one of the most exciting dishes I've ever tasted. Now it's a piece of Salvadoran cooking we can hold on to, thanks to Isabel and her family.

Sourcing rooster isn't as easy as going to the local grocery store, but it was not a challenge for me. You shouldn't have any trouble sourcing it at a specialty poultry place. In L.A.—the Westside, Downtown, Chinatown, almost every direction in the city—I was able to find a place that sold it. Similar to gallina, the animal protein here is a more mature animal, which means the meat may have a stronger flavor and the muscles may be much firmer than in a young chicken. This is what makes the chicha so valuable in this recipe. The bromelain in the pineapple tenderizes the meat and allows for a very succulent finished product.

The spices are similar to the relajo in panes con pollo, or chompipe, and are echoed in a lot of Salvadoran cooking. Extra points if you can find dulce de panela, or a chocolate tablet used for hot chocolate, from El Salvador. These special ingredients can all be purchased at Latin markets, and especially at Salvadoran markets.

●

continued

GALLO EN CHICHA

continued

16 ounces light beer
½ cup pitted prunes
½ cup capers
½ cup raisins
½ cup pitted green olives
2 tablespoons vegetable oil
2 Yukon gold potatoes, peeled
    and cut into 1-inch cubes
2 large carrots, peeled and
    sliced into 1-inch rounds
¼ bunch cilantro, coarsely
    chopped
½ cup finely chopped
    pineapple
Arroz Frito (page 51), pan
    francés, and Ensalada
    Verde (page 50) for serving

Pat the gallo pieces dry with paper towels.

Set a comal or griddle over medium-high heat. Once it's hot, sprinkle with a little water to check if it is ready; the water should quickly evaporate. Add the tomatoes, bell pepper, onion, celery, and garlic and grill until the vegetables darken on the outside, about 15 minutes. Using tongs, flip them over several times throughout so that they cook evenly. Transfer the vegetables to a plate and set aside. Turn the heat to medium.

In a small bowl, combine the sesame seeds, pumpkin seeds, chiles, star anise, cloves, peppercorns, bay leaves, and cinnamon stick and stir to incorporate. Transfer the spice mixture to the comal and toast until it turns fragrant, about 2 minutes, making sure to stir it so it doesn't burn. Transfer the toasted spices to a blender and add the grilled vegetables, consommé, salt, chocolate, and dulce de panela. Blend on high speed until a smooth sauce forms, about 2 minutes, adding a few teaspoons of water to keep the mixture moving as needed.

Set a fine-mesh strainer over a medium bowl and pour the blended sauce through the strainer. Add the Worcestershire, cumin, thyme, and chicken bouillon to the bowl and stir to mix thoroughly. In a very large bowl, combine the gallo pieces, chicha, beer, and sauce, making sure the gallo is evenly coated. Stir in the prunes, capers, raisins, and green olives. Cover the bowl with aluminum foil, transfer to the refrigerator, and let marinate overnight or up to 24 hours.

In a large pot over medium heat, warm the vegetable oil until it shimmers. Working in batches, add the marinated gallo pieces and sear on both sides until there is browning on all sides. Add all of the gallo pieces back to the pot and any remaining marinade in the bowl and let simmer until the internal temperature registers 165°F on an instant-read thermometer, about 45 minutes. Add the potatoes, carrots, cilantro, and pineapple and cook until they are tender, about 15 minutes more.

Serve the gallo with arroz, pan francés, and ensalada verde.

"Siempre vuelvo a el pasado," says Isabel. (I always return to the past.) Leaving El Salvador was no different from when she left her small hometown. Both times, she fled toward opportunity. Both times, she didn't say goodbye to her mother.

Leaving home brought her the freedom she always wanted but now, in her adult years, she realizes the high cost. "When you get here [the United States] and see that here is also hard and oppressive, you think, 'Well, I never should have left.' Because while there were no toys, and it was all poverty, there was happiness. You can laugh, you can bathe in the rivers, and when fruit ripens, the whole gang goes running to pick it. When you get here, you see there is none of that," she says.

"Once you're in the United States, the truth settles in that you've left your family. You say, 'In two years, I'll be back.' Then years go by. Five years go by, then ten, and then it's not so easy because you start a family and you don't have papers."

I should never have left. It's a thought Isabel can't escape. The reality of her decision hit her like a blow when she finally went home after a decade away. At the airport in El Salvador, she was able to embrace her siblings and see them for the first time in years. She also saw that they'd grown older. "No, I didn't see my siblings grow up," she says wistfully. "I didn't see my parents get older. I never imagined that I'd be told over the phone that my mother and father passed away and then realize I couldn't go attend their funerals. That's one of the bitter traumas that life gives you—to be told your family member has died and to not be able to go because of the lack of a document."

What comforts Isabel is that she was able to change the lives of her siblings because of her sacrifices. "My greatest pride is that my siblings are professionals. My brothers tell me, 'Thanks to you, we studied because of the help you gave us.'"

Isabel was eventually able to return home because "Tu corazón no puede renunciar a su tierra." (Your heart can't give up its land.) When she arrived this time, she was so anxious to disembark. "I could smell that earthy fragrance and hear the melodies the birds were singing. I couldn't believe it. When you're experiencing difficult times, you think you'll never see home again and that you're going to die and never return. I said I have to go back. And it was beautiful."

TORTITAS DE CAMARÓN

MAKES 4 TO 6 SERVINGS

1 pound 26/30-count raw
    shrimp, peeled, deveined,
    and tails removed
3 eggs, separated, at room
    temperature
¼ cup sliced green onions
½ bunch cilantro, finely
    chopped
1 garlic clove, chopped
1½ tablespoons dried shrimp
½ teaspoon baking powder
½ teaspoon baking soda
¼ teaspoon ground cumin
½ teaspoon kosher salt
6 ounces prepared masa
Grapeseed oil for frying
Arroz Frito (page 51) and
    lemon wedges for serving

The first time I ate this dish was in Miriam's galley kitchen. We had already met once, chatting about her El Salvador stories during my search for women to interview for this book. This time we were going to cook. So as soon as we said our greetings, we got to work. I witnessed her ease in her kitchen, how she glided from one end to the other. As she went from chopping shrimp to slipping outside to grab herbs from her garden and coming back in to wash them, she shared even more stories with me. "I promise you that you're going to love these tortitas," she said. She was right.

When you're itching for something savory, filling, and easy, tortitas de camarón is it. Shrimp is chopped and mixed with herbs and corn masa for a savory tortita, a plump shrimp cake. Some cooks finish these in tomato sauce, like other rellenos, but Miriam prefers them just like this, with a sprinkle of lemon juice. Here, she utilizes masa for the tortitas, so have some prepared masa ready. A good ratio is about 1:1 of masa harina to water.

●

In a large colander, rinse the shrimp under cold running water. Transfer to a cutting board and pat dry with paper towels. Chop the shrimp into bite-size pieces.

In a large bowl, using an electric mixer on high speed (or a whisk), whip the egg whites until soft peaks form. Add the egg yolks and continue to whip until stiff peaks form, about 2 minutes. Set aside.

In a large bowl, combine the chopped shrimp, green onions, cilantro, garlic, dried shrimp, baking powder, baking soda, cumin, salt, and prepared masa and mix well. Fold in the egg mixture and mix until thoroughly combined.

Line a large plate with paper towels or put a wire cooling rack in a baking sheet and set near the stove. In a large skillet over medium heat, warm the grapeseed oil until it shimmers. Using two large spoons, shape some of the shrimp mixture into two tortitas, each 2 to 3 inches wide. Fry until golden and crispy, about 2 minutes per side. Transfer the fried tortitas to the prepared plate to drain. Repeat with the remaining shrimp mixture.

Serve the tortitas immediately with arroz and lemon wedges.

MEET CUTE

Whoosh. It was the sound of compressed air being released, along with the squeaking and hissing from buses arriving at and departing from the bustling bus terminal in San Salvador. Buses were the easiest, most accessible, and fastest way to get around the country, especially if you needed to go to La Unión, on the coast.

The exhaust fumes in the air and wide range of loud noises inside the terminal created an urgency in everyone, especially during the agitated hours of rush hour. The auditory volume of the place alone was something—a whole level of sensory overload ratcheted up by the fleet of colorful autobuses decorated with designs and dichos proclaiming "Dios te ama" and "el dinero da movimiento": "God loves you" and "money gives movement." Adding to this was a flurry of people going every which way, with some leaving San Salvador and others arriving—not to mention the fifty or so folks sitting on bus rooftops.

Miriam had fought the traffic to get to the terminal, but now making her way through the place was a whole other thing. She was in the middle of searching for her bus, heading to La Unión for her vacation. Many buses were so distinctive in appearance that you didn't have to read the route number to know which one you needed. Then she felt the unmistakable hand of a man trying to touch her backside. Instantly she felt her blood boil. It wasn't uncommon for this to happen on buses,

A bus en route to Santa Tecla.

especially in a packed terminal such as this. Never one to shy away from conflict, she quickly stood up to the man: *whack, whack, whack.* Before she knew it, she had clobbered him with her large beach bag. Miriam didn't stay long enough to see what happened to him.

Still trembling, she found her bus and climbed aboard. Once inside, she sat down and cried from el enojo, anger. She hated that these ambushes happened all the time. As she tried to calm down, a young man approached her. "Disculpe, ¿que le paso?" he asked. (Excuse me, what happened to you?)

He looked kind, so she explained how she'd had to defend herself just minutes before. He sympathized with her. During the next three and a half hours to La Unión, she learned that he was also on a trip. He

was a college student all the way from the University of California, Santa Cruz. She liked that he had told her he enjoyed cooking. His family was from Mexico, but he had been raised in California—"un lugar gipi," a hippie place.

Entertained and absorbed by their easy conversation, they were both surprised by the bus attendant who came to collect their paid tickets. *Oh yes, the ticket is in the bag,* Miriam thought. Then she winced when she opened her bag, only to remember all over again the incident at the terminal. When she defended herself by hitting the man with her bag, she had forgotten everything she had in there. A jar of beautiful tangy Salvadoran crema, her clothes, and a camera. A camera that she meant to use on her vacation. Now it was covered with goopy streaks of crema and guishtes, shattered pieces of glass everywhere.

CONCHAS RELLENAS

MAKES 50 STUFFED CLAMS

1 tablespoon unsalted butter
1 tablespoon extra-virgin olive oil
8 ounces ground pork
1 large yellow onion, diced
1 medium green bell pepper, cored and diced
1 large tomato, diced
2 large carrots, peeled and diced small
1 large russet potato, peeled and diced
25 blood clams, opened, cleaned, separated from their shells, and diced; shells reserved (see Consejo)
5 tablespoons coarsely chopped fresh flat-leaf parsley leaves
2 tablespoons coarsely chopped fresh cilantro leaves
5 garlic cloves, minced
1 teaspoon garlic powder
Kosher salt and freshly ground black pepper

continued

Blood clams can be found from northernmost Mexico all the way down to Peru and are a beloved seafood in El Salvador, both raw and cooked. Carolina is the one who introduced me to this dish, and this is her recipe.

Carolina says, "When I was a little girl, we went to Tía Carmen's house in Cojutepeque, and the most exciting part of our visit would be sitting down to feast with the adults and my adored primas. I used to think how lucky they were that in their house, el almuerzo was so special—everyone in that household came home for a few hours during the day to eat and connect. Food preparation at Tía Carmen's began right after breakfast and was ready by noon or one in the afternoon, in time for lunch, which is El Salvador's biggest meal of the day. Tío Alex's discriminating taste for good food demanded that at least three main dishes be prepared daily. One memorable one for me was conchas rellenas."

This dish is as much fun to make as it is to eat. It was quite a beautiful experience for me. Breaking open and cleaning the clams, making the filling, washing each individual half shell, stuffing them, making the egg batter, frying them, finishing them in the tomato sauce, and then seeing the people I love at the table enjoying them—the best part—was amazing. It's a lengthy process but so enjoyable. It is perfect for a special occasion (a dinner party or anniversary) or for sharing with those you love with your whole heart.

In this recipe, after you open the clams for the filling, reserve the shells. Brush each shell thoroughly so that it is nice and clean when you're ready to fill it.

•

In a large saucepan over medium heat, warm the butter and olive oil. When the butter melts, add the pork and cook until it changes color from pink to brown, about 5 minutes. Add the onion, bell pepper, tomato, carrots, and potato and cook until the potato is tender, about 7 minutes. Add the clams and cook until they are firm, about 3 minutes. Add 3 tablespoons of the parsley, 1 tablespoon of the cilantro, the minced garlic, and garlic powder, and season with salt and pepper. Stir to thoroughly mix the herbs and seasonings into the filling. Remove the pan from the heat and set aside.

Preheat the oven to 350°F.

To make the sauce: Place the tomatoes, bell pepper, onion, and garlic in a roasting pan and roast until the skins on the vegetables have burst and have darkened, about 30 minutes. Using a large spoon, transfer the roasted vegetables to a blender. Add the oregano and chicken broth and blend until smooth, about 2 minutes. Season with salt and pepper. Set aside.

CONCHAS RELLENAS

continued

Salsa de Tomate para Conchas Rellenas

3 large tomatoes, stemmed

1 medium green bell pepper, cored

1 large yellow onion, coarsely chopped

2 garlic cloves, left whole

1 tablespoon dried oregano

2 cups chicken broth

Kosher salt and freshly ground black pepper

5 eggs, separated

¼ cup vegetable oil

On a large plate or baking sheet, arrange all the clean clam half-shells. Add a heaping 1 tablespoonful of filling to each shell and place on the plate.

In a large bowl, using an electric mixer on high speed (or a whisk), whip the egg whites until soft peaks form. Add the egg yolks and continue to whip until stiff peaks form, about 2 minutes. Set aside.

Line a large plate with paper towels or put a wire cooling rack in a baking sheet and set near the stove. In a large skillet over medium heat, warm the vegetable oil until it shimmers. Using a large slotted spoon, immerse each filled shell in the egg batter, thoroughly coating the filling. In batches, carefully place the shells in the hot oil and fry until the egg turns golden and starts to look fluffy, about 2 minutes. Turn the shells over and cook for 1 minute more. Transfer these conchas to the prepared plate to drain.

Wipe the skillet with a paper towel and place over medium heat. Arrange the conchas in the skillet, place a large colander over the skillet, and pour the tomato sauce through the colander over the conchas. Let simmer until the conchas have warmed through and all the flavors have infused, about 10 minutes. Place the conchas on a clean platter and drizzle the sauce over them. Sprinkle with the remaining 2 tablespoons parsley and 1 tablespoon cilantro.

Serve the conchas immediately.

CONSEJO

If you've never opened or worked with raw clams or oysters, you might need some practice before beginning this recipe. Once the clams are opened, be sure to remove the coarse "husk" and dirt from within the shell of each. Separate the meat and scrub the shells (which will be stuffed later with filling) with a small scrub brush.

PESCADO SECO ENVUELTO

When my mom and I are in the kitchen, it's a party. There are so many laughs and plenty of "No jodas, Karla." It's usually because I've asked for clarification or we're testing something and I've just explained to her that I need to stop and write down the five steps she's already completed. It happens. I love it.

This dish is extremely popular in El Salvador during Easter. It makes me feel like my grandmother is in the kitchen with us. So many of her recipes make us emotional. This one gives us pure joy because of the salted fish. The story goes that every time my grandmother made this, she was so worried that the fish would be too salty that she'd oversoak it and it would come out bland. This is so hilarious to us that we break into big belly laughs, straining abdominal muscles we don't know we have. It hurts so good.

When we make this dish, we often do the same thing my grandma did and totally forget when we started soaking the fish. A series of questions follow as we investigate and retrace our steps. But there have been a few times when we really did forget and the fish was not salty at all, which means that when you're preparing it, you need to add salt. Just don't oversalt it. But if you do, just laugh.

When I'm making this dish, the type of salted fish that I use is robalo. If you're in a Salvadoran market, like El Turco Meat Market in Los Angeles, you'll find different types of imported salted fish from El Salvador, such as mackerel, boca colorada, tilapia, and corvina. I will always go to the meat market so that I can use fish from El Salvador. However, if a Salvadoran market isn't available, salted fish can also be found in Caribbean markets and even certain grocery stores. On the day you want to serve this meal, soak the fish in a large bowl of water for at least 3 hours, or up to 12 hours. Note that the longer the fish soaks, the less salty it will be. If you prefer a longer soak, drain and change the water every 3 hours. If leaving overnight, simply change the water in the morning and keep changing it while it soaks.

For the eggs to be at the proper temperature for beating, leave them out at room temperature overnight.

●

MAKES 12 SERVINGS

1 pound dried garbanzo
   beans, rinsed and soaked
   in 8 cups water overnight,
   then drained
1 garlic clove, left whole
1 fresh bay leaf
One 3-pound salt fish, soaked
   and drained (see headnote)
12 Roma tomatoes, stemmed
1 medium green bell pepper,
   cored and halved
½ medium red onion, peeled
4 garlic cloves, left whole
6 eggs, separated, at room
   temperature
1 teaspoon all-purpose flour
1 cup canola oil
6 small Yukon gold potatoes,
   peeled and quartered
Arroz Frito (page 51) and
   Ensalada Verde (page 50)
   for serving

continued

PESCADO SECO ENVUELTO

continued

In a medium pot over medium-high heat, bring 8 cups of water to a boil. Add the garbanzos, garlic, and bay leaf; turn the heat to medium; cover; and let simmer until the beans are tender, about 45 minutes. Remove from the heat and drain. Set aside.

Using a sharp knife, scale the fish by scraping the blade back and forth across the skin until the scales slough off. Rinse the fish under running water and then pat dry with a paper towel. Using a knife or kitchen shears, cut the fish into twelve pieces and set aside.

In a large pot, combine the tomatoes, bell pepper, onion, and garlic and add enough water to cover the vegetables. Set over medium-high heat and cook until the vegetables are soft, 8 to 10 minutes. Using tongs or a large slotted spoon, transfer the vegetables to a blender, in batches if needed, and blend until smooth. Set aside.

In a large bowl, using an electric mixer on high speed (or a whisk), whip the egg whites until soft peaks form. Add the egg yolks and the flour and continue to whip until everything is incorporated. Set aside.

Line a large plate with paper towels or put a wire cooling rack in a baking sheet and set near the stove. In a large skillet over medium heat, warm the canola oil until it shimmers. Using your hands or tongs, dip each piece of fish in the egg mixture, making sure that all sides of the fish are coated. Working in batches, fry three pieces at a time, carefully placing the fish in the oil and frying until golden brown, about 1 minute per side. Transfer the fried fish to the prepared plate to drain.

Wipe the skillet clean with a paper towel and turn the heat to medium-high. Add the fried fish, tomato sauce, garbanzos, and potatoes; cover and cook until the potatoes are tender, 10 to 15 minutes.

Serve the pescado with arroz and ensalada.

MOJARRA FRITA

When I was growing up, mojarra frita was the epitome of a Saturday meal. I was in charge of setting the table for dinner, so I would make sure we had enough napkins for the bones, since each of us got a whole fish. My brother would trade his fishtail for my two fish eyes, and, personally, I think I got the better deal. He loved the crunchy eyeballs, but those never appealed to me. This dish was a funny meal to me because we loved that my mom would make it and the only thing that she asked of us was to be mindful eaters and not talk. Her fear was that if we were talking, we'd lose focus and accidentally swallow a fish bone. So my brother and I would silently and happily eat our fish, curating perfect bites of fried fish, frijoles licuados, rice, and fresh radish—all with extra lime on top. It was magnificent.

This rendition is from Rosa Elvira. She adds chicken bouillon and Sazón to her mojarra, making it even more savory. She is the mother of Yenny, my oldest Salvadoran friend, whom I met when I was fourteen. Rosa Elvira is from a coastal town, where she was also a fisher for some time.

●

Rinse each tilapia under running water and pat dry with paper towels. Using a sharp knife, score each fish by cutting diagonal slashes, about 1 centimeter deep, into the thickest part of the flesh. Be careful not to make the incisions too deep, or the fish may fall apart once it's cooked.

In a small bowl, combine the mustard, garlic powder, chicken bouillon, Sazón, and salt and stir to mix thoroughly into a paste. Rub the mustard paste all over each fish until they are well coated. Allow the fish to marinate at room temperature for 10 minutes.

Line a large platter with paper towels or put a wire cooling rack in a baking sheet and set near the stove. In a large skillet over medium heat, warm the vegetable oil until it shimmers. Using tongs, carefully place a single fish in the oil and fry until it turns golden brown, 5 to 8 minutes per side. Transfer the fried fish to the prepared platter to drain. Repeat for the remaining three fish.

Serve the mojarra with ensalada, arroz, frijoles, and tortillas.

MAKES 4 TO 6 SERVINGS

4 whole fresh tilapia (10 to 12 ounces each)
¼ cup yellow mustard
2 tablespoons garlic powder
1 tablespoon chicken bouillon powder
1 tablespoon Sazón
1 tablespoon kosher salt
2 cups vegetable oil
Ensalada Verde (page 50), Arroz Frito (page 51), Basic Olla de Frijoles (page 40), and Tortillas Salvadoreñas (page 36) for serving

A TRIBUTE TO LAS NECIAS

I first met Yenny as an awkward fourteen-year-old. I was the new girl in school. Previously, I planned to transfer with my friends from middle school to Los Angeles High, but that didn't happen. My parents decided to send me to a different school far from the friends I'd worked so hard to make, and now I didn't know a soul. My insecurity and anxiety made me want to disappear into the walls. I don't know exactly what day it was, where I was going, or where I was on campus but I do remember the moment I first spotted Yenny. I will never forget how seeing her immediately made me feel like the sun had come out on a cloudy day. She had the most brilliant smile and such even teeth. She wore glasses like me. She had hair like mine. Not really curly, not really straight—it just made a statement with volume and a touch of frizz. She looked happy.

She was also wearing green from head to toe. You couldn't look away. Her JanSport backpack was a bright emerald-spruce green, her Converse high tops were a Nickelodeon-slime green, her khaki pants were a muted army green, and her T-shirt (the bluest green she had on) was a nice aqua. The last thing I noticed was her iconic (at least to me) green zip hoodie with white and black pinstripes, like Adidas stripes. Even her jacket was the color of a four-leaf clover. She looked like the coolest girl ever. Not long after I first saw her, we became acquaintances and then close friends. I remember the moment when we realized that we were both Salvadoran. With a big smile, Yenny exclaimed, "Oh what? No way, I'm Salvi too." She became my first Salvi friend.

Years later, I find myself in Yenny's home. She's an adult now, married. We're still friends. Rosa Elvira, her mother, has prepared a feast of mojarra frita for us. After eating, we move to the living room. Yenny sits on a pouf on the floor, her mother sits on the couch closest to Yenny, and I'm in a reading chair across from them. We speak about Rosa's life—or rather, Rosa shares and we listen. She explains that she will never stop using her maiden name, Zelaya, out of the enormous love she has for her father. We also talk about the early mornings that Rosa experienced growing up in El Salvador. When she was seven, she worked with her father and sisters on the land, planting corn, rice, sorghum, beans, and all kinds of other crops. They would often wake up at three in the morning and work until five or six in the evening. The farm labor she started at a young age didn't stop until she moved to the United States at the age of twenty.

We briefly talk about the time when Rosa and her family traveled north and got caught in Mexicali. Rosa says, "Aja, alli nos dieron frijoles duros y una tortilla."

"Tortilla Mexicana?" I ask. She replies, "Si. En Mexicali, ahi, nos pusieron el dedo. Es que alli, en Mexico, es dificil caer." She explains that someone ratted them out and Mexico is a tough place to land. Every so often, Yenny reminds her mom about certain details of her story by gently asking her questions like, "That was the Mexican police?" Eventually, we land on the topic of the sometimes tense relationship they've had over the years. Rosa was too strict, she herself acknowledges. "Too hard, maybe."

Yenny says with a laugh, "She's a very strong woman, which is good . . . most of the time." She adds, "But we butt heads a lot, too, and it's because I've been told we're the same person." I ask her in what ways. She thinks for a moment. "Somos bien . . . necias. Strong. Independent."

CEVICHE DE PESCADO

MAKES 6 TO 8 SERVINGS

1½ pounds rockfish, cleaned,
    boned, and cut into ½-inch
    pieces
1½ cups lemon juice
1 cup peeled, seeded, and
    chopped tomatoes
1 cup chopped Persian
    cucumbers
1 cup peeled, pitted, and
    chopped mango
½ medium red onion, chopped
2 green onions, chopped
1 jalapeño, chopped
1 tablespoon rice vinegar
1 tablespoon extra-virgin
    olive oil
2 teaspoons sea salt
Crackers or crispy tortillas
    and hot sauce for serving
    (optional)

"You can't really fuck it up" is what Carolina says about her ceviche recipe. Carolina and her family own a small bed-and-breakfast in La Libertad, on the coast of El Salvador. It's called Surf y Sol, and ceviche is one of the dishes that they serve at their restaurant. It captures "todo es playa," the spirit of beach life, where everything is done with ease. Ceviche is playa life—meant to be quick and celebratory.

After getting revolcadas en el mar—spit out from the rolling ocean waves—the body is spent and calories are needed. Ceviche is the answer: mouthwatering bits of fresh food with a little acid, some protein, and spice. It's heavenly with a cool agua de coco or fresco de ensalada. Ceviche es playa.

Carolina's method is to cure the fish in the lemon juice and then just add whatever vegetables you like. Ceviche is versatile, so it's forever easy. Ask your fishmonger to clean your fish and remove the bones for best results. Ceviche should be prepared the same day the fish is purchased. If rockfish isn't available, Carolina suggests halibut.

In a large bowl, combine the rockfish and lemon juice. Allow the fish to marinate until the flesh has turned opaque, 15 to 30 minutes. Add the tomatoes, cucumbers, mango, red onion, green onions, jalapeño, rice vinegar, olive oil, and salt and mix well, until all the ingredients are evenly seasoned and coated.

Serve the ceviche with crackers or crispy tortillas and hot sauce, if desired.

MAKING FRIENDS IN L.A.

Carolina doesn't like super-lemony things. But she loves ceviche, and she's known for making a great one. Her friends beg her to make it whenever an opportunity comes up. "I learned how to do it, and I made it for my friends, and they were just like, this is the best ceviche we've ever had. We love it. One friend said, 'I'm standing over the dish eating it because I can't stop.'" That's how good it is. The only catch: It never comes out the same way twice.

"They're like, every time you make it, it tastes different," Carolina says. "I say, 'Oh, that's funny.'" Then she tells me, "It's still good, but sometimes it's better than other times." Either way, this group has always made Carolina feel special. She points to the photographs on her fridge. "That's my friend Diana, who's right there . . . the girl in the skirt, yeah, that's one of them." They're some of her closest friends from college.

Carolina doesn't disagree with her friend's assessment. She does always make ceviche differently. Sometimes the ratio of vegetables to fish is different. Sometimes she uses Meyer lemons from her tree; other times, lemons from the store. "Maybe the reason why it tastes different is that I use different types of fish," she says. "When I want to be extra extravagant, I'll use halibut. But when it's a big, huge amount, I'll make it with rockfish."

Learning to cook is something Carolina loves and has always found enjoyable. Whether she cooks for her family, two people, or just one person, she finds immense joy in it, and it's a tool that's helped her find friends. This means a lot to her because finding friends hasn't ever been easy. "I just remember their parents saying things like, 'Oh, she's a bad influence and don't hang out with that little girl,' that kind of thing."

It was 1972 in Los Angeles when she arrived. Change and tension were in the air. New buildings were being added to the skyline, and the Vietnam War and the US presidential election were dominating the news and conversations. The buzz of life was happening all around. Carolina was grappling with the tension of a new life when she came to live in Echo Park. She was eight years old and had been raised by her grandmother in El Salvador for the past six years, since her mother had to leave when Carolina was two.

"I grew up pretty much on my own with my grandmother, who wasn't really nurturing. I felt betrayed because I felt abandoned by my mother when she came to this country and left me behind. And when my son was born and I had to take care of him, I would be like, 'God, I didn't have anyone taking care of me when I was this age.' And then as I realized things, it was like, no wonder I'm so fucked up. And I mean, miraculously, I made it through."

Leaving El Salvador for the east-central L.A., northwest of downtown, was a big change for Carolina. Her new normal was a neighborhood where all the Cubans and Puerto Ricans she knew did not embrace her. "I don't know, I felt like they weren't very nice to me. I was always an odd person, and they made fun of me because I was really skinny and ugly with big teeth."

It wasn't until college that making friends got easier, and cooking for them became a way to know herself. "It's like that side of me that they get to say, 'Oh yeah, this is a girl from El Salvador we've known,' because I have a group of friends that I've had for the last twenty, twenty-five, thirty years. When I think about it, it's a way for me to express that side of me that people don't see all the time."

"It makes me proud, you know, like, this is my culture, and look how delicious this is. I've never been a very nurturing person. So with cooking, it gave me a chance to express that love."

PUNCHES CON ALGUASHTE

**MAKES 6 SERVINGS
(2 CRABS PER PERSON)**

2 large tomatoes, minced

2 medium green bell peppers,
cored and chopped

1½ cups water

1 cup alguashte (see page 55)

4 green onions, chopped

¼ bunch cilantro, chopped

¼ bunch flat-leaf parsley,
chopped

1 tablespoon seafood bouillon
powder

1 tablespoon kosher salt

1 teaspoon yellow mustard

1 teaspoon ground cumin

8 tablespoons unsalted butter

3 garlic cloves, minced

12 punches, cleaned (see
Consejo)

Arroz Frito (page 51), Ensalada
Verde (page 50), and
Tortillas Salvadoreñas
(page 36) for serving

CONSEJO

*Humanely kill the
punches by piercing a knife
through their eyes. Use a large
scrub brush and a toothbrush to
pull apart their abdomens using
your thumb and forefinger. Pull
the bottom shell away from their
bodies. Rinse the insides of the
punches until the water
runs clear.*

Walking through the outdoor Salvadoran market in Los Angeles is always a good idea. In fact, any time you can visit a market backed by an immigrant community, you're bound to find something new, fun, and worthwhile. This was exactly the case when I came upon punches, a type of crab. In coming to this market for years, I'd always seen them hanging live in the vendor stalls, ready to be taken home. And I'd always been intimidated by them.

I decided to face my insecurity about cooking this particular seafood and went to buy some. When I finally arrived at the market, all the courage I'd worked up was almost misspent because the vendors were already sold out. It was only nine in the morning, but I hadn't left home early enough. To be honest, I felt relieved but also disappointed; I'd wanted to try something new and cook something special for my family. That is, until I found one vendor at the very end of a long row of stalls who was selling the last dozen crabs in the entire market. Once again, that mixture of relief and disappointment set in. I was happy I'd get to try this, but I was feeling a tiny bit of dread.

The punches are cooked in a sauce made from alguashte, a pumpkin-seed powder. The sweetness of the punches along with the nuttiness of the alguashte and herbs makes this a wonderfully pleasant dish with a great depth of flavor. Make this for a special occasion—it's a showstopper for a small, intimate family dinner or a celebration with friends, a cumpleaños, a promotion, or an anniversary.

Punches are mud crabs from the Salvadoran mangroves. They vary from a blue-purple color to an orange-purple color. The punches should be alive when you buy them. If you can't get them, substituting a different type of crab will work fine.

●

In a blender, combine half of the tomatoes, half of the bell peppers, the water, alguashte, green onions, cilantro, parsley, seafood bouillon, salt, mustard, and cumin, and blend on medium speed to a smooth sauce. Set aside.

In a large saucepan over medium heat, melt the butter. Add the garlic and cook until it is soft, about 2 minutes. Add the remaining tomatoes and remaining bell peppers and cook until tender, about 5 minutes more. Add the punches, stir well, and turn the heat to low.

Add the sauce to the pan and cook until the sauce thickens and turns an opaque green and the crabs' color brightens, about 15 minutes.

Place two punches with plenty of sauce on each individual plate and serve with arroz, ensalada, and tortillas.

CHUMPE CON RECAUDO

Most Salvadorans speak Salvadoran Spanish, which differs from conventional Spanish. The name of this recipe is a good example; while most Spanish-speaking folks say *pavo* when referring to turkey, we call it *chompipe* when referring to the animal, and *chumpe* when referring to the meat. In the Nahuat language, the word is *tzunshipetz*, which translates to "cabeza pelada" in Spanish, or "bald head" in English.

Chumpe is very popular in El Salvador, and it's an obvious choice for a holiday meal. I grew up enjoying this kind of turkey for all the special holidays, and I looked forward to it all year because it's delicious. This particular recaudo, or salsa criolla, is very similar to the one made for panes con pollo or even a guisado. However, the chompipe's distinctive flavor is what makes it extra special. It must be Christmas or New Year's Day if I smell this dish.

I associate chumpe with a cumbia song that always plays during our New Year's family gatherings. Its lyrics always get me in the heart because it's nostalgic AF and reminds me that there is always much to be grateful for and that good times are ahead too.

Yo no olvido al año Viejo / Oh, I can't forget the last year

Porque me ha dejado cosas muy buenas / Because it has left me with great things

Ay, yo no olvido al año Viejo / Oh, I can't forget last year

Porque me ha dejado cosas muy buenas / Because it has left me with great things

Carmen is known for her chumpe con recaudo, to the point that she's famous in her church for bringing this dish every holiday season. She marinates the turkey in wine, which is a different method than what I was raised with. Marinating the turkey in wine overnight helps tenderize the meat. I recommend using a good wine for cooking, like a Pinot Noir, Merlot, or lighter Cabernet, because their moderate tannin levels make them less dry and astringent.

Most cooks use a very specific oval-shaped roasting pan, called a chompipera, for this dish. It's as important as any of the ingredients in the recipe, and as you'll see in Carmen's story, it's absolutely integral to the end result. You can find chompiperas in Latin American markets and online; if you can't source one, a very large oval roasting dish, along with aluminum foil to cover the turkey, also works.

●

continued

MAKES 10 TO 12 SERVINGS

One 14-pound turkey, thawed, neck and giblets removed, and the bird patted dry

One 750ml bottle red wine (see headnote)

8 tablespoons unsalted butter, at room temperature

1 cup yellow mustard

Sea salt

1 tablespoon raw white sesame seeds

1 tablespoon raw pumpkin seeds

1 tablespoon cumin seeds

1 tablespoon black peppercorns

1 pasilla chile

3 dried bay leaves

15 Roma tomatoes, stemmed

1 medium white onion, peeled

6 garlic cloves, left whole

4 cups water

1 tablespoon achiote powder

One 9½-ounce jar Spanish olives

2 tablespoons capers

CHUMPE CON RECAUDO

continued

Place the turkey inside a chompipera or roasting pan and add the wine. Transfer to the refrigerator and let the turkey marinate for at least 12 hours or up to overnight. The next day, discard the wine.

In a small bowl, combine the butter, mustard, and 1 tablespoon salt to form a smooth paste. Rub the paste over every part of the turkey, including under the skin and in all the crevices. Cover the turkey with plastic wrap and refrigerate for 2 hours. Before roasting, let the turkey sit at room temperature for 1 hour.

Preheat the oven to 400°F.

In a small dry skillet over medium-high heat, combine the sesame seeds, pumpkin seeds, cumin seeds, peppercorns, pasilla chile, and bay leaves and toast until they turn fragrant, about 5 minutes, making sure to stir and shake them in the pan so they don't burn. Remove from the heat and set aside.

In a large skillet over high heat, combine the tomatoes, onion, and garlic and roast until the tomato skins have split and the onion is translucent, 15 to 20 minutes. Working in batches, transfer the toasted spices and roasted vegetables to a blender and blend at high speed into a smooth sauce, about 3 minutes. After blending each batch, transfer the sauce to a large container (I use a pitcher). To the last batch, add the water, achiote powder, and 1 tablespoon salt and blend until thoroughly incorporated. Adjust the seasoning, if necessary; it should just taste pleasant.

Position the turkey, breast-side down, in the chompipera. Pour all the sauce over the turkey, sprinkle with the olives and capers, and cover with a lid or aluminum foil. Place in the oven, turn the temperature to 350°F, and roast the turkey for 3 hours, basting it with the sauce in the chompipera every hour. When 45 minutes of roasting time remain, carefully turn the turkey breast-side up and re-cover. During the last 10 minutes of roasting, carefully taste the sauce (it will be hot) and season with salt, if necessary, then remove the lid so the top of the turkey turns a deep golden brown.

The turkey is done when an instant-read thermometer inserted into the thickest part of the breast registers 150° to 155°F, and the thickest part of a thigh registers 165° to 170°F. If desired, carve the turkey and then add it back to the chompipera with the sauce.

Serve the turkey with the pan sauce.

CONSEJO

The turkey can be safely marinated in the wine for up to 2 days in the refrigerator before cooking. During the marinating process, the turkey should be rotated so that the marinade can penetrate as much of the meat as possible.

"No, no . . . casi todos hacen seco el turkey. Nadie lo hace como en El Salvador." Having tried several kinds of turkeys, Carmen insists that no one makes it like they do in El Salvador. Almost everyone makes a dry turkey, she says. But she thinks Salvadoran chumpe is the best—hers especially.

You need several things to make it properly. Tomatoes are of the utmost importance, as is achiote, for its rich color and earthiness. Sesame seeds are imperative, as well as toasting the seeds until they are fragrant. Olives, of course, are essential, and she wouldn't serve this dish without them; although she has never particularly enjoyed them, they are crucial for creating that well-rounded, savory, bright, umami flavor of the dish. However, when it comes to salt and other ingredients in her recipe, "tantear" is her philosophy. Tantear is neither a metric of measurement nor a direction. It's quite literally a feeling, a call to action, asking oneself, *Is this the flavor I want? Does it feel like that's enough?*

When it comes to her secret ingredient for her famous turkey, it's not an ingredient but a tool—her olla, or pot. It makes all the difference, she says. "Como se conserva el jugito en mi olla"—her roasting pot conserves the sauce so well that the turkey stays juicy. She uses her special olla only twice a year, and only when she is making her turkey.

"Los Americanos, quizás les gusta asi séquito, pero nosotros no. Nosotros así comemos el pavo, así con salsita," she says. (The Americans, maybe they like their turkey dry. But not us—we eat it like this, with its sauce.) Her family isn't the only one who has marveled at her skill in making Salvadoran chumpe. Many at her church have made a comment or two: "Wow, hermana, this is delicious." "Hermana, please give us the recipe." Once, an hermana from the congregation fell ill, so Carmen made her a holiday turkey. As Carmen retells the story with shock, "Hermana Silvia says to me after trying the turkey, 'Wow, Hermana, so delicious. Did you buy it?'"

Nowadays, she doesn't cook it as much because of her other love. Typing at her office job of thirty-three years has left her with carpal tunnel syndrome, which makes it hard to maneuver the turkey and, most of all, her special pot.

CHAO MEIN SALVADOREÑO

MAKES 4 TO 6 SERVINGS

1 pound boneless, skinless chicken breasts, sliced into 1-inch pieces

2 tablespoons apple cider vinegar

2 tablespoons lemon juice

2 tablespoons canola oil

3 medium white onions, thinly sliced

1 medium red bell pepper, cored and sliced

1 medium green bell pepper, cored and sliced

1 medium orange bell pepper, cored and sliced

1 bunch celery, thinly sliced

8 tablespoons unsalted butter

2 large carrots, peeled and sliced into 2-inch matchsticks

2 güisquiles, sliced into 2-inch matchsticks

12 ounces egg noodles

1 teaspoon kosher salt

1½ pounds 26/30-count raw shrimp, peeled, cleaned, and deveined

1 tablespoon soy sauce

Arroz Frito (page 51) and Tortillas Salvadoreñas (page 36) for serving

When I was a kid, I never questioned our culinary history. So when we ate chao mein, I just naturally thought it was Salvadoran food. Of course, once I grew up and put two and two together when we dined at Chinese restaurants, I knew better. No one is really sure how this dish made it into the recipe lexicon of Salvadoran cuisine, but it is a favorite of many homes. Chao mein is beloved by the world; it's delicious, it's versatile, and, here, you'll find a great option with vegetables that offers a Salvadoran twist.

There aren't many noodle dishes in Salvadoran cuisine, but this one is important. My grandfather is a chao mein fan, and he makes sure there are tortillas and rice to go with it. This is one of Marta Rosa's favorite dishes to prepare for her family.

In a large bowl, combine the chicken, apple cider vinegar, and lemon juice and mix well.

In a large skillet over medium-high heat, warm 1 tablespoon of the canola oil until it shimmers. Add the chicken and cook until its raw appearance is gone and each piece is nicely browned, about 7 minutes. Transfer the chicken to a plate.

In the same skillet over medium-high heat, warm the remaining 1 tablespoon canola oil until it shimmers. Add the onions and cook until they turn golden brown, about 5 minutes. Add all the bell peppers and the celery and the salt, cover, and cook until the vegetables have softened, about 2 minutes. Turn the heat to low and add the butter. When the butter has melted, add the carrots and güisquiles and cook until they turn tender, 10 to 15 minutes.

Meanwhile, in a large pot over high heat, bring enough water to cover the noodles to a boil. Add the noodles and cook until al dente according to the package directions. Drain the noodles and add to the skillet with the vegetables. Turn the heat to low, add the chicken and the shrimp, cover, and cook until they have turned pink and opaque, about 2 minutes. Stir in the soy sauce and mix well.

Serve the chao mein with arroz and tortillas.

CONEJO PARRILLADO

When I traveled to El Salvador to learn about its food history, I was lucky enough to try this dish. We drove the famous Ruta de las Flores, or Flower Route, to the western part of the country to get to the Feria de Gastronomía—Gastronomy Fair—in Juayúa. The smell of grilled meats filled the air, vendors called us to their stalls, and a multitude of glorious colors and textures jumped out at us; all overwhelming in the best way possible.

My only goal at the fair was to try something new. I had my eye on a few options, but after making several rounds, I went with the grilled rabbit. Its smell alone was enough to tell me it was the right choice. Served with fresh tortillas, casamiento, fresh cheese, and chirimol, it was a memorable meal, especially because while I was eating a separate nearby vendor was selling live pet bunnies from a cage. The vendor had taken one outside of its cage and it was so tiny that it fit in the palm of their hand. Every time someone came near their table, they stretched out their hand so patrons could see this ball of cuteness.

Rabbit is a protein frequently enjoyed by Salvadoran and early Indigenous communities. The flavors in this recipe taste different from what I had back in El Salvador, but that dish at the feria inspired me to do my own take, and rabbit is a fantastic reason to fire up the grill. This recipe requires prep ahead of the grilling. Prepare the brine four hours before you intend to grill.

●

In a large container, combine the rabbit, water, onion, celery, three of the garlic cloves, the bay leaves, lemon juice and lemons, and ½ cup salt; cover; transfer to the refrigerator; and let brine for 4 hours.

Meanwhile, in a blender, combine the mustard, cilantro, parsley, basil, oregano, olive oil, honey, and 1 teaspoon salt and blend on medium speed into a uniform green sauce. Set aside.

Once the rabbit has finished brining, transfer to a plate and pat dry with paper towels. Rub half of the herb sauce all over the rabbit until it is well coated.

Prepare the grill to 350°F, or medium-high heat.

Place the rabbit on the grill, close the cover, and grill for 20 minutes. Open the cover, baste the rabbit with the remaining sauce, turn it over, and continue cooking until an instant-read thermometer registers 160°F when inserted into the thickest part of the meat, about another 20 minutes. Transfer the rabbit to a plate and let rest for about 10 minutes before cutting into pieces.

Serve the conejo with casamiento, ensalada, and lime wedges.

MAKES 4 TO 6 SERVINGS

One 3-pound rabbit, left whole
8 cups water
1 medium white onion, quartered
3 celery stalks, sliced into 2-inch pieces
6 garlic cloves, left whole
3 fresh bay leaves
2 lemons, halved and juiced
Kosher salt
½ cup yellow mustard
½ bunch cilantro, coarsely chopped
¼ bunch flat-leaf parsley, coarsely chopped
6 basil leaves
2 sprigs fresh oregano, leaves picked
2 tablespoons extra-virgin olive oil
1 teaspoon honey
Casamiento (page 59), Ensalada Verde (page 50), and lime wedges for serving

BEBIDAS

A fruit and vegetable street vendor in La Libertad.

Salvadoran beverages are never afterthoughts, but emblems of pride and identity. And they truly reflect the bounty of their country's markets. The drinks in this chapter are as much a part of Salvadoran food culture for the diaspora as the entrees. One common experience shared by many Salvadorans is a drink known as ensalada. In Spanish, *ensalada* means "salad," which confuses some non-Salvadorans. This beverage contains various ingredients, but it is made mostly from fruit—sometimes eight or more varieties, depending on the season and region.

FRESCO DE MARAÑÓN

MAKES 8 SERVINGS

Two 14-ounce bags frozen
    marañón (see Consejo),
    thawed and chopped
    into bite-size pieces
¼ teaspoon kosher salt
8 cups water
1 cup granulated sugar
Ice cubes for serving

Marañón, or cashew fruit, is often described as *tetelque*, which, apart from being a fun Spanish word to say, isn't a term you want to use for food. It means "astringent," or "acidic and bitter," with a mild stickiness that stays on the tongue. Even though its astringency is known across El Salvador, marañón is beloved for its indescribable taste, which is sweet and has a satisfying tropical freshness to it.

Laura, who also shares her sopa de res recipe on page 134, made this drink for me when we were doing recipe testing. It paired wonderfully with her sopa, adding delightful flavor to our meal.

•

In a blender, combine three-fourths of the marañón, the salt, and 1 cup of the water. Blend on high speed in 10- to 30-second bursts until the fruit begins to turn into a coarse pulp, 2 to 3 minutes. Add the sugar and blend until it dissolves and the fruit is completely pureed, about 2 minutes. Transfer the sweetened, blended marañón pulp to a large pitcher.

Add 1 cup water to the blender and turn on the blender again to rinse any pulp off the blender walls, and pour this liquid into the pitcher. Add the remaining 6 cups water to the pitcher and stir in the remaining marañón. Refrigerate the fresco for 30 minutes to 1 hour before serving.

When ready to serve, fill individual glasses with ice and pour in the fresco. Make sure each has some of the chopped marañón.

CONSEJO

Since fresh marañón is hard to find outside of Latin America, the frozen fruit is a great option. It is available in the frozen food aisles in most Latin American grocery stores.

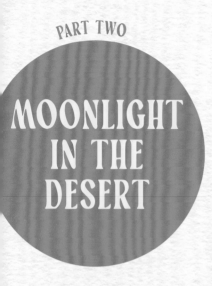

PART TWO

MOONLIGHT IN THE DESERT

In the darkness, under the bed, Laura could hear her thoughts so clearly. Why did I leave? Why did I let Mamá Mila convince me? Elisabeth's shaking was worsening. Her aunt was no better. They had to get out of that bedroom. Even though it had been a few minutes since the DHS officers had knocked on the front door, they could still be outside. Laura closed her eyes and remembered her Mamá Mila.

"Siempre esperaba el día domingo." Sundays were Laura's favorite day as a child, because they were also her grandmother Mamá Mila's favorite. "Seeing my grandmother smile and be content and happy made me feel the same way," she explained to me. Her grandmother's good mood was contagious. Sundays were for family and adventure. Of course, it was also a day filled with good eating. To prepare for the hour's journey to El Majahual, the famous playa of El Salvador, they made snacks for the road. Panes con frijoles. Or panes con pollo y repollo, the perfect foods for an excursion.

Laura would help her grandma pack all the items into Laura's uncle's car. Nestled in the back seat between her grandmother and her cousins, Laura felt so rich. Gazing at the street vendors selling fresh tortillas, and the lush greenery of La Libertad along the way, she knew they'd be arriving soon. And then it would be time for lunch, with cócteles, mariscos, and the fresh catch of the day. The family would order la mojarra frita, her grandmother's favorite.

At this moment, Laura was terrified. Breathing into the dingy carpeted floor beneath the bed they were all hiding under, she could almost taste that fresh fish she grew up eating every Sunday with her grandmother. Now she was so far removed from both. It was that wonderful feeling after playing and running around for hours in the hot sun that Laura craved the most. The friendly waves of El Majahual were always gentle enough for her to enjoy as an eight-year-old playing in the sea. And the feast that awaited them at her grandfather's family home was the perfect way to end their excursion. There, they were treated like royalty. Fresh coconuts upon arrival. Hot bowls of sopa de res for dinner. Fresh cuajada, fresh tortillas, and plenty of hugs to go around.

Taking a deep breath, Laura wriggled herself out from under the bed. One never knew who was dangerous. They were trapped in a room in the house of a male stranger, and her gut instinct told her to keep watch and rotate shifts to stay vigilant. Laura looked out the window at the bright moon. She knew it was past midnight, and they would need to keep watch for at least six hours until sunrise. "Vaya, Elisabeth y Tía. Salganse de allí. Vamos a tener que vigilar la puerta. Quién sabe si ese hombre es bueno o malo, pero hay que estar listas por si acaso," said Laura, pep-talking to her two compañeras. They could trust only their intuition and one another to protect themselves. They would keep an eye on the smooth metal doorknob. Whatever awaited them in the morning, they would face together. "I'll keep the first watch. Both of you sleep," said Laura.

When Laura awoke, her tía was keeping watch. It was still dark, but early-morning light was beginning to seep into the sky. It was time to open the door. "Tía, Elisabeth, sea lo que sea, vamos a salir de aquí," whispered Laura. Elisabeth and Laura's tía nodded their heads in agreement. They were exhausted but needed to leave to stay alive. They expected to face danger when they opened the door. Instead, sitting on the floor in front of them was a basket filled with clean clothes, towels, and soaps. Laura was confused. So was her tía. The mystery man appeared. Now, in the daylight, he looked much different from the ominous shadow of the night before. In Spanish, he said, "Hurry. Here are some supplies. Wash up in the bathroom. I've gone looking for a coyote to take you safely out of here."

"Señor . . . ni se que decirle . . . gracias . . . que Dios se lo pague." Laura could barely speak. She didn't know what to do but give the man her thanks. Here they had suffered a sleepless night filled with panic, and all the while he had been trying to help. "A red car will be here to pick you up," he said. He approached Elisabeth, who had been crying, and as he grabbed her hand, he said, "Apúrense, hijas." A short time later, just as he had promised, a red car pulled up. In it was a couple. "They're going to take you all to Los Angeles," the man said.

Laura, her tía, and Elisabeth piled into the trunk. After showering and changing clothes, they were already feeling safer and better. The man set a backpack inside the trunk by their feet. "Here are some sandwiches, clothes, medicines, and a map," he said kindly. All three women teared up. As they were driven away, Laura savored the safety of the moment. Their journey wasn't over, but they had lived to see a new day.

FRESCO DE ENSALADA SALVADOREÑA

MAKES 16 SERVINGS

4 cups finely chopped
   pineapple, in ½-centimeter
   pieces

1 cup firmly packed brown
   sugar

16 cups water

8 ounces marañón, finely
   chopped, in ½-centimeter
   pieces

1 Pink Lady apple, finely
   chopped, in ½-centimeter
   pieces

1 large ripe mango, finely
   chopped, in ½-centimeter
   pieces

2 cups finely chopped fresh
   mamey in ½-centimeter
   pieces

One 14-ounce bag frozen
   whole jocotes

1 teaspoon pineapple essence
   (optional)

3 medium romaine lettuce
   leaves, chopped into
   thin ribbons

Sprigs from 1 bunch watercress

In some ways, ensalada as a beverage is very variable, which means its flavors are also variable. Versions across El Salvador feature everything from nances, jocotes, and marañón to just about every other tropical fruit you can find in the country. Within the diaspora are a few other options: grapes, apples, peaches, and even plums. The essentials seem to be pineapple as a base, along with apples and jocotes. And don't forget the fresh watercress or lettuce!

This beverage is special for many reasons. It's a refresco (or fresco for short), but it also makes sense as an ensalada because it's basically a liquid tropical fruit salad—tangy and sweet, with a wonderfully well-rounded flavor. In this recipe, Isabel adds pineapple essence, which she says is optional. With most of these ingredients, whatever options that are available are always the go-to, but that being said, if you have access to all fresh fruit, feel free to use. Same goes for the pineapple—if you can't access fresh, some Salvi cooks suggest canned. Just make sure to grab the pineapple that's in juice, not syrup.

●

In a blender, combine 3 cups of the pineapple, the brown sugar, and 2 cups of the water. Blend on high speed until smooth, about 2 minutes.

Transfer the pineapple mixture to a jug or beverage dispenser that will be large enough to hold all the water and chopped fruit. Add the marañón, apple, mango, mamey, jocotes, pineapple essence (if using), remaining 1 cup pineapple, and remaining 14 cups water and stir to mix well. Add the lettuce and stir. Allow the beverage to sit for 10 minutes so the flavors mingle.

When ready to serve, fill about a third of each glass with fruit, then top with the fresco. Garnish with a sprig of watercress. Offer a spoon along with a straw so that guests can spoon out the fruit as they sip.

HORCHATA DE SEMILLA DE MORRO

Horchata's history can be traced to West Africa, where the original beverage was made from tiger nuts and consumed more as a health elixir than the sweet drink we enjoy today. Depending on the region, at least ten different ingredients are used in Salvadoran horchata. But the one indispensable ingredient are small, round dark-brown seeds called semillas de morro. Lending depth, a distinctly earthy flavor, and an enjoyable grittiness, these seeds capture the essence of this beverage. This drink has body! I have read that semillas de morro have a taste similar to that original horchata recipe from West Africa.

●

In a small dry skillet over medium heat, toast the morro seeds, sesame seeds, peanuts, pumpkin seeds, cacao seeds, and cinnamon stick until they turn fragrant and have deepened in color but are not too dark, 5 to 7 minutes. Remove the toasted spice mixture from the heat and let cool for 5 minutes.

In a blender, combine ½ cup of the cooled spice mixture, 2 cups of the water, and ½ cup of the sugar. Blend on high speed until smooth, about 1 minute. Strain this blended horchata through a manta or a fine-mesh sieve into a large jug or beverage dispenser. Repeat the blending and straining until the remaining spice mixture, water, and sugar are used. Using a long ladle, stir the horchata and adjust the sweetness as necessary.

When ready to serve, fill individual glasses with ice and pour in the horchata.

MAKES 16 SERVINGS

1 cup morro seeds
1 cup raw white sesame seeds
1 tablespoon raw peanuts
1 tablespoon raw pumpkin seeds
7 raw whole cacao seeds
One 6-inch cinnamon stick
16 cups water, or as needed
2 cups granulated sugar, or as needed
Ice cubes for serving

CHICHA DE PIÑA

MAKES 2 LITERS

Peel of 1 large pineapple
    (see Consejo), cut into
    4-inch strips
8 ounces dulce de panela
8½ cups water
Ice cubes and granulated sugar
    (optional) for serving

When I was growing up, my mom made fresh frescos for our regular weekday dinners. Sometimes we had bottled orange juice, but mostly it was the fresh stuff that was available. We also enjoyed chicha, a fermented pineapple drink. ("Fermented" means that it has low levels of alcohol.) What I love most about this recipe is that we use the entire fruit; pineapple is so important in Salvadoran cuisine that we even use the peel to make a beverage.

When I was researching curtido, chicha became increasingly significant to me. The rare, older cookbooks I found always referred to vinegar as *vinagre casero*, "homemade vinegar." Chicha is fruit based, made from apples and most often from pineapple peels. Then I learned that chicha was also used to make vinegar. I thought this was so cool. In some ways, chicha is like homemade wine, so it makes perfect sense that if it ferments longer, it becomes vinegar.

In this recipe, we are making the chicha. Some recipes add tamarind or other fruit to their mixture. The important thing to remember is that, depending on the weather, you might need to adjust how long it sits at room temperature. I've tested this in Southern California year-round, and the fermentation time has varied. So, as with most things, experiment and have fun with it.

You know you've done it right if, after a few days, you see little bubbles and some movement in the liquid. This means it's fermenting. It is also normal to see white bits forming on the surface of the liquid. But if you start seeing black spots, this means bad bacteria have contaminated it. This can largely be prevented if you cover your container with a tea towel and secure it with a rubber band around the lip. The beverage needs to breathe, but it also needs to stay covered.

●

In a large container, combine the pineapple peel, dulce de panela, and water and stir to mix well. Cover with a manta or other thin fabric that allows the chicha to breathe and secure with a rubber band. Set the container on a counter at room temperature, away from direct sun, and let ferment for 3 days. If the chicha looks bubbly, taste it; it should have a pleasant sweetness and acidity. If it's not bubbly, keep fermenting and taste it after another 24 hours.

Set a strainer over a large pitcher and pour the chicha through the strainer; discard the pineapple peel. Store in the refrigerator for up to 3 days.

When ready to serve, fill individual glasses with ice, pour in the chicha, and stir in sugar to sweeten, if desired.

CONSEJO

Wash the pineapple peel with your preferred fruit wash. If your chicha is not fermenting, the environment might be too cold. Leave it outside, not in direct sunlight. Warmer temperatures will help the fermentation process.

SALVISOUR

MAKES 1 SERVING

2 teaspoons alguashte
(see page 55), plus more
for garnish
1 lime wedge, the juice of 1 lime,
plus 1 thin lime slice
3 ice cubes, plus more for
shaking
1 ounce Tíc Táck
3 tablespoons Mango Verde
Syrup (recipe follows)
⅛ teaspoon kosher salt

This is a beverage that I traveled far to try. Years ago, Nómada, a very hip bar in San Salvador, posted a photo of a drink that contained mango verde, alguashte, and lime. When I was finally in El Salvador to do research, I was thrilled to go there with my dear friend Maya, a fellow Salvadoran friend and screenwriter. We ordered a round of drinks and I was blown away. The taste was just as exquisite as I had hoped it would be when I spotted it online years earlier.

This bar's vibes were wonderful. It was my second night in the country. Maya and I were catching each other up on our projects, dreaming out loud, and enjoying our drinks. I ordered another because it was worth repeating, and this time I savored it.

This is my interpretation of what I tasted that night and what I now call a SalviSour. I use Tíc Táck, which is the national spirit of El Salvador. It is a lower-proof cane vodka that has been distilled multiple times to make it smoother. If you can't find it, use any vodka you have on hand. You can order Tíc Táck on several websites. Or when you go to El Salvador, buy a large bottle and pack it in your checked luggage.

●

Pour 1 teaspoon of the alguashte onto a small plate.

Slice the lime wedge through the middle, stopping before you cut the peel. Place the slit of the wedge on the rim of a lowball glass and run it around the rim to moisten. Turn the prepared glass upside down in the alguashte to coat. Place the three ice cubes in the prepared glass and set aside.

Fill a cocktail shaker two-thirds of the way with ice, then add the Tíc Táck, mango verde syrup, lime juice, salt, and remaining 1 teaspoon alguashte. Shake well, about 10 seconds, then pour into the prepared glass.

Garnish the SalviSour with the lime slice and enjoy right away.

continued

MANGO VERDE SYRUP

Mango verde, or green mango, is an addiction of mine. What I find endearing is that among the Salvadorans who I know have gardens, they often have a mango tree but they almost never pick ripe fruit from it—they always buy from the store. It's comical. The reason is that they're too busy eating the super-tart, acidic, unripened fruit, which is why it's called mango verde. Obviously, you'd lose out on perfectly delicious green mangoes if you just let them ripen on the tree.

Mango verde is a popular snack that is made even more sour by adding lime, salt, alguashte, and, sometimes, hot sauce. A bag of mango verde with these fixings is the Flamin' Hot Cheetos equivalent in the homeland. This recipe turns that sour-tart flavor into something sweet. Enjoy this syrup with mineral water, drizzled on a piece of toast, or, like my family does, by the spoonful directly from the jar.

If you don't have a mango tree, you can source unripe mangoes from markets that specialize in foods from Latin America, Central America, or Asia.

●

In a medium saucepan over high heat, combine the mango verde, sugar, and water and bring to a boil. Turn the heat to low and let simmer until the mango starts to soften and turns from a bright green to a muted yellow color, about 10 minutes. The syrup is done when it has thickened and coats the back of a spoon. Allow to cool completely before using.

Store the syrup in an airtight container in the refrigerator for up to 2 weeks.

MAKES 2½ CUPS

1 pound mango verde, peeled and quartered
1 cup granulated sugar
1 cup water

Green mangoes, avocadoes, roasted cashews, and limes for sale at a rural market in La Libertad.

CHILATE

During my online searches on Salvadoran food history, I once came across a screenshot that someone took of a webpage in Spanish. It showed text that described chilate as chilate del guerrero, since this was a favorite beverage of Indigenous fighters from El Salvador in pre-Columbian times. The drink was believed to give those warriors the energy to maintain their activities throughout the day. I have not verified this information, but I love the idea of chilate as the beverage of warriors. It often gets a bad rap because it's not sweetened. Its muted flavor is not a loud presence in the room—more a supporting actor than a leading star.

Chilate is a Salvadoran ritual usually enjoyed in the afternoon or hot with a sweetened accompaniment, typically Nuegados de Yuca (page 245), Torrejas (page 255), or even Plátanos Asados (page 252). It's a lifestyle that's delicious. Like many other beverages, chilate is served in a guacale. These bowls are made from the round grapefruit-size fruits of the morro tree; the fruits are not eaten but are turned into hard shells that are the go-to vessel for serving most beverages in El Salvador.

This recipe is from Estela. She learned it from her mother-in-law; together they made a living for many years selling food. One of her mother-in-law's specialties was chilate with nuegados de yuca. The chilate's subtle corn flavor and spice is the perfect complement to the nuegados.

●

Set a comal or griddle over medium heat. Once it's hot, sprinkle with a little water to check if it is ready; the water should quickly evaporate. Add the maíz and toast until fragrant, about 10 minutes.

Line a fine-mesh strainer with fine cheesecloth and set over a large pot.

In a blender, combine 1 cup of the toasted maíz and 5¼ cups of the water and blend until all the kernels are pulverized, about 3 minutes. Pour the blended mixture through the prepared strainer. Grab the corners of the cheesecloth and twist to expel any additional liquid into the pot. (Discard the strained maíz.) Repeat with the remaining maíz and water.

Set the pot over medium-high heat; add the ginger, anise seeds, and allspice; and bring to a boil. Turn the heat to medium-low and stir constantly until the chilate thickens, about 10 minutes, making sure to not let it stick to the bottom of the pot and burn.

Pour the chilate into mugs and serve immediately.

MAKES 12 SERVINGS

1 pound dried maíz
10½ cups water
One 1-inch chunk peeled
    ginger, smashed
½ teaspoon whole anise seeds
½ teaspoon whole allspice

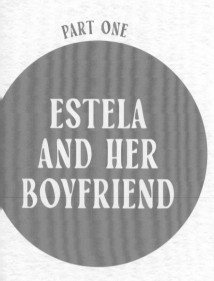

PART ONE

ESTELA AND HER BOYFRIEND

It had started innocently enough, with high school girls talking about boys. They met at a fiesta rosa. Usually her mother didn't allow Estela to attend outings, much less parties, but to Estela's surprise, her mother said yes to a cousin's request to take Estela along. Estela knew that here she'd meet the young boy her cousin had told her about a few times already. When her cousin finally introduced them, she displayed her boldness once again by suggesting that Estela and Manuel dance together.

"Baile con el," her cousin said. "Dance with him. No tiene pareja. He doesn't have a partner." So they did. Estela wasn't shy, and she liked Manuel. But she had her mother to think about, the one who had worked hard for her. Who had asked her daughter not to date and not to have boyfriends: "Con solo que no vayas andar de novia." Her mother's words echoed in Estela's head. But it was the 1980s, there was a war, and she was fifteen. So they danced. Manuel looked at her sweetly, showing interest. "Where do you go to school?" he asked. She answered. Another moment passed as the music played and they swayed their bodies to the beat. "Do you think I could pick you up one day from your school?" he asked. Estela knew the answer to that question in an instant. "No!" she exclaimed.

From then on, he made an effort to see her. He'd walk by her school or where she lived, just for a chance to see her. It would often come with an invitation: "Let's go out for un chocolatito y galletas." Some time went by before he finally mustered the courage to share with Estela his true feelings. "I want to tell you something," he said earnestly. "I . . . I don't want to offend you, but I have been thinking about this a lot, so I can tell you. I know that you haven't had a boyfriend, and well, I don't want to offend you, but I like you. I want to be your boyfriend." Estela, swept away by his words, knew she liked him too. She felt it in her blood. But she couldn't say that to him. Instead, she said, "Let me think about this because I've never gone with anyone."

"Aja, bueno ¿te puedo estar veniendo a ver?" he said. (Well, can I come by to see you, then?)

"Sí," she replied. Estela remembers these details as she recalls her time in the cafetales, where her mom had sent her as punishment for having a boyfriend. Estela wept and wept when her mother found out that she had been with Manuel for a year. If it hadn't been for one of the neighbors telling her mother, Estela would have still been undercover.

In her anger, Estela's mom took her out of school for an entire month and sent her to work on the finca, doing hard manual labor and digging holes deep enough to plant coffee trees. Estela developed calluses on all her fingers and more blisters than she could count. Her mother intended to make Estela's deception a lesson for her. "Vas aprender lo que cuesta ser una mujer en El Salvador que no es profesional, que le toca andar trabajando en el campo," she said. (You're going to learn what it's like to be a woman in El Salvador who isn't a professional and who has to work the land.)

Estela understood her mother. She believed in her. Estela would tell her mother her dreams of becoming a nurse, a designer, or whatever else, so long as she became an accomplished woman. And her mother would warn her, "Don't go being a girlfriend, because if you do, everything you want will go away." Estela felt the weight of her mother's words. But she didn't know what to do—she was completely in love. After one year of being with him, she didn't think she could ever leave him.

Coffee farmer picking coffee in Finca El Aguila, Ahuachapán.

ATOL DE PIÑA

MAKES 6 TO 8 SERVINGS

2 cups uncooked white rice
8½ cups water
4 cups pineapple: 3 cups cut
    into 1-inch pieces, 1 cup
    chopped bite-size
One 3-inch cinnamon stick
½ cup dulce de panela

Pineapple has got to be one of my favorite fruits. Like the tomato, it's essential to Salvadoran cuisine. It's everywhere—in our pickles, cold beverages, stews, proteins, and, of course, hot beverages such as a traditional atol. When I was talking to Isabel over the phone about her recipes, I asked if she had any sweet dishes. Her excitement was palpable when she said, "Oh bueno, el atol de piña me queda super rico." That's exactly what I was hoping for as I explained that we wanted to curate a good list of both sweet and savory recipes for the cookbook. She went on to describe how she made it, and once again, it blew my mind how important it is to ask about all dishes. This recipe celebrates the pineapple's classic flavor in one of El Salvador's most iconic beverages.

●

In a large dry skillet over medium heat, toast the rice until it turns fragrant, about 5 minutes, making sure to stir it so it doesn't burn. Transfer the toasted rice to a large bowl and add 4½ cups of the water. Let it soak until the grains look plump, about 20 minutes.

Line a fine-mesh strainer with fine cheesecloth and set over a large pot.

In a blender, combine the 3 cups pineapple pieces and remaining 4 cups water and blend on high speed until no solid pieces of pineapple remain. Transfer to a large pot. Place the soaked rice in the blender and blend on high speed until the rice is completely pulverized. Pour the blended mixture through the prepared strainer. Grab the corners of the cheesecloth and twist to expel any additional liquid into the pot. (Discard the strained rice.) Add the remaining 1 cup chopped pineapple, the cinnamon stick, and dulce de panela.

Set the pot over medium-high heat, bring to a boil, and cook the pineapple mixture, stirring constantly, until it has completely dissolved and the atol has thickened, about 10 minutes. You'll know it's ready when you feel increasing resistance as you stir.

Serve the atol hot, in big mugs, with a spoon to scoop out the chunks of pineapple at the bottom.

PONCHE SALVADOREÑO

The heat was blistering, and all I really wanted was something cold. Something icy. A Salutaris—a Salvadoran mineral water brand—would have been magnificent. Or even better, a cold beer.

However, there was none to be had at the Feria de Gastronomía in Juayúa, which I had attended because I was told it had incredible food, and that was absolutely true. But the heat was oppressive, and I needed refreshment. I had very little cash, so I hoped to find something that fit my budget. And that's when I finally saw her—a vendor selling ponche Salvadoreño. I was immediately intrigued. I had $2 left in cash. But as I walked toward her stall, I noticed there was no ice at her station, no cold bottles of any beverage. Instead, there was fire, and above the flames, a beautiful steaming clay pot. Inside was a tawny-colored beverage, which I assumed was the ponche. I greeted her and asked her how much it was, and when she said $1.50, I knew then and there I was going to drink this hot beverage. She had a few bottles of alcohol for the piquete, a splash of alcohol, each one infused with a different fruit. I chose the marañón tequila. It was amazing. I was already so full, and I had only wanted something to help me cope with the heat, but it was a lost cause once I saw her. When you can't beat 'em, join 'em.

This is my version of what I tasted that hot day. For the piquete, I like to use a Salvadoran rum, like Cihuatán, which you can find in specialty liquor stores.

●

In a medium saucepan over medium-high heat, combine the milk, cinnamon stick, nutmeg, and orange zest and cook, stirring occasionally, until steaming, 5 to 6 minutes.

Meanwhile, in a medium bowl, combine the egg yolks, sugar, and salt and whisk into a thoroughly combined paste.

Whisk ½ cup of the steaming milk mixture into the egg mixture to temper it. Then slowly whisk the tempered mixture into the milk mixture in the saucepan. Turn the heat to medium-low and cook, whisking continuously, until thickened and it coats the back of a wooden spoon, 10 to 15 minutes. Turn off the heat and stir in the vanilla.

Pour the ponche into mugs, leaving about ½ inch at the top of each. Add a generous splash of rum, if desired; the amount depends on how big of a piquete each person prefers. Garnish with a sprinkle of ground cinnamon and serve warm.

MAKES 8 SERVINGS

8 cups milk
One 6-inch cinnamon stick, plus ground cinnamon for garnishing
½ teaspoon grated nutmeg
Zest of 1 medium orange
4 egg yolks
½ cup granulated sugar
⅛ teaspoon kosher salt
½ teaspoon vanilla extract
Rum for serving (optional)

ATOL DE ELOTE

MAKES 6 SERVINGS

1 teaspoon kosher salt
7½ cups fresh corn kernels
5 cups milk
½ cup granulated sugar
One 4-inch cinnamon stick
2 teaspoons cornstarch
    (optional)
1 teaspoon ground cinnamon
    (optional)

When the fresh corn season begins in El Salvador, which can be as early as April, this traditional food appears everywhere—including restaurants, street corners, and homes. *Atol* is a word derived from the Nahuat language, and it means "aguado" or "soft." In this recipe, it's a thick beverage made from fresh corn, milk, sugar, and cinnamon, and its flavor is pure corn. Many folks who make tamales de elote eventually make atol de elote because they already have all the ingredients for it.

In this recipe, feel free to use your preferred milk. Whether the milk I've used is low-fat dairy, whole, lactose-free, almond, or even oat, they've all worked nicely.

●

In a small pot over medium heat, bring 1 cup of water to a boil. Add ½ teaspoon of the salt and 1 cup of the corn kernels and cook until the corn is tender, about 2 minutes. Drain the corn and set aside.

Working in batches, if needed, add the remaining 6½ cups corn to a high-powered blender and blend until smooth, about 3 minutes.

Set a fine-mesh strainer over a stockpot and pour the blended corn into the strainer, discarding the kernel skins left behind. Add the milk, sugar, cinnamon stick, and remaining ½ teaspoon salt to the pot; set over medium heat; and bring to a boil, stirring constantly. Cook, stirring constantly, until thickened, about 20 minutes. You should encounter some resistance as the atol thickens. If necessary to help it thicken, in a small bowl, combine the cornstarch and a bit of the hot liquid and stir to dissolve. Stir this mixture into the pot.

Ladle the atol de elote into large mugs and spoon about 1 teaspoon of the cooked corn kernels on top of each. Garnish with a sprinkle of ground cinnamon, if desired, before serving.

ANTOJITOS DULCES

Shaved ice bicycle cart vendor at El Palmarcito, a public beach in La Libertad.

Desserts and sweet treats are naturally defined by the resources of a people or their country. El Salvador is no different. One principal ingredient native to the land is panela. Inside this package is the dulce, which is made from the juice that's extracted and cooked from sugarcane. A popular way to enjoy it is to cook various foods such as plantain, mango, and squash and then boil them in panela syrup until they turn fork-tender.

Another dessert ingredient is corn—masa, to be precise. Corn is a Mesoamerican staple, and while it's famous for its savory uses, it's also featured in many sweet dishes. The philosophy around desserts and sweets in El Salvador differs from that of traditional Western cultures in that sweets are considered not just superficial additions but regular foods in their own right—eaten as appetizers, breakfast, and snacks. And, if people are very hungry, they can also be enjoyed after meals.

EMPANADAS DE PLÁTANO CON LECHE

MAKES 8 TO 10 EMPANADAS

8 ripe plantains
4 cups Leche Poleada
   (page 238), cooled
4 cups vegetable oil
¼ cup granulated sugar

Salvadoran empanadas de plátano con leche is a dessert made from plantains that are boiled, mashed, and molded into oval shapes, then filled with a custard, fried, and finished with a coating of sugar. It is an indulgent treat loved by many. Some replace the poleada with refried beans.

When you shop for plantains for this dish, look for ones that aren't too ripe and mature; they should have some yellow coloring with darker spots. (Those used for fried plátanos are completely dark with no yellow.) Also, the plantains for this recipe should never be green. If they are, place them in a paper bag and store in a dark place, like a cupboard or an oven.

This recipe is by Maria. In her story, she relates how she learned to cook Salvadoran food working in a restaurant in the United States, not in her home country.

•

Cut the ends off the plantains. Slice each plantain crosswise into four equal pieces. In a large pot over medium-high heat, combine the plantains and 5 cups water and bring to a boil. Turn the heat to medium-low, cover, and cook until the peel separates from the flesh, about 25 minutes.

Using tongs or a large slotted spoon, remove the plantains from the water, peel them, and place in a large bowl. Using a fork, a potato masher, an immersion blender, or even the paddle attachment for a stand mixer, mash the plantains until there are no clumps. Let cool to room temperature.

Take ¼ cup of the mashed plantain and flatten it between your palms, using your fingers to create an even 4-inch-thick disk. Place about 2 tablespoons of poleada on one half of the disk. Fold over the other half of the plantain, like a clamshell, and press on the edges to securely seal the empanada on all sides. Shape the empanada into an oblong form. If any tears occur, patch them with additional dough. Repeat with the remaining plantain and poleada.

Line a large plate with paper towels or put a wire cooling rack in a baking sheet and place near the stove. In a large stockpot or Dutch oven over medium-high heat, warm the vegetable oil until it reaches 375°F. Add a pea-size portion of plátano; if the oil sizzles, it's ready for frying.

Add four empanadas to the oil and fry until crispy and caramelized deep brown, about 2 minutes per side. Transfer the fried empanadas to the prepared plate to drain and let cool to the touch.

Roll each empanada with some of the sugar and serve.

DISH–WASHING

The aroma of fried food clashed with the fragrance of liquid detergent. It was the smell of clean, sudsy hot water that brought Maria's focus back to the dishes. She washed soiled plates, glasses, bowls, and serving dishes as fast and efficiently as she could. With all the clanging of dishes and the blaring noise of the sink sprayer, Maria could barely hear when Rina, the principal cook at El Migueleño, a popular Salvadoran restaurant, came in with an urgent plea.

"Maria, la otra cocinera no llegó. ¿Cree usted que me puede ayudar?" she asked. (Maria, the other cook did not come. Do you think you can help me?) *Of course*, Maria thought. Be it dishes, cooking, or cleaning, she was prepared to do whatever she needed to earn her pay so that she could send money back to her family in their small village in Morazán. She had learned so much about Salvadoran cooking since working at this Los Angeles restaurant, and it was one of the first jobs that she actually liked since arriving in the United States. She was determined to do anything to help her coworkers.

Maria was fearless. Her motto in life was "No hay nada fácil, pero no hay nada difícil." (Nothing is easy but nothing is difficult.) She could face anything. She could do anything. What Rina needed most at that moment was tortillas, the Mesoamerican flatbread that accompanies every single dish in her Salvadoran restaurant. Fresh ones. Round. Plump. Evenly thick throughout. And she needed them immediately.

The afternoon shift cook had not arrived, and Rina could not afford to wait any longer. The flow and rhythm of the kitchen had been sabotaged by the lack of hands. Servers had already filled the 48-inch stainless-steel slide ticket-rack mounted on the wall. Each ticket represented a hungry customer expecting tortillas with their meals—perfectly round, thick, sweet-smelling Salvadoran tortillas. There was only one problem. Maria had never made a tortilla in her life. Of all the things she knew how to do in this world, making tortillas was not one of them. She had only just arrived from El Salvador, and she was coming to terms with the reality that the war had taken away her chances of learning recipes and kitchen knowledge from her own culture. Back home in Morazán, she was lucky if they got pastelitos once a year. Arroz y frijoles were the staples of her diet.

Removing her grubby dishwashing apron and latex gloves, she headed to the handwashing station. How many times had she seen her mami make tortillas back home? She could figure it out. "Ahorita le salen las tortillas, Rina. Ahorita, no se preocupe," she said. (The tortillas will be out soon, Rina. Right now, don't worry.) After working at the restaurant for a few months, Maria had yet to tell any of her coworkers that she had never eaten certain Salvadoran foods, much less made any.

Now was not the moment for disclosures. She washed her hands, made her way to the cooking station, and touched the masa. The cool feel of the mound pleased her. *I can do this*, she thought, holding on to her instincts and memories. "¿Cuántas va querer, Rina?" she asked. (How many will you want, Rina?)

"Hmmnnn ay mamallita, usted sólo tortée, hay le aviso," Rina answered. By the high-pitched sound that Rina made, Maria knew her question was foolish. There was no set amount—just an endless procession of flatbreads.

LECHE POLEADA

MAKES 4 TO 6 SERVINGS

2 cups milk
Two 4-inch cinnamon sticks
¼ cup cornstarch
¼ cup granulated sugar

Leche poleada is that welcome hug from the person you love the most, the epitome of comfort and sweetness. This Salvadoran custard comes together with just a few ingredients, and its smooth creaminess is perfect. You can't say no.

This can be enjoyed on its own, topped with raisins or with a sprinkle of cinnamon, or used, cooled, in Empanadas de Plátano con Leche (page 234).

In a medium heavy pot over medium-high heat, combine the milk and cinnamon sticks and let scald, about 7 minutes. (Little bubbles will form around the edge of the pan, and the milk should register 180°F on an instant-read thermometer.) Remove the cinnamon sticks and turn the heat to medium-low.

In a small bowl, whisk together the cornstarch, sugar, and ½ cup of the cinnamon-milk until thoroughly incorporated. Add the cornstarch mixture to the cinnamon-milk in the pot, turn the heat to low, and cook, stirring constantly so no lumps form, until the mixture thickens, 5 to 7 minutes. Remove from the heat, cover, and let cool for a few minutes.

Serve the poleada on its own, like a pudding.

CONSEJO

Once the poleada has cooled completely, it stiffens, which makes it workable to use as a filling for empanadas. If you want to enjoy it soft, add ½ cup milk to the poleada and warm over low heat until it becomes like a custard again.

I DIDN'T KNOW HE HAD A WIFE

Coming to the United States was not an easy process, but it wasn't difficult, either. "Thank God I came with papers," Maria says. Life in the United States was different. For starters, in El Salvador she had lived with her mother and siblings. Her mother had a little tiendita where they sold groceries, fruits, cheese, and cream. As one of the oldest children in the family, Maria dedicated herself to helping her mother. If Maria was needed to work early in the morning at the store or help her siblings, she was always willing and ready.

When she arrived in the United States, she knew she would be living with some of her sisters and her father, but she never suspected she'd also be sharing the house with her father's new wife and her children. That last part was the shock of her life—her father's other family. "My father had not told us that he had a wife, an official woman in the house," she says. "And that she would be at the airport to pick us up. When we landed, he introduced us, saying, 'Her name is Virginia.' I felt a big pain in my heart all at once."

She tells me about sitting next to her father on the airplane as they were about to land in Los Angeles and looking out the window at all the lights of the city. She'd never seen so many lights before. Not in their cantón de Agua Blanco, and not in Cacaopera. After all, Morazán was the departamento hardest hit by the civil war, a conflict that forced countless families to flee their homes and villages and find refuge elsewhere. After Maria's family moved to Cacaopera, they stayed for a year, slept on the floor, and suffered profoundly. Then, after receiving a warning from soldiers that they needed to leave in seventy-two hours, they were displaced once more, this time to the municipality of San Francisco Gotera, where they endured constant violence and nearby gunshots. Soon, the sight of disembodied pieces of human flesh became normal.

In her new life in California, Maria began living a different reality. The first thing that she ate in Los Angeles was, of course, at McDonald's. "It was a breakfast. I don't even remember, but it was a little hamburger, with egg." Her family soon moved to MacArthur Park, which had once been a highly desirable neighborhood, with a genteel suburban feel and streets lined with Victorian-style houses. Now it offered glimpses into a different, faded world. They lived near the corner of South Alvarado and South Mountain View Avenues, but there was no mountain view. Now, instead of helping her mother with her younger siblings, she began helping Virginia, her father's new wife, with the chores of the house. Because fourteen people lived there, Virginia had gotten good at

making schedules for what needed to be done—laundry, cooking, shopping, everything.

Maria found this new life overwhelming. She had never been separated from her mother, not even during the war. This was the first time they were not together. "I spent a year crying," Maria admits. Missing her mother and her siblings was almost unbearable. At that time there was no telephone, so all communication was done by writing letters once a month. "I told Mamita, 'If you get a letter from me, money is going to come to you.' Each letter contained money, $50 or $100. I sent her money so that my two younger brothers could at least get to go to high school."

Paternas, a type of tropical fruit in El Salvaor, is very seasonal at the market.

HOJALDRAS

MAKES 12 COOKIES

8 tablespoons unsalted butter, melted, plus more for greasing the pan
1 cup cuajada (see page 57)
2 cups masa harina
½ teaspoon baking soda
½ teaspoon baking powder
½ teaspoon kosher salt
1½ cups water
1 cone dulce de panela

These corn cookies go by many names, including hojaldras. They are sprinkled with dulce de panela and known primarily as a treat from Concepción de Oriente, in the eastern part of El Salvador. The base for this cookie is masa. In Chinameca, every day, abuelitas make these along with a similar cookie called totopostes, and it takes them about five hours from start to finish. Between making the masa from scratch and mixing the dough to shaping the cookies and getting the clay oven to the right temperature, it's a laborious process. This cookie is special not only because of its process but also because its ingredients are different from the traditional European ones that were adopted by the pan dulce culture of El Salvador. I personally love a sweet corn moment—it feels true to the land to transform corn into a cookie.

Making designs in hojaldras allows you to make them your own. The bottom of each cookie should be thick enough to support pinching or pressing in the center. These pinched designs act like miniature mountain ranges across the cookies, capturing and dispersing the melted panela into sugary pools. And if you decide to skip making designs, that is completely fine; just be sure the bottoms of your cookies aren't too thin, otherwise holes might form during baking.

If your panela is newer or fresher, you shouldn't have much trouble breaking it up. If it takes a lot of effort to break the cone into shards and powder, it only means that panela is dehydrated and has been on the shelf for a while. I've seen my mom repeatedly swing a bag of panela into the kitchen door frame with all of her strength, leaving many dents behind. Do what you have to do. Don't worry, it will still come out delicious.

•

Preheat the oven to 375°F. Butter two baking sheets or line with parchment paper or a silicone baking mat and set aside.

In a small bowl, combine the melted butter and cuajada and stir to thoroughly mix. In a large bowl, combine the masa harina, baking soda, baking powder, salt, and water and mix until thoroughly incorporated. Add the butter-cheese mixture to the dry ingredients and mix until evenly combined and the consistency of cookie dough.

Divide the dough into twelve equal portions. Using the palms of your hands, roll each portion into a ball and then flatten them into disks about 4 inches in diameter. Pinch the edges of each disk to make a small outer wall. Then pinch or press designs in the disks, if you like.

Place the disks on the prepared baking sheets, spaced about 2 inches apart to allow space for the cookies to spread as they bake. Cover with a manta or kitchen towel and set aside.

Wrap the panela in a towel and tie the ends of the towel together, or seal the panela in a ziplock bag. Using a hammer or mallet, smash the panela into small shards—the smaller the better. Sprinkle the panela shards into the center of each hojaldra.

Bake the hojaldras until the outer edges are crispy and golden brown and the panela is melted and bubbly, 20 to 30 minutes. Remove from the baking sheets, transfer to a wire rack, and let cool completely.

Store the cookies in an airtight container at room temperature for up to 8 days.

NUEGADOS DE YUCA

MAKES 6 TO 8 SERVINGS

Nuegados de yuca are like fritters. The difference is that these savory yuca-based ones are finished in a syrup called miel de dulce de panela. Some folks grate the yuca while it's raw, while others cook it first, like Estela instructs here. I appreciate both since they lend different textures. The grated version is similar to hash browns or even latkes, while the cooked one is esponjadita, spongy and light. And wherever there are nuegados de yuca, chilate (see page 223) is almost always nearby. It's very common to see a vendor in a park in El Salvador selling both of these items. Together, they make the perfect sweet and savory snack.

These particular nuegados are made in a unique Apopense style. Estela learned to make them as they do in Chayito, a super-famous chilateria in Apopa, a neighborhood in San Salvador. There they make them round and plump, with a hole in the center.

2 large yuca, peeled and cut into 2-inch pieces
4 ounces queso fresco
¼ cup rice flour
2 cups canola oil
2½ cups water
1 cone dulce de panela

●

In a large pot over medium heat, bring 5 cups of water to a boil. Add the yuca and cook until it turns tender, about 20 minutes. Using tongs, transfer the yuca to a plate and let cool for 30 minutes. Remove the fibrous vein from the center of each piece of yuca.

In a large bowl, combine the yuca, queso, and rice flour and mix thoroughly until a dough forms. Take 2 ounces of the yuca dough and shape it into a small donut with a hole in the center. Repeat with the remaining dough.

Line a large plate with paper towels or put a wire cooling rack in a baking sheet and place near the stove. In a medium pot over medium-high heat, warm the canola oil until it registers 350°F on an instant-read thermometer. (Add a tiny piece of yuca dough; if the oil sizzles, it's ready for frying.) Using a slotted spoon, carefully add one or two nuegados at a time to the hot oil and fry until they're golden brown, about 2 minutes per side. Using tongs, transfer the fried nuegados to the prepared plate to drain.

In a small pot over medium heat, combine the water and panela. Allow the panela to melt and come to a boil, about 8 minutes. Turn the heat to low and let simmer, stirring occasionally, until the panela becomes a syrup, about 15 minutes. Add the nuegados and let them absorb some of the syrup for about 1 minute.

Place the nuegados on a plate and drizzle additional panela syrup over the top before serving.

PART TWO

ESTELA AND HER HUSBAND

It happened so quickly. Estela heard the banging on the thin barras of the zaguan—someone was pounding at the entrance. Rosita, her five-year-old daughter, who was at the table doing homework, was quick to jump up from her seat but Estela stopped her and said, "Eh, no vayas. Yo voy a abrir." (Hey, don't go. I'm going to open.)

As Estela exited the little house that she shared with her husband and Rosita, she could make out a few people gathered at the zaguan. They weren't friends but more like "Hi, bye, send my saludos a la familia" people. People you barely knew, but it was polite to at least say hello to them. "¿Como estan?" asked Estela.

"Decile. Decile," said a young man urgently to a woman at the gate. (Tell her. Tell her.) When el joven said this, Estela immediately sensed something was wrong. "¿Decime, que es lo que me vas a decir?" she asked. (What is it you want to tell me?)

"No se ni que decirle. Mire, su esposo, lo acaban de matar," said the woman. (I don't even know what to say. Look, your husband, they've just killed him.)

"No te equivocas. No te has equivocado," gasped Estela. (No, you're mistaken. No, you have made a mistake.)

"Como no," the woman replied. "Of course, he told me soon after it happened. My mother went out running to see if there was anything we could do for him, but it was too late." The woman paused. "¿Usted esta embarazada?" (Are you pregnant?)

"¿Y porque?" asked Estela. (Why?)

"Porque el, estaba agonizando, decia, 'mi hija, y mi mujer va a tener un bebe.'" The woman explained that while Estela's husband was slowly dying, he could be heard saying in agony, "My daughter . . . and my wife is going to have a baby." Only in that moment did Estela realize what was being said about her husband. Between her tears, she shouted, "Lies! What you're saying are lies!" Her screams at the zaguan alerted the rest of the family inside the house.

In a blur and barely able to assess the situation, Estela saw her father-in-law rushing to the zaguan. She heard him asking in a voice heavy with concern, "¿Que paso? ¿Que paso?" The neighbors began to explain that they had just witnessed his son's murder. He was being chased on his motorcycle when men stopped him, dragged him off his motorcycle, shot him there in the road, and fled, leaving him mortally wounded and barely breathing. According to this neighbor's mother, Estela, Rosita, and their unborn baby were in his last thoughts.

It was wartime, and death and grief were also their neighbors. But it wasn't civil war that killed Estela's husband—it was bad business partners. Estela was devastated. They had been saving for a house of their own, and recently they had finally found the one they wanted. It had taken them five years to save thirty-two thousand colones, and they needed only eight thousand more to buy their dream home. Inside the house, her husband's carne asada was getting cold. Before he had left for the day that morning, Estela had asked him what he wanted for almuerzo, and he had said carne asada. He always came home for lunch, and this was the first time he had missed it.

BUDÍN DE PAN

MAKES 4 TO 6 SERVINGS

12 pan francés, or 1 bag sliced
    bread
3 cups milk
1½ cups granulated sugar
4 tablespoons unsalted butter,
    melted
¼ cup Salvadoran rum
1 teaspoon vanilla extract
One 1-ounce box of raisins
Finely grated zest of ½ lime or
    orange

Budín de pan is our version of bread pudding. It's a food that finds new life with pan francés. When I asked my family if they ever saw a budín de pan made with bagged bread, there was a very loud and dramatic "No!"—it has to be pan francés. For some Salvadorans, it can be controversial to make this dish with a different kind of bread. What I will say is that once you have the bread, make sure you've mashed it well enough. Since this recipe doesn't use any eggs, you can taste it to make sure the flavor is just right. You score extra points if you use a quality Salvadoran rum, like Cihuatán.

    This recipe is by Suyapa. When I was introduced to her years ago, she was the only SalviSoul mom who knew exactly what recipe she'd be contributing the minute we met. Most of the moms had ideas only after we talked and strategized together. But with Suyapa, there was no doubt it was going to be budín de pan. She is also one of two Salvi moms ever to give me her recipe in written form. The second was Carolina (see page 182 [Conchas Rellenas]).

●

Preheat the oven to 350°F.

    In a large bowl, tear the bread into bite-size pieces. Add the milk and, using a wooden spoon or your hands, mix until each piece of bread is completely soaked in the milk. Add 1 cup of the sugar, the butter, rum, vanilla, raisins, and citrus zest and mix well. Set aside.

    In a small heavy saucepan over low heat, sprinkle a thin layer of sugar on the bottom of the pan. As the sugar starts to melt, gradually add more sugar, using a rubber spatula to gently mix the melted parts with the dry sugar. Repeat with the remaining sugar, being careful not to stir too much, until this caramel is an amber color. This happens quickly and has a high risk of burning, so keep a close watch on it.

    Pour the caramel into a 9-inch round baking pan. Using a wooden spoon or spatula, transfer the soaked bread mixture to the baking pan over the caramel.

    Bake the budín until it turns golden brown, about 1 hour. Let it cool for about 10 minutes and then run a knife along the edges of the pan to loosen the budín. Place a large plate or cutting board on top of the pan and invert the budín onto the plate to reveal the caramel-coated bottom.

    Serve the budín de pan immediately.

TRUST THE PROCESS

It was necessary to make a disguise. If one has naturally very dark hair, lightening it to a platinum blond—or any kind of blond—is risky. And such a dramatic color change with no real professional guidance is even more risky. Suyapa's mother had no time to waste. Inmigración officials were detaining people left and right in Los Angeles, and sospecha, suspicion, alone was enough to get you picked up off the streets. Papers were needed, and her daughter did not have them, at least not yet.

Suyapa had been cooperative with the idea of dyeing her hair. She had just arrived in Los Angeles and needed to walk to work. Any effort to blend in with other people around her seemed like a good idea. From her point of view, looking like Americanos meant blond hair; standing out as a newly arrived young inmigrante was not a good idea. No one present for the bleaching took into account just how dark her hair was, or studied it long enough to see what undertones she had or how they interacted with her skin tones. New hairdos like this required a certain amount of trust in the process, but no amount of trust was going to fix what happened. The only way to describe how her hair turned out was pelo de zanahoria—carrottop. It was dry, damaged, and so far from the disguise they had all imagined.

Managing her new life in Los Angeles, reuniting with her mom, and adjusting her expectations of how things were going to be in L.A. were already taking up so much of Suyapa's mental space, and now *this*. She had already dealt with being removed twice from home. Born in Honduras to Salvadoran parents who moved to Honduras for work opportunities, they had to return to El Salvador because of a war that started between the two countries. This forced Suyapa to leave the only place she knew and then to suffer from incredible homesickness.

Years later, she traveled to Mexico to cross the border into the United States, only to get thrown in jail for two weeks, and deported to Guatemala. Then she returned to Mexico and survived the winter in Mexico City; this time she stayed to work in a restaurant to learn Mexican slang, the Mexican anthem, and Mexican culture in hopes of convincing immigration officials that she wasn't a Central American but a Mexicana. She reattempted the border crossing into the United States, making the final stretch of the journey to reunite with her mother in Los Angeles and endure other dangerous feats. All this to come to the country where she expected an opportunity to finally go to school, study, and make a new life, only to end up in this vulnerable place with brittle orange hair.

PLÁTANOS ASADOS

MAKES 8 SERVINGS

8 plantains, unpeeled

What's the best thing after enjoying a family backyard barbecue? When all the savory items have been devoured, the drinks have been finished, we're on to the coffee round now, the food has settled in our bellies, and the eventual encore is expected. Plátanos asados. That's the best thing.

Nothing paints a picture of a good time more than feeling full from delicious food and seeing Mami, tía, or my cousin with a tray of ripe plátanos, teasing the crowd: "Ya van estar los plátanos." It's not so much a dessert as a sweet finishing note to a splendid meal.

Leave the plátanos on the grill while you get the coffee going, make a joke with your tía, and take a tally of who wants a whole plátano and who wants to share one. Then come back to the grill to see vibrant yellow peeking from darkened peels. And wait to hear the eventual praise—"Wow, so simple and so delicious." Serve with Leche Poleada (page 238) on the side.

●

Prepare your grill to cook at high heat.

Place the plantains directly on the grill rack and grill until their skins have darkened and the flesh has burst through, about 25 minutes. The insides should be a vibrant yellow and soft, tender, and creamy with a hint of tropical tang.

Serve the plátanos asados immediately.

TORREJAS

Thick slices of pan de yema are transformed into torrejas, which are dipped in egg batter, fried, and then cooked in a syrup made from dulce de panela. I remember once walking into my grandmother's kitchen and seeing a very tall pot on the stove. She asked if I wanted torrejas, and I said sure. I can't remember if this was my first time eating this dish, but I wondered about two things in this exchange. The first was how were the torrejas still whole and not complete mush, since she pulled them out from that tall pot full of syrup? And second, why was I being given food soaked in syrup? I felt as though I was getting away with something or sneaking a treat.

I still enjoy eating torrejas, and the sweetness is never cloying. It's always just right, especially paired with Chilate (page 223) or hot coffee.

●

In a medium pot over medium heat, combine the water, dulce de panela, cloves, and cinnamon stick and bring to a boil. After the dulce dissolves, turn the heat to low and let simmer, stirring occasionally, until the syrup that has formed is still liquid but with all the ingredients combined, 5 to 7 minutes. Remove from the heat and set aside.

In a medium bowl, using an electric mixer on high speed (or a whisk), whip four of the egg whites until stiff peaks form, about 1 minute. Add four of the egg yolks and whisk thoroughly.

In a large skillet over medium-high heat, warm ¼ cup of the neutral oil. Swirl the oil so it coats the entire surface of the pan.

Using a spatula, slide one slice of the pan de yema into the egg mixture to coat completely and then transfer gently to the skillet. Fry until the edges and bottom of the bread turn golden brown, about 2 minutes, then flip it and cook the other side until golden, about 2 minutes more. Place the fried bread on a baking sheet or baking pan. Repeat with another five bread slices. Pour about half of the syrup over the bread.

Repeat the whipping, coating, and frying with the remaining egg whites, egg yolks, bread slices, and neutral oil. Add the second batch of fried bread to the first layer, pour the remaining syrup on them, and let soak for 30 minutes.

Serve the torrejas immediately.

MAKES 12 SERVINGS

2½ cups water
1 cone dulce de panela
2 whole cloves
One 4-inch cinnamon stick
8 eggs, separated, at room
    temperature
½ cup neutral oil
    (such as canola oil)
12 slices Pan de Yema
    (page 260)

Dulce de panela stacked at the market in San Salvador.

QUESADILLA

MAKES ONE 9-INCH CAKE

8 tablespoons unsalted butter, melted , plus more for greasing

3 eggs, separated, at room temperature

1 cup granulated sugar

1 cup grated queso duro blando or Parmesan cheese

½ cup milk

½ cup crema Salvadoreña, or crème fraîche

1½ cups all-purpose flour

1 teaspoon baking powder

¼ teaspoon kosher salt

2 teaspoons raw white sesame seeds

In El Salvador and much of Central America, *quesadilla* refers to a sweet cheese pan dulce, where the cheese is incorporated into the batter. Many folks use Parmesan cheese (for its funk) and pancake batter. I have also heard of Salvis in the southern United States using a cornbread adaptation of the recipe. I have made quesadillas countless times, and I have used only Salvadoran cheeses because they were the first items that revealed to me how obsessed Salvi folks are with food. Why? Well, my relatives always bring back pounds of cheese from El Salvador—queso duro blando, queso duro viejo, and queso morolique. These aged cheeses must be excellent if it's worth leaving your belongings back in the homeland to make room for cheese in the suitcase.

If you cannot source Salvadoran cheese, you may use Parmesan cheese; in place of crema Salvadoreña, crème fraîche. This pan dulce is usually served with hot coffee. My relatives who recently visited from El Salvador, where they can get all kinds of quesadilla at any hour of the day, loved this recipe so much that they requested it two days in a row.

●

Preheat the oven to 350°F. Lightly butter a 9-inch cake pan or cast-iron skillet.

In a large bowl, combine the egg yolks and sugar and beat until thoroughly combined. Add the queso, milk, and crema and mix well. Gradually add the melted butter to the cheese mixture and mix until fully incorporated. Set aside.

In a medium bowl, sift together the flour and baking powder. Add the salt and mix well.

In another medium bowl, using an electric mixer on high speed (or a whisk), whip the egg whites until stiff peaks form, about 1 minute. Set aside. Clean the mixer beaters.

Add one-third of the flour mixture to the cheese mixture. Using the electric mixer on low speed, mix just until combined. Repeat with half the remaining flour and then the remaining flour, scraping the bowl and beaters after each addition.

Using a rubber spatula, fold the egg whites into the batter until no streaks remain and they are combined thoroughly. Pour the batter into the prepared pan and sprinkle the sesame seeds over the top.

Bake the quesadilla until golden brown and a toothpick inserted in the center comes out clean, about 45 minutes. (If the toothpick comes out with any moisture on it, continue baking for 5 minutes more.) Let cool for 5 minutes.

Cut the quesadilla into squares or wedges to serve.

MINUTA DE TAMARINDO

You're at the balneario or la toma, or water park, having fun splashing around and enjoying the sights and weather. But there is one thing missing; across the way, you spot the answer. It is el minutero, the shaved-ice vendor, pushing a wooden cart filled with tall bottles of brightly colored, thick syrups neatly lined up next to a big ice block.

Minutas are El Salvador's version of shaved ice. Sweet and cold, this treat takes it up a notch by featuring the brightness of lime, the earthiness of alguashte, and the tartness of tamarind. It's legit when you see the minutero swat away the bees. It's that good—even the bees want in on it.

●

In a medium bowl, combine the shaved ice and jalea, then sprinkle with the alguashte, salt, and lime juice (if using).

Serve the minuta de tamarindo with a spoon.

1 cup shaved ice
½ cup Jalea de Tamarindo
    (recipe follows)
1 tablespoon alguashte
    (see page 55)
½ teaspoon kosher salt
Juice of ½ lime (optional)

JALEA DE TAMARINDO

Sour, punchy, tart, and pucker-inducing tamarindo has a flavor profile very representative of Salvadoran food. Tamarind is definitely one of those tropical tastes that take you on a journey of sensation and joy.

●

Peel the tamarind, then rinse the pulp with running water to remove any lingering pieces of peel.

In a medium bowl, combine the tamarind and 2 cups of the water and let soak for at least 30 minutes or up to 4 hours.

In a medium saucepan over high heat, combine the remaining 2 cups water, tamarind and its soaking water, and sugar and bring to a boil. Turn the heat to low and cook until most of the water has evaporated and the liquid has thickened into a syrup that coats the back of a spoon, about 25 to 30 minutes. Let cool. (You can strain the liquid, but most Salvadoran cooks don't, as the tamarind seeds create a more pleasurable sensory experience.)

Store the jalea de tamarindo in an airtight glass jar in the refrigerator for up to 2 weeks.

MAKES 3 CUPS

1 pound tamarind
4 cups water
1½ cups granulated sugar

PAN DE YEMA

MAKES 1 LOAF

½ cup milk

1 teaspoon active dry yeast or
  instant yeast

2 teaspoons granulated sugar,
  plus ½ cup

2 cups bread flour, plus more
  for the work surface

1½ teaspoons crushed
  cinnamon stick
  (see Consejo)

¼ teaspoon kosher salt

1 teaspoon yellow food coloring
  (optional)

3 egg yolks

¼ cup vegetable shortening,
  plus more for greasing

1 teaspoon raw white sesame
  seeds

1 egg white, beaten

A few of the recipes in this book made me cry during the testing process, and this is one of them.

From the beginning of this project, I wanted to show off the brilliant pan dulces of El Salvador. Gabby from Panadería Cuscatleca signed on immediately to be a part of the project, therefore legitimizing the pan dulce recipes of this book. But when she sent me the ingredient quantities, they were the largest I had ever seen. They were the amounts required for her family panadería, located on the corner of Pico and Union in one of the most densely populated Salvadoran neighborhoods in Los Angeles. Fifteen pounds of flour. Five pounds of eggs. Two ounces of baking powder. This would not do for a home cookbook.

Through a series of texts, notes, phone calls, photos, and videos sent back and forth, as well as hours-long visits behind the scenes at their bakery, we worked together to create a recipe that would be usable and wouldn't break the bank or anyone's spirit like it did mine through the process.

This bread is very popular during Semana Santa (Easter) because it is used to make torrejas (see page 255). While I was developing this recipe, I had an epiphany that this bread is similar to challah. So many bread-baking traditions in El Salvador connect the cuisine to Sephardic and Arabic cultures.

●

In a small saucepan over low heat, warm the milk until it registers no more than 110°F on an instant-read thermometer. Remove the pan from the heat, add the yeast and 1 teaspoon of the sugar, and stir to dissolve. Cover the pan with plastic wrap and let it sit in a warm area for about 15 minutes to activate the yeast mixture; it should foam.

Place the flour in a large bowl or on a clean work surface and make a well in the middle of it. Pour the ½ cup sugar, cinnamon, salt, food coloring (if using), yeast mixture, and egg yolks into the well. Using a wooden spoon or your hands, slowly mix the ingredients until everything is thoroughly combined into a shaggy dough. Add the vegetable shortening and thoroughly mix it into the dough.

Lightly grease another large bowl. On a clean, lightly floured work surface, knead the dough until it is smooth and no longer sticky, about 10 minutes. Using a bench scraper, transfer the dough to the prepared bowl and cover with plastic wrap and a kitchen towel. Place the bowl in a warm area and let the dough rise until it doubles in size, 45 to 60 minutes.

Lightly grease a 9 by 5-inch loaf pan or line it with parchment paper. Lightly flour the work surface. Transfer the dough to the prepared surface and stretch it into a

Starting the fire to prepare pan dulce for baking in a clay oven.

9 by 13-inch rectangle. With the long side nearest you, roll the dough into a log. Tuck in the ends so it will fit inside the pan and pinch any seams together. Place the dough in the prepared pan, cover with plastic wrap, set in a warm place, and allow it to rise again, about 60 minutes.

Preheat the oven to 350°F.

In a small bowl, combine the remaining 1 teaspoon sugar and the sesame seeds and stir to mix.

Using a pastry brush, lightly brush the loaf with the egg white. Using kitchen scissors, snip the dough, less than 1 centimeter deep, from the center down each length of the loaf in a crisscross pattern. Sprinkle the sugar-seed mixture into the crevices.

Bake the pan de yema until the crust is a deep golden brown and the internal temperature registers 190°F on an instant-read thermometer, about 45 minutes. Let it cool for 15 minutes before cutting and serving.

CONSEJO

For this recipe, I advise using Ceylon cinnamon. Break away a few pieces and pound them in a mortar and pestle. If necessary, break them further using your fingers.

Use the pan de yema for torrejas, or enjoy it by itself. If you plan to use it for torrejas, Gabby recommends baking it the day before.

SEMITA PACHA DE PIÑA

If we follow the etymology of the word *semita*, it inevitably leads us to the Spanish language. It derives from the word *acemite*, or "oil," and from what I understand, when it comes to pan de semita, we are generally speaking about afrecho, or wheat bran. This is an example of the influence of Sephardic Jewish food traditions in Salvadoran cuisine. Many types of pan de semita exist in Latin America, and in those different versions, wheat bran is not necessary. However, in El Salvador, the bran is crucial—it's not semita without it.

When I learned this recipe and practiced it, I could not help but notice how much it reminded me of making pie, since it has a pastry shell with a yummy fruit filling. It's more similar to a slab pie, although not exactly, as this dough also has yeast and baking powder and so it will rise, unlike a pie dough. But the connection is undeniable.

Either way, this semita is *pacha*, which means "shallow," and filled with pineapple. Back in the homeland, a piece of semita is an anytime kind of thing, but it's also popular for an afternoon cafecito break—enjoying a hot cup of coffee and a pan dulce while people-watching at the bakery.

For this recipe, you will need to use a hammer or mallet to crush the dulce de panela into small shards or pieces (but not powder).

●

Preheat the oven to 350°F. Tear two pieces of parchment paper the length of a baking sheet.

In a large bowl, using an electric mixer, or a stand mixer fitted with the hook attachment, combine the flour, wheat bran, ½ cup sugar, baking powder, yeast, and ½ teaspoon salt. Turn the mixer to low and blend the dry ingredients, about 2 minutes. Add the butter, 4 cubes at a time, and mix until the dough has a sandy texture, about 3 minutes. With the mixer running, use a rubber spatula to scrape the bowl so everything gets a chance to incorporate. Gradually add the water, 3 tablespoons at a time, and continue to mix until the dough is moist. Cover the dough and let rest for 15 minutes.

Flour a rolling pin so it doesn't stick to the dough. Divide the dough in half and place one portion on one of the sheets of parchment. Shape the dough into a ball and roll it out into a large thin layer that will fit a baking sheet. Make sure the dough extends to the edges of the baking sheet and trim to fit. (Save the trimmings.) Slide this first layer along with the parchment paper onto the baking sheet.

4 cups all-purpose flour, plus more for rolling
1 cup wheat bran
½ cup granulated sugar, plus 2½ teaspoons
2 teaspoons baking powder
1 packet active dry yeast
Kosher salt
16 tablespoons cold unsalted butter, cut into 1-inch cubes
1 cup water
2 cups canned crushed pineapple, drained
2 cups crushed dulce de panela

continued

SEMITA PACHA DE PIÑA

continued

Spread the pineapple evenly over the dough, leaving a ½-inch border around the edges. Sprinkle the dulce de panela over the top of the pineapple, making sure it is evenly distributed.

On the second sheet of parchment, roll out the second portion of dough into a large thin layer that will fit a baking sheet. Flip this onto the pineapple and dulce de panela and trim to fit. (Save the trimmings.) Using your thumbs and forefingers, pinch the edges of the dough to seal. Using a fork or a knife, poke the top layer of dough about eight times across the whole surface.

Using your fingers, gently roll and stretch the dough trimmings into two large strips measuring 16 inches long, four medium strips measuring 12 inches long, and four small strips measuring 7 inches long, each about 1 centimeter thick.

Lay one of the large strips diagonally across the semita so it reaches from corner to corner. Then lay two medium strips in the same direction, equally spaced out from the large one, trimming to fit. Repeat with two of the small strips. Then repeat in the other direction with the remaining five strips, so they form a crisscross pattern. Gently pat the tops of the strips where they meet so they all touch one another. Sprinkle the remaining 2½ teaspoons sugar over the top of the semita.

Bake the semita until golden brown, about 45 minutes. Let it cool for about 10 minutes before serving.

Front door of a
home in Panchimalco,
San Salvador.

PART ONE

PAN DULCE, A FAMILY LEGACY

"¿Adónde estás?" Don Humberto yelled as he walked into the back room of the bakery. "¡Te dormistes!" Gabby had once again been caught taking a nap on the giant flour sacks there. Quick to defend herself, Gabby protested: "Yeah, we already did the semita. And, and . . . what else am I supposed to do, Dad? What else am I supposed to do?"

"Okay, bueno ve con el muchacho. El te va enseñar lo que está haciendo en su estación." Begrudgingly, Gabby climbed off the sacks and dusted the flour from her clothes. She listened to her father and went to ask the young worker to show her a new task. It was summer in L.A. She was twelve. Instead of going to movies, visiting water parks, and shopping, like her classmates, she was helping out at the bakery again. A punishment, according to Gabby. She was constantly bored.

Everything in her life was the bakery. Her dad always smelled like the bakery. He wore only white, his baker's uniform. He missed family functions, parties, and everything because of the bakery. They had to get up super-early so he could drop her and her siblings off at school in Echo Park. She and her brothers would ride in the back of the van, where their dad had installed a mattress for sleeping on the way to school. They'd get dropped off at six in the morning and were the last kids to get picked up because of the bakery. All of the United States would eat Thanksgiving dinner in the afternoon or evening, but they'd be eating at ten at night because of the bakery. Her uncle was also a baker. When they were together, they'd start talking about life, fun things, and family. Then eventually, the conversation turned into talking shop about . . . the bakery.

Its smells were second nature to her. She could quickly tell what kind of pan dulce had just come out of the oven. When pan francés finished baking, there was a yeasty fragrance in the air. If semita pacha de piña was coming out of the oven, the smell of sweet sugar, tangy pineapple, and cooked flour filled the bakery. When someone came in asking for pan dulce, she knew what they really meant was they wanted a concha. If they wanted to try a new pan dulce, she knew just what to recommend. She had picked up on all these distinctions after spending countless hours at the bakery. And she could name every variety of pan dulce sold there, whether they were from El Salvador or other countries.

One woman who worked at the bakery was her friend. She would tell Gabby the secrets of certain pan dulce recipes and share what made their pan better. Gabby would pull up a milk crate or anything she could find to get comfortable and listen. It was comforting, relaxing, and engaging to learn by her side. Seeing the

layers of semita come together was enough to entertain Gabby. It was remarkable to watch this woman roll out the dough, spread the pineapple and sugar inside, roll out a second layer of dough, and carefully place it on top of the jam filling. Finally, she would roll five feet of dough into a thin, ropelike string. It was delicate enough to look dainty on the outside of the semita but sturdy enough that it wouldn't break when rolled out and moved to the pastry.

Eventually Gabby's dad would appear. "Okay, me voy hacer ruta," he would say before going off to deliver pan dulce to liquor stores around the area. And Gabby, too, would be off again, hitting a new wall of boredom. A pan dulce would be finishing baking while another was going into the oven. It wasn't all bad. Even though she couldn't have a summer break, she could look out from the bakery counter onto the world. At least, she knew her world well.

TORTA MARIA LUISA

MAKES 12 SERVINGS

Poleada for Maria Luisa

3 cups milk

6 tablespoons granulated
    sugar

One 3-inch cinnamon stick

2 tablespoons unsalted butter

6 tablespoons cornstarch

2 eggs

16 tablespoons unsalted butter,
    at room temperature

1¼ cups granulated sugar,
    plus 1 tablespoon

4 eggs, at room temperature

3 cups cake flour, sifted

1 tablespoon baking powder

1 teaspoon baking soda

½ teaspoon kosher salt

1¼ cups milk, plus more as
    needed

1 teaspoon crushed cinnamon
    stick (see Consejo,
    page 261)

3 or 4 drops red food coloring

Sugar Glaze

2 cups confectioners' sugar

¼ cup milk

The first time I came across torta Maria Luisa was not in a bakery but in a social media zodiac poster created by a popular Salvadoran cartoonist, on a webpage called Dichos de un Bicho. It was around 2017, and Salvi creators were finding one another online. This poster matched different Salvadoran panes dulces to different zodiac signs. Needless to say, the one matched to my sign was this torta—a tall creation with two layers of cake, a creamy layer of poleada, frosting, and bright pink sugar. My interest was piqued! As with any zodiac, I was very curious to see what this exact match said about my sign.

I could not recall hearing about or seeing this particular pan dulce before, so I went searching for it. When I found it at Panadería Cuscatleca, Gabby's family bakery, she said they'd been making it for a long time, I had just never noticed it before. But once I did, it kept popping up everywhere. After trying it at Gabby's family bakery, I was hooked.

Now that I've learned how to make it with Gabby and how they've adapted the recipe, I've discovered many different ways of preparing it. The topping is different in El Salvador, where some bakers make it with a meringue layer. At Panadería Cuscatleca, they have simplified the process; instead of adding a meringue layer, they finish it off with a sugar glaze, as I've done here.

The leche poleada for this recipe is different from the one that Maria uses for empanadas. This one has eggs and butter, making it like a pastry cream, which holds better when the Maria Luisa goes in the oven. It is best to make the poleada right before making the cake, since it needs to be soft in order to spread on the cake.

●

To make the poleada: In a medium saucepan over medium heat, combine 2½ cups of the milk, the granulated sugar, cinnamon, and butter and let scald, about 7 minutes. (Little bubbles will form around the edge of the pan, and the milk should register 180°F on an instant-read thermometer.) Turn the heat to low.

Meanwhile, in a medium bowl, combine the remaining ½ cup milk and the cornstarch and whisk until the cornstarch has dissolved. Add the eggs and whisk again until well combined into a paste.

Whisk ½ cup of the scalded milk mixture into the egg mixture to temper it. Then slowly whisk the tempered mixture into the milk mixture in the saucepan. Keep whisking until the poleada starts to become more creamy and less liquid, 3 to 4 minutes. Remove from the heat and set aside.

continued

TORTA MARIA LUISA

continued

Position a rack in the middle of the oven. Preheat the oven to 350°F.

Coat a 13 by 9-inch baking pan with nonstick cooking spray. Line the bottom of the pan with parchment paper.

In a stand mixer fitted with the paddle attachment, combine the butter and 1¼ cups granulated sugar and mix on medium-high speed until fluffy, about 3 minutes. Using the attachment, scrape the bowl to evenly incorporate and then continue to mix for 2 minutes. Turn the speed to low, add the eggs one at a time and beat until combined. Scrape the bowl again.

In a large bowl, combine the flour, baking powder, baking soda, and salt. Add the dry ingredients to the mixer bowl and mix on medium speed until smooth, about 5 minutes. Scrape the bowl again.

With the mixer on medium speed, add the milk and cinnamon. Scrape the bowl again and continue mixing until the batter is soft and looks almost like pancake batter, about 2 minutes.

Pour half of the batter into the prepared pan, making sure it evenly covers the bottom. Using an offset spatula, spread the batter to all the corners of the pan. Carefully pour the poleada over the batter to completely cover it. (If the poleada has cooled and stiffened, stir in 1 tablespoon milk or water so it becomes pourable again.) Pour the remaining batter evenly over the poleada. Using the spatula, spread the batter and smooth the top.

Bake the cake until golden brown (it's okay if some small cracks appear), 50 minutes to 1 hour. Let cool completely in the pan, then place a lightweight cutting board on the top and carefully invert the cake onto the board. Peel off the parchment paper, then place a second cutting board on the cake and invert once more. Avoid handling or cutting the cake while it is still hot because the poleada layer needs to set.

In a small bowl, combine the remaining 1 tablespoon granulated sugar and the food coloring and stir to make a bright-pink topping. Set aside.

To make the glaze: In a small bowl, combine the confectioners' sugar and milk and whisk until a smooth paste forms.

Pour the glaze over the top of the cake, allowing it to drip over the edges. Let rest for 5 minutes, then sprinkle with the pink sugar topping. Once the glaze has set completely, about 5 minutes more, using a serrated knife, cut all four outer edges off the cake, just like you were cutting the crust off a sandwich; the layers should be visible from the side.

When ready to serve, cut into 2 by 2-inch pieces.

Walking out of Panadería Cuscatleca, Gabby picks up on the smell, that bakery smell. Out of habit, she panics. It's all over her clothes, her hair, everywhere. For a long time, she hated it because it was a reminder that despite her attempts at creating boundaries between herself and the family business, she couldn't beat the force that was the bakery. All roads led there. She's not bothered by it anymore, though. She's used to it. People walk into her family's Los Angeles establishment every day and, like clockwork, someone brings up the aroma. "Wow, que rico huele." (Wow, it smells so good here.)

Gabby had just finished restocking the case of her little pan dulce trailer, a concept she had been itching to do for years—sell her family's pan dulce at different festivals, on streets all over L.A., and even at movie studios. "Everyone loves pan dulce," she says. Gabby figured that plenty of Latino people attended these festivals and events, and while there were always burgers, tacos, and even pupusas, the only desserts she'd noticed were churros, funnel cakes, and ice cream. Why not offer some of her family's pan dulce at these events?

So, Sweet LA Mobile was born, and "pan dulce on wheels" became a reality. Her father, an "old-fashioned Salvadoran dad" as Gabby describes him, was skeptical. He'd been a baker for most of his life and didn't think putting pan dulce on wheels was the way to go. He also didn't believe that offering vegan options at their bakery was worth the effort, but now after years of doing so, he is more supportive.

One night, Gabby was in Koreatown with her trailer. A woman walked by, then stopped and turned around. "Can I ask you a question?" she said.

"Yeah, of course," responded Gabby.

"This pink one? You know what. I saw it as I walked by and it reminded me of my childhood." The moment Gabby heard that, she lit up. She loves such stories. "My grandma used to make this when I was a little girl," said the woman. "And lately I've been very emotional. I was just walking by and it caught my eye. So yeah, I want to take some home." After she bought them, she told Gabby, "Thank you for bringing a memory that I just completely forgot. It's not that I blocked it out, but it was just there and you brought it to the surface."

"Oh my God, you're welcome," Gabby said. The women were both emotional for a moment before the customer walked away. Gabby packed up her trailer, cleaned up, and made her way back to the bakery. When she saw her dad, she said, "Hey, guess what happened today?"

ACKNOWLEDGMENTS

I am overwhelmed with gratitude to so many people who have taken care of this project and taken care of me. My life has improved thanks to their love in both words and actions. I want to thank the following:

My parents, Teresa and Carlos. Ma, thank you for being who you are. Our relationship has given me so much strength. You've cooked with me, talked with me, cried with me, and shared so much. I don't think I'll ever have enough of your stories or food. Papito, you have been the best dad to me, and I can't thank you enough for seeing me through as a writer, from reading my published pieces, asking me about the details of my career, and trying to understand what it is I do, to motivating and celebrating me. I hope both of you know how important you will always be to me. Ustedes siempre seran mis primeros amores, los amo para siempre. My brother, David, hermanito, I appreciate you so much for your encouragement throughout these years. You have always been ready to tell me a good word that snaps me out of doubt and fear, reminding me that I am a "no-bullshit-taking powerful Salvi woman."

My husband, John. I knew I was in good hands with you, mi cielo, when I first shared a dream and you said, "How can I help make it happen?" I found you, you found me, and now it's a constant conversation about how we can make the life we want happen. So many people were instrumental in getting this book into existence, but I felt I could start only because of your immense and loving support. Your presence in my life makes me feel healthy, loved, and capable. This love has been my safe place, a balm, and shown me what is possible.

My family—Tía Patty, Stephany, Samantha, Juliancito, Luis, Abuelo, Iris, Mario, Tía Gladis, Juan, Iris (la de la Samantha), Tío Mario, Tía Cristina, Tío Javier, Tío Roberto Carlos, Cassandra, Yoyo, Tía Morena, Karen, Estela, Kelly, and Jennyfer—I love you all. You have supported this book, loved it with me, let me use your houses for a cooking class, picked up ingredients for recipe testing, and answered so many questions about food and about our family's history. At every corner you've shown up, and it's meant everything to me.

The SalviSoul women, without whom this project and book would literally not exist. I am so glad that fate brought us together. I didn't know what I was doing when I started this, but you still all believed in it and for that, you'll always be my heroes.

My community, Yenny Urquilla and Sanobar Sajan, our friendship has kept me grounded. Maddie, thank you for your support mujer. Maya Salomé, mujer, you get me. I sent you pages early on, and it was the excitement in your voice after reading them that gave me so much confidence to keep going. Our talks on WhatsApp, IG, phone calls, everything we've shared has shaped me for the better and made me a better writer and person. Gracias por ser quien eres. Victor Interiano, you were one of the first people to understand this project. From the first Facebook post you shared about my project, hyping it up, you were all about SalviSoul, and I am forever grateful for our conversations, your counsel, and your friendship. Yeiry Guevara and Anita Abassi, you are Salvadoran women whom I admire immensely—thank you for reading through my proposal, tweaking it, and rooting for me. Anita, thank you especially for reminding me to "just let it rip" when it came to writing this book. Yesika Salgado, thank you for your poetry. Your words gave me an idea of how to teach the mountain to kneel. To my Salvadoran community, thank you for receiving SalviSoul and championing this work together.

The SalviSoul community on Instagram, Facebook, YouTube, TikTok, and Twitter, without you, this book would not have happened. One voice grew into thousands, and that's what's made all the difference. Every like, every comment, and every share has nurtured this work, and the growth we see is because you've all cared for it.

Andrianna deLone, you were the only agent who didn't make me feel like I had to convince you that a Salvadoran cookbook was a worthwhile pursuit and that it deserved to exist. Your words and actions reassured and validated me. Thank you.

The Ten Speed Press family, thank you for bringing this book to life. Dervla Kelly and Emma Campion, both of you always made me feel better when it came to understanding this process as a debut author. There was never a feeling of "don't ask this because it's silly," and you were always helpful in the most kind and available ways. Emma, thank you especially for helping me with all the details concerning the visual aspects of the book. Your help was invaluable. Felix Cruz, you slid into my DMs and literally changed my life. Things aligned, and before we knew it, we were both Salvi kids working on the first Salvadoran cookbook published in this country. I'm so happy it happened the way it did.

Gracias Dra. Claudia Moisa, usted fue parte clave para terminar este libro. Mi agradecimiento nunca será suficiente.

Lastly, my production team—Ren Fuller, Caroline Hwang, Nidia Cueva, Ty Ferg, David Koung, Jessica Darakjian, Hina Mistry, Monica Torrento, and crew—you are responsible for the beautiful photos in this book. When I first started this project, the photo shoot that would eventually happen was just a daydream that comforted me when I was working odd jobs and trying to inch my way forward. You all helped make that dream come true. An enormous thanks also to Kathleen Blakistone for having us at Moonwater Farm in Compton. This project started with my Mamá Lucy, who lived in Compton, so to find your farm at which to shoot the photos was a wonderful way to end the project back in the same neighborhood. And thank you, Proplink Studio, for having us and taking care of us.

Gracias de corazón.

ABOUT THE CONTRIBUTORS

KARLA TATIANA VASQUEZ is a food writer, recipe developer, and food stylist based in L.A. Her writing has been published by *The Los Angeles Times*, *San Francisco Chronicle*, and *Teen Vogue* among others. Her recipe development work can be seen in *Food & Wine*, *Serious Eats*, *BuzzFeed Tasty*, and *Tastemade*. She is also a food justice advocate and an active member in her community to increase healthy food accessibility in low-income communities, previously working with Hunger Action Los Angeles and Los Angeles Food Policy Council. She founded SalviSoul to preserve her family's recipes, and since then it's expanded to focus on cultural memory and intergenerational healing for the Salvadoran diaspora.

REN FULLER is a food and lifestyle photographer and director based in L.A. Born in the former USSR, her upbringing has influenced her love of food, culture, and exploration. She translates this into the way she captures stories for her advertising, editorial, and cookbook clients.

MONICA TORRENTO is a portrait and candid photographer, as well as a strategic designer, based in El Salvador. Growing up in El Salvador has deeply influenced her approach to capturing everyday life, people, and their stories. While Monica delves into various creative and photographic realms, she specializes in working with commercial and editorial clients, expertly weaving narratives from advertising campaigns to intimate personal stories.

INDEX

Text copyright © 2024 by Karla Vasquez
Photographs copyright © 2024 by Ren Fuller

Published in the United States by Ten Speed Press, an imprint of the Crown
Publishing Group, a division of Penguin Random House LLC, New York.
TenSpeed.com

Ten Speed Press and the Ten Speed Press colophon are registered trademarks of
Penguin Random House LLC.

Typefaces: Grilli Type's GT Alpina, Pangram Pangram Foundry's Neue Montreal,
and Taylor Penton's TAY Makawao.

Library of Congress Cataloging-in-Publication Data is on file with the publisher.

Hardcover ISBN: 978-1-9848-6142-9
eBook ISBN: 978-1-9848-6143-6

Printed in China

Editor: Dervla Kelly
Designer: Emma Campion
Production designers: Mari Gill, Faith Hague, and Mara Gendell
Production and prepress color manager: Jane Chinn
Food stylist: Caroline K. Hwang | Food assistant: Jessica Darakjian
Prop stylist: Nidia Cueva | Prop assistants: Hina Mistry and Reb Rich
Photo assistants: David K. Peng and Ty Ferguson
Copyeditor: Mi Ae Lipe | Proofreader: Rachel Markowitz
Indexer: Elizabeth Parson
Publicist: Felix Cruz | Marketer: Brianne Sperber

10 9 8 7 6 5 4 3 2 1

First Edition